CONTENTS

Inclusive Learning

PREFACE

Report of the Committee on Students with Learning Difficulties and/orDisabilities

I have great pleasure in submitting my committee's report for the consideration of the Council. We thank the Council for the opportunity to take part in the enquiry which was occasioned by the new responsibilities placed on both the Council and the colleges in the *Further and Higher Education Act 1992.*

We have gathered a substantial body of evidence and believe that our proposals are well found and far reaching. If adopted, our proposals would improve existing provision and extend opportunities to many who do not now participate in further education, to their loss and to that of our economy and the wider society. We therefore urge the Council to set in hand ways of implementing our recommendations.

I wish to place on record my admiration for the time and effort so unstintingly given by members of the committee, over a period of three years. Our report is presented to the Council unanimously.

The committee's work was made possible by the unfailing support of many individuals and organisations. We are grateful to colleges, many of which have worked hard for many years to develop provision for students with learning difficulties and/or disabilities, and many of which gave their time and thought unstintingly to help us. We are grateful to parents, who told us clearly what they want from further education. We are grateful to the students who shared with us so generously their experiences of further education. In many ways, this report is theirs.

No praise can be too high for the work of the staff team led by Elizabeth Maddison, Merillie Vaughan Huxley, Pat Hood, Peter Lavender and Lisa Young. They supported and guided us at all stages and have undertaken the main burden of drafting the report.

John Tomlinson

John Tomlinson
Chairman
June 1996

Introduction by the Chairman, Professor John Tomlinson

In this introduction I try to convey an idea of the informing spirit of the committee and our report. I touch upon the values and perspectives which we brought to bear, some main lines of analysis and argument, and our pivotal insights and recommendations. It is not a substitute for the report; there can be no substitute for reading the careful analysis and interlocking recommendations in the body of the report. It is only the key to the door. Please tour the house and enjoy its design and furntiure in your own way.

The Further Education Funding Council (the Council) had asked the committee to examine current educational provision for those with learning difficulties and/or disabilities and to say whether the new legal requirements of the *Further and Higher Education Act 1992* were being satisfied and, if they were not in any respects how that could be remedied. Tackling these questions has been a major undertaking. There was not any complete description of existing provision as inherited from the former local education authorities (LEAs) and in the specialist residential colleges. There were no agreed definitions by which to set the boundaries of the enquiry. There had been very little research into appropriate ways of learning, curriculum or management. Means by which to assess the learning achieved, by stages to assist in further learning or summatively to register achievement, were comparatively under-developed. Progression from school to college was not managed to the same depth in all areas. And, although many LEAs, colleges, health and social services authorities, and voluntary organisations had collaborated successfully in the interests of students with learning difficulties, progress countrywide had been very uneven and everywhere the sudden lifting of the further education colleges out of the local government system had left jagged edges.

In consequence, we have had to undertake some fundamental research. We commissioned a review of the research literature (Bradley *et al.*, 1994) and a report on the law as it bore upon both the Council and other agencies or authorities. We commissioned a nationwide mapping of the provision for students with learning difficulties and the incidence of disabilities and learning difficulty. We arranged for evidence to be submitted in ways that gave all concerned opportunities to put their views and recommendations; and we commissioned a unique series of workshops in which the students themselves and their advocates could speak directly (SCPR, 1996).

As a result of these enquiries, and our visits, oral evidence and discussions, we have a great deal of robust quantitative and qualitative data on which we have based our findings and recommendations. Most important of all, we have thought our way through to an approach to learning which represents another step forward, perhaps the final step, on the long march towards embracing students with learning difficulties and/or disabilities fully and unequivocally within the general approach to learning appropriate for all students.

The intellectual challenge set the committee was considerable. So also has been the excitement of finding ways to meet it as perennial educational dilemmas and problems of effective management have been faced, argued out, and resolved into clear and realistic proposals.

Like any human group who spend three years together on a daunting task, we ourselves learned a great deal and therefore were changed people by the end. Likewise the world moved on as we worked. The new further education system called into being in 1992 not only expanded rapidly but grew more self confident as new relationships between a national funding council and college corporations became established. This confidence and capacity to cause effective action will be needed if the Council and its collaborators decide to implement our report. Change is easier in a period of expansion and that period is virtually at an end so that resources are likely to become more scarce, at least in the immediate future. Our contacts with colleges and others in the further education world and especially the results of the testing we arranged for our proposed approaches, in some 20 colleges, convince us that there is a hunger in the system to move forward and that a lead from the Council and others in authority will be welcomed and acted upon, if the conditions we recommend can be created.

The report

The immediate purpose of this report is radically to improve educational opportunities for about 130,000 of our citizens who are currently attending further education colleges and other centres. To that end we make a number of proposals that can be put in hand in the next two years within current resources. Its deeper purpose is to extend further education to thousands not now included. To that end, we make structural proposals requiring a five- to ten-year timescale and the reordering of some priorities. The combined effect would be to transform the further education system of this country to the immeasurable benefit of future generations, our economy and the quality of our whole society.

The background

When I first entered educational administration, nearly 40 years ago, some of our citizens were deemed ineducable and never offered any formal educational opportunity or stimulus, seeing out their childhood and adult lives in families (who received little help or advice), in hospitals or in occupation centes (later called training centres). That regime was brought about by the terms of the *Mental Deficiency Act 1913,* and the attitude it betokened was altered in law only in 1970 (1980 in Northern Ireland) and then only so far as schoolchildren were concerned. Those who experienced that regime, at least for some of their lives, may still be as young as 30. If they are over 45, it will have covered what for other children would have been their whole experience of school.

For those with disability or learning difficulty who *were* permitted to attend school, the starting-point was usually the description of their condition given by doctors. Whatever may have been the intentions of those passing the *Education Act 1944*, the effect was to define special educational need as springing from physical or mental disability. The formal process that was required in order that an LEA could 'ascertain' the need for special education often entailed resort to compulsory medical examination or the use of intelligence testing and invariably meant assigning the child to one of the statutory categories of handicap. It was not until 1959 that parents were given a right to appeal against the LEA's decision. Once ascertained as needing special education, children were for the most part taught in separate schools or classes. The term 'educationally sub-normal' remained in law until 1981. Such rigidities and perceptions perpetuated the isolation of children receiving special education, even though they were technically within the education system.

However, attitudes and understanding were changing rapidly in the post-war years. In 1976 an Education Act declared that as far as practicable all children with special educational needs should be educated in ordinary schools. In 1978, the Warnock committee, in a landmark report, broke through with proposals to achieve this and much more which led to the *Education Act 1981*, now amended and extended by the Act of 1993. As a result, the lives and expectations of very many have been transformed. They include not only the children themselves, who have experienced a more sensitive and effective education, but also other children who have had the experience of working alongside them, and teachers, who had hitherto not worked in these ways; and not least, the families of the children and the organisations and services that collaborate with the education service.

Those working in further education need to remember this history and that our adult society contains at least three layers of experience. Depending on the period in which you grew up and the nature of your disability or learning difficulty, you may have been excluded altogether from education, included but isolated within it, or increasingly regarded as part of the whole work of the education service.

While these developments in attitudes towards children of school age were taking place, further education, in the post-war years, became a more recognised and vigorous part of the education service. It was thus better able, when called upon from the 1970s, to play a part in providing for older people with learning difficulties and/or disability. Section 41 of the *Education Act 1944* had placed a duty on every local education authority 'to secure the provision for their area of adequate facilities for further education, that is to say, full-time and part-time education for persons over compulsory school age'. Growth was slow and achieved with difficulty. Immediately after the war, resources were concentrated on rebuilding and extending the school system. From the mid-1950s, governments began to emphasise the need for technical education and during the next 20 years building programmes were introduced and numbers grew dramatically so that in 1974 there were 335,000 full-time day students compared with 52,000 in 1953; and 727,000 part-time day students compared with 333,000 (Bristow, 1976). However, the general expectation was that students who entered further education courses would have the required minimum standard of educational achievement and be able to take the courses as offered. A survey of 1973, which did not include those with severe learning difficulties who had not been in the school system up to that time, found that only 10% of those leaving special schools entered further education. A further 9% entered special residential courses, an important reminder of the historical significance of specialist residential colleges and the foundations which supported them. Some 51% of those considered 'suitable' for further education were without any provision at all.

The impetus for change came from two directions. Some LEAs encouraged and funded provision, often spurred on by colleges themselves, by expert advisory staff and the experience of implementing the 1970 and 1981 Education Acts in schools. And the Manpower Services Commission, formed in 1974, promoted a series of youth training schemes as youth unemployment rose dramatically. Courses in basic education became a significant element in the programmes, as those with learning difficulties were increasingly disadvantaged in the changing labour markets. A survey of 1987 identified some 250 courses of this kind, in approximately half the colleges of further education in England (Stowell, 1987).

This, crudely summarised, was the situation at the passing of the *Further and Higher Education Act 1992* in which students with learning difficulties and/or disabilities are the only group of students specially mentioned. It not only places these students fully within the scope of further education, itself a powerful message, but also signifies the importance attached by government and parliament to provision for them. It is a landmark in the development of education policy. The Act says that the Further Education Funding Council 'shall have regard to the requirements of persons having learning difficulties' in the course of carrying out its general duties to provide full-time and part-time education. 'Have regard' is a relatively flexible duty in law and gives the Council room for the exercise of judgement as to what should be done for any individual according to circumstances. It is thus the starting-point of the Council's turning to the committee for advice and of the advice we now offer.

Our approach to learning

Central to all our thinking and recommendations is the approach towards learning, which we term 'inclusive learning', and which we want to see adopted everywhere. We argue for it because it will improve the education of those with learning difficulties, but believe it is also true that such an approach would benefit all and, indeed, represents the best approach to learning and teaching yet articulated. When we tested our approach in a number of colleges, that is what we were told.

Put simply, we want to avoid a viewpoint which locates the difficulty or deficit with the student and focus instead on the capacity of the educational institution to understand and respond to the individual learner's requirement. This means we must move away from labelling the student and towards creating an appropriate educational environment; concentrate on understanding better how people learn so that they can better be helped to learn; and see people with disabilities and/or learning difficulties first and foremost as learners.

It may sound simple, even obvious; but it has profound consequences. There is a world of difference between, on the one hand, offering courses of education and training and then giving some students who have learning difficulties some additional human or physical aids to gain access to those courses, and, on the other hand, redesigning the very processes of learning, assessment and organisation so as to fit the objectives and learning styles of the students. But only the second philosophy can claim to be inclusive, to have as its central purpose the opening of opportunity to those whose disability means that they learn differently from others. It may mean introducing new content into courses, or it may mean differentiated access to the same content; or both.

Let it be clear that this approach does not involve glossing over disability or learning difficulty, still less pretending that given some change to the ways we teach they make no difference. Many individuals with disabilities and/or learning difficulties told us bluntly that we should not seek to minimise still less ignore the real difficulties or differences that a disability or learning difficulty can bring into a person's life. I recall vividly, for example, at one of the many conferences I have addressed since we started, a man who had been blind from birth telling me emphatically:

I am blind, I have always been blind and always will be. I don't mind people knowing that: in fact I want them to know it. What I do not want is their pity or condescension. And what I do want is to be able to learn the same kinds of things as sighted people learn.

I have not forgotten. However, that instance and many others in the evidence we received only serve to re-emphasise that for a teacher the focus should not be on the disability itself but on what it means for the way that person can learn, or be helped to learn even more effectively.

Moreover, all students in further education bring with them a history of earlier educational experiences of more or less success in learning. That is especially true for those with disability or learning difficulty because of the history I have already outlined of our changing approaches to their education over the last 50 years. Since so much of the burden a disability or learning difficulty places on individuals is thus socially constructed — the result of attitudes and attributions by those who deem themselves without disability or able to learn normally — all the more reason for all those in education, governors, managers and teachers, to make their central concern the ways an individual learns and how they can be accommodated.

A key element in reconceptualising provision for students with learning difficulties is the recognition that their needs are cognate with those of all learners. Ensuring that all pupils or students make progress demands that teachers do not treat them uniformly, but differentiate their approaches according to the previous experience and varied learning styles of those pupils or students. Providing audio-tapes for a blind learner, amplification or photographs for a deaf person or simplified text for a hesitant reader are matters of degree rather than kind. Moreover, teachers have to select materials and methods appropriate to the subjects being taught: artists must encourage visual awareness and skill with colour, shape and texture, scientists must foster observation and an experimental approach, historians must learn how to use evidence from the past. Each domain of knowledge has its different procedures for examining the world, different tests for truth. Each student must learn the ways needed to proceed in the chosen study and adjust their learning styles accordingly. The task of teachers is always to effect a marriage between the requirements of particular subject-matter and the predispositions, stage of development and capacities of those who would learn. The wider the spectrum the greater the insight and ingenuity called for. We extend this view to the learning strategies adopted by people with disabilities and/or learning difficulties and their teachers.

One more thing needs to be said about this approach to learning, for the removal of doubt. Our concept of inclusive learning is not synonymous with integration. It is a larger and prior concept. The first step is to determine the best possible learning environment, given the individual student and learning task. Colleges told us, in evidence and when we tested this approach with a few, that this was increasingly their approach to all students. For those with a learning difficulty the resulting educational environment will often be in an integrated setting and, as in schools, increasingly so as the skills of teachers and capacities of the system grow. Sometimes it will be a mixture of the integrated and the discrete. And sometimes, as in the specialist residential colleges, it will be discrete provision. We envisage a system that is inclusive and that will require many mansions. Each element of the system will need to play its part: the teacher and learner; the institution or college; and the whole further education system. We acknowledge that this will require a degree of sector-wide and regional planning and collaboration so that scarce resources are best matched to estimated needs; and for this purpose the Council's regional committees and the colleges will need to co-operate and agree on sensible divisions of labour.

This is consonant with the proposal we also make that the time has come when colleges must share with the Council the legal duty 'to have regard' to the requirements of these students and thus assist in building a system that is 'sufficient' and 'adequate' for all who come forward. It also is realistic. Some colleges have made great strides over the last

10 years or so towards the inclusive approach. The different stages of development can be a basis for planning for the future, but in a way that can allow all who so wish to develop new capacities.

But there is also clear evidence that the quality of the provision made for these students is less good than that to be found in colleges generally. The work seldom features in college-wide systems of strategic planning, quality assurance or data collection and analysis. Few questions are asked about the purpose or relevance of what students with learning difficulties and/or disabilities are being asked to learn. Monitoring and evaluation of students' achievements is less common in this work than elsewhere and managers often lack awareness or understanding of what is required. We recognise fully that there is good provision with skilled teachers and knowledgeable managers, but remain concerned about the overall quality of provision nationally.

So much remains to be done, even in the best served areas, especially in terms of enfranchising those now mainly excluded — those with mental ill-health, with emotional and behavioural difficulties, and those with profound and multiple disabilities — that no college or service which may wish to develop its provision need be denied the opportunity. With so much still needing to be done, a co-operative and interdependent approach is essential.

Increasing participation

An inclusive approach to the education of those with learning difficulties and/or disabilities has two aspects. The approach to learning just outlined would raise the quality of the educational experience of students in the colleges. But we must also find ways to increase participation and ensure that all who may want further education can be welcomed on terms they can accept. This means both trying to understand the underlying dynamic of current patterns of participation and creating ways to help the Council and colleges to know better how far they may be satisfying the potential demand. There is no escaping the fact that this requires clear definitions of who may be included in the phrase 'learning difficulties and/or disabilities'. A process that allows us to know in broad terms for how many we should be providing does not require the definitions that used to be attached to individuals once they are within education, and we have demonstrated that it is more effective to concentrate on providing the education environment needed to meet an individual's learning goals.

We commissioned major research projects to map existing provision and participation and also to create an instrument — a practical guide — for measuring how far need is being met in a locality, which could be placed in the hands of the colleges. While we were doing this, the Council's committee on widening participation in further education, chaired by Helena Kennedy QC, began its work and we have shared our thinking and results closely with it. A general strategy to widen access and participation can only be of benefit to those with learning difficulties and would create a strong framework for the more specific strategies we recommend.

The mapping exercise provided the best data now available about the number of students with learning difficulties in sector colleges (Meager *et al.*, 1996). The figure is 131,000, roughly 5% of the total student population. This figure is about three times the number found by a survey in 1985, allowing for the addition of sixth form colleges to the sector since and remembering that our definitions were more fully thought through and the data collected more rigorously, thanks to the quality of the work by the researchers at the Institute for Employment Studies and the co-operation of the colleges. There is little difference between type of college in the 'average share' per college of students, evidence that most colleges are strenuously seeking to extend their work in this field.

There is, however, considerable variation between regions. In future, the individualised student record (ISR), if adapted in the ways we suggest, will allow both colleges and the Council to maintain statistics on a consistent basis so that for the first time, we shall have a reliable picture of how provision and participation may be changing over time.

Turning to the other question, of how many ought we to be providing for, it is far more difficult to make progress. The Council's statisticians examined carefully the large national data sets that are available, but each has been compiled on a different basis from the rest, relating to its prime purpose. Regretfully we have had to conclude that it is possible at the moment only to make incomplete estimates of the incidence of learning difficulties and/or disabilities in the population. The data we would need in order to do better have not been collected, presumably because public policy has not hitherto embraced the desire to offer further education to adults with learning difficulties. Only now is it possible to think of an entitlement and hence to ask how far policy is providing it.

The data that are available, however, are thought-provoking. The 1991 census records just under 3,000 16 to 19 year olds with a limiting long-term illness living in communal establishments and a further 69,000 living in private households. This is considerably higher than the estimated 46,000 16 to 19 year olds with a disability estimated from the OPCS disability survey of 1995. The 1991 census records nearly 2 million aged 16 to 59 with a limiting long-term illness, while the labour force survey of 1993 gives a figure of just over 3 million based on answers to questions about health problems or disabilities which affect the kind of paid work the person can do. The general household survey (GHS) of 1992 gives the highest figure for 16 to 64 year olds with health problems, namely almost 6 million. This is likely to be due to the phrasing of the question in the GHS which relates to any long-standing illness, disability or infirmity that limits the activities of the respondent. The general impression seems inescapable: there must be many more who could benefit from education than the 130,000 now involved. The statistical instrument that we have had devised, if used by colleges in the future, should allow them to make useful estimates of the incidence of learning disabilities and/or difficulties in their area, as part of a strategic approach to needs analysis, itself one of the many approaches needed to widen access.

The student

Our proposals are rooted in the belief that students with learning difficulties should be helped towards adult status. This requires the achievement of autonomy, and a positive self-image realistically grounded in the capacity to live as independently as possible and contribute both to the economy and the community.

The case for providing further education for those with learning difficulties is fundamentally no different from that for providing it for anyone, just as the Warnock Report declared 20 years ago (HMSO, 1978, para. 1.4). Moreover, the economic case for improving educational opportunities for those with learning difficulties and/or disabilities should loom much larger in public policy than it has done hitherto. Involvement in productive economic activity of people of working age with disability is one half that of those without disability (40% compared with 83%). Two-fifths (41%) of disabled people of working age have no educational qualifications compared with under one-fifth (18%) of non-disabled people; but for those who are economically active the proportion is 26% (compared with 16% for non-disabled). The economic advantage of education for both individual and society is manifest. Yet, unemployment rates (on the International Labour Organisation definition) among people with disabilities are around two and a half times those for non-disabled people (21.6% compared with 9%), and this is about the same for both men and women. (Sly *et al.,* 1995, and Institute of Manpower Studies, 1995). There can be little doubt that many of our citizens are failing to contribute as they and society would wish because low educational opportunities have reinforced the difficulties presented by disability.

We developed strategies to meet our concern for the involvement of the students. The call for evidence was couched so as to encourage responses in many modes and we received audio- and video-tapes, drawings, paintings and artefacts as well as text in many languages and in Braille, amounting to over 1,000 items many of which could be deemed the direct voice of the student. In addition, we organised 10 workshops in various parts of England through which students and their advocates could speak directly. Their testimony is vibrant, direct and often moving. It has been an important shaper of our recommendations (SCPR, 1996). Many of our recommendations are designed to ensure a continuing place for students in both their own learning and the management and review procedures of the colleges.

A further essential feature of an improved service will be extended collaboration with other services, especially health, social work, the LEAs, TECs and voluntary organisations. Where such arrangements already exist, their value and effect speak for themselves and we recommend that time is found to work at the many inter-disciplinary relationships which are necessary for a comprehensive further education service, from counselling and assessment, through teaching and assessment on course to transition from further education into work or other settings. Not least, such inter-disciplinary co-operation and the development of mutual understanding and support will need to suffuse the enhanced programmes of staff training for both teachers and managers, which are another major feature of our recommendations.

Quality: Management; teaching and assessment; inspection

The part played by college governors and managers in colleges and services is one of the constant factors determining the quality of what the student receives. Evidence from all parts of further education confirms that unless senior management is knowledgeable, committed and energetic in the pursuit of creating a good service for students with learning difficulties, the work and dedication of middle management and teachers is diminished or frustrated. Likewise those holding departmental, faculty and similar senior but middle-range positions of responsibility must ensure that teachers are supported in making the provision intended by college plans. Their role is crucial also, and we were given evidence from many quarters that strong and sympathetic middle managers can help create the optimum conditions for learning and teaching.

It is clear beyond all doubt that those teaching students with learning difficulties bring a dedication and humanity to the task that is admirable and deeply appreciated by the students. To join a class or workshop session, or to observe an assessment or review is often to see a range of human understanding and giving and receiving (by both teacher and student) which is at a level of emotional intensity greater than the common modes of teaching require. Moreover, as those with disability and learning difficulty have increasingly become members of the 'ordinary' classroom or workshop, so both teachers and other students have had the humanising experience of these extended relationships and procedures in the pursuit of learning. Just as in the school system over the last 15 years, so increasingly in further education, the system and the experience of all in it has been enriched as those with disability have taken a full place and made a unique contribution.

However, the existing levels of training of teachers working with those with learning difficulties are not sufficient, taken overall, and urgently need improvement.

Some salients have been made in the recent past so the system does not lack the seed corn now needed. The Further Education Unit produced several key documents in the 1980s which show the way to a richer curriculum. *A Special Professionalism* (Stafford, 1987), an enlightened clarion call, was produced by a joint committee following a report by the Advisory Council on the Education and Training of Teachers (ACSET) in 1984. There are some regional organisations offering training and a few interested universities.

It also needs to be acknowledged that those in the colleges, whether rightly or wrongly, feel that they have made the many improvements we have noted despite rather than because of FEFC requests for information and the government's requirements for efficiency savings. It must not be forgotten that, whatever structural changes may be made or opportunities for staff development may be offered, the transformation we wish to promote is dependent ultimately on changes in attitudes and practices of staff which challenge many aspects of current thinking and organisation.

We are clear that a major, carefully planned and adequately funded programme of staff development supported by ear-marked national funding is essential. Its purpose will be not only to train the current cohorts of managers and teachers, but also to transform provision so that universities and others continue to offer teacher training and curriculum development of the highest order. We place the improvements needed in the training of managers equal in importance with that needed by teachers for the classrooms or workshops. And we place this total necessity for a nationally-planned and funded development of staff in our group of most essential and urgent recommendations.

It will be necessary for the development programme to attend concurrently to three aspects. These are 'teacher training', 'management training' and 'organisational development'. Some programmes of educational innovation have approached only one or other of these, with less than satisfactory results in consequence. Teachers who have been trained in new approaches have continued to work in unsuitable organisational structures, managed by people who had not been given the opportunity to understand their changed role in supporting the new purposes and methods of teaching. Or managers and organisations have been 'developed' according to general theories which were not sufficiently related to the educational purposes of the organisation. In designing the recommended national development programme there will be the opportunity to adopt an integrated approach.

These better trained teachers and managers will need to work in a stronger framework which has higher expectations. Inspection arrangements should be strengthened so they can provide evidence of the match between student needs and a college-wide inclusive environment. Monitoring of provision, the use made of funding and analyses of future needs must become a regular feature of both college and Further Education Funding Council management, notwithstanding the fact that, in the educational process itself, students need not, and should not be labelled. Inspection reports on the specialist residential establishments should be published, as are those for sector colleges. In their self-assessments, which will increasingly become a feature of a more mature system, all colleges should vigorously measure their progress towards inclusive learning.

Further Education Funding Council

The Council has access to four levers on the further education system: funding, audit, college development plans and inspection. The Council should require that, in future, colleges should accept a responsibility to have regard to the requirements of students with learning difficulties and/or disabilities. The Council and colleges should use the new statistical instruments to establish the extent of need and monitor progress towards meeting it. The Council, through its regional organisations, should ensure that the system is trying to be inclusive and monitor progress towards it. That may mean, in a few cases, a more interventionist policy; but we doubt it, given the concern for the work we have found throughout the system. Inspection also has a key role to play in the way just described by clarifying standards of high quality, the evidence that may be gathered for their presence and the use made of additional units of funding.

The funding methodology will remain the bedrock of the Council's policy. It not only provides the resources, but sends signals about priorities. When we started our work the methodology was brand new. Both Council officers and college staff were learning what it meant. There was a good deal of anxiety, even some suspicion in places. Three years on, our conclusion is that the basic concept of providing additional units on a mounting scale of need is appropriate and has helped most colleges to improve their provision. We do not suggest a radical re-design, though as we worked, the Council made some changes that we recommended and in the report further significant detailed amendment is proposed. We do think, however, that there is a need to explain the system more clearly so that colleges may realise its potential value. Amendments to the interpretation of schedule 2(j) to the *Further and Higher Education Act 1992* are strongly recommended, which should meet the most urgent concerns put to us by colleges, students and voluntary organisations. Individual equipment and learning technology should be brought within the scope of the additional support bands. And, as local or regional development plans are approved, so new funding arrangements will be needed to set up new provision in key places, because the present system cannot provide for the quantum leap, especially in the capital funding, that is required. Development planning needs to promote co-operation between specialist colleges and sector colleges backed by continued convergence between fee levels for comparable provision. For at least five years there must be ear-marked central funding for the staff development programme. Our most radical proposal is that the Council should urge the government to establish a common funding base for all post-16 education whether in schools or further education. We have been convinced that current differences affecting students with learning difficulties make no sense in educational terms and are not in the public interest because they only add to the anxieties of students and their families or advocates at times when choice should be based solely on the quality and appropriateness of educational provision.

The Council asked the committee: 'Is the system properly "having regard" to students with learning difficulties and/or disabilities and is the provision made "adequate" and "sufficient"?' The answers must be 'no' in enough respects to require concerted action. Whilst the sector is, we believe, complying with the law as it is written, a more generous interpreation is clearly needed in the light of changing conditions. The volume of provision is probably meeting demand as currently expressed, but there is clear evidence that many groups are under-represented, including adults with mental health difficulties, young people with emotional and behavioural difficulties and people of all ages with profound and multiple disabilities. For those who *are* taking part, the quality of provision is not good enough, and as a result student experience is too often unacceptably inferior. A combined effort to improve management, teaching, support systems and collaboration with other services is essential to build the framework for learning and the inclusive system we could now create. The levers for doing that are largely already in the hands of the Council. Others require action by government and other authorities and agencies. Our proposals set out a programme of immediate action and middle-term structural change, all dependent on increased expertise in the managers and the teachers. To deliver all this would not only transform the opportunities for the students, but would also release a vital flow of further talent into the economic life of the country.

The British ought to feel some pride in the approach they have made to the education beyond school of those with disabilities and/or learning difficulties. Without the structure of a formal constitution bestowing rights on individuals, we have yet found a powerful way in which to promote the enfranchisement of those with learning difficulties. During school age this is done through formal requirement for a statement, now backed up by a transition plan, and access to special education for up to about 20% of the age group as may be required by individuals from time to time. In the USA, for example, a similar legal framework brings between 14 and 16% of the school population within reach of the Individual Education Plan. Beyond school in the USA, however, the individual has no rights under any education law. He or she must claim a right to 'reasonable accommodation' under laws to do with disability or rehabilitation. In the USA the system shifts its basis abruptly from paternalism relying on professional expertise during the compulsory school period to individualism, relying on the student's strength in the market, thereafter. And there is much concern in that country about the extent of exclusion from education, training and employment of adults with disabilities, considerable though the provision for those brought within scope may be in many respects. In England by contrast, the *Further and Higher Education Act 1992* required the Further Education Funding Council 'to have regard' to students with learning difficulties in all aspects of discharging its responsibilities. The more we have examined the implications that follow from this formulation, coupled with the requirement that further education should be 'adequate' and 'sufficient', the more we have come to appreciate how strong the foundations of an excellent further education service for such students are. Our report and its recommendations are, in an essential way, designed to reveal them and provide the blueprint for the building.

Everything we propose is within the grasp of the system if we all want it enough, because its full growth or its seeds are already present somewhere: we are not recommending an idealistic dream, but the reality of extending widely the high quality which already exists in pockets, locked in the minds and actions of the few who must become the many.

Postscript

'Reports are not self-executive', Florence Nightingale, an energetic writer of reports for government, continually reminded herself. And indeed some good reports have only gathered dust and some good ideas in others have not been taken up.

We urge that if the Council sees merit in some or all of our analysis and recommendations, it will set up mechanisms to attend to their implementation. Every step needs not only resourcing, but monitoring and evaluating so that we learn from our new experiences. It is the strength of an executive agency that it has executive authority.

John Tomlinson

John Tomlinson
June 1996

References

Beachcroft Stanleys (1996) *Duties and Powers: The Law Governing the Provision of Further Education to Students with Learning Difficulties and/or Disabilities: A Report to the Learning Difficulties and/or Disabilities Committee*, London, HMSO

Bradley, J., L. Dee and F. Wilenius (1994) *Students with Disabilities and/or Learning Difficulties in Further Education: A Review of Research Carried out by the National Foundation for Educational Research*, Slough, National Foundation for Educational Research

Bristow, A. (1976) *Inside the Colleges of Further Education*, London, HMSO

Stafford, D.V. (1987) *A Special Professionalism: Report of the Further Education Special Needs Teacher Training Working Group*, London, HMSO

HMSO (1978) *Special Educational Needs. Report of the Committee of Enquiry into the Education of Handicapped Children and Young People* (Warnock Report), London, HMSO, Cmnd 7212

Institute of Manpower Studies (1995), *Equality for Employment Targets: A Consultative Document*

Johnstone, D. (1995) *Further Opportunities: Learning Difficulties and Disabilities in Further Education*, London, Cassell

Meager, Nigel, Ceri Evans and Sally Dench (of The Institute for Employment Studies) (1996) *Mapping Provision: The Provision of and Participation in Further Education by Students with Learning Difficulties and/or Disabilities: A Report to the Learning Difficulties and/or Disabilities Committee*, London, HMSO

SCPR (1996) *Student Voices: The Views of Further Education Students with Learning Difficulties and/or Disabilities: Findings from a Series of Student Workshops Commissioned by the Learning Difficulties and/or Disabilities Committee*, London, Skill: National Bureau for Students with Disabilities

Sly, Frances, Robert Duxbury and Christine Tillsley (1995) *Disability and the Labour Market: Findings from the Labour Force Survey*, London, HMSO

Stowell, R. (1987) *Catching up? Provision for Students with Special Educational Needs in Further and Higher Education*, London, NBHS/DES.

PART ONE

Framework and Findings

Chapter 1: Main Findings and Rationale

In this chapter, the committee describes its terms of reference; the early work by the Council and its concerns; the committee's evidence strategy; and the committee's main findings. The committee argues that the weaknesses it finds in the quantity and quality of provision can be explained in part by the history of the provision; and that the weaknesses can only be addressed if there is a renewed focus on learning.

INTRODUCTION

1.1 The decision to set up the committee was one of the earliest taken by the Council. In doing so, the Council recognised:

- extensive public concern and expectations about the learning opportunities available for these students, expressed in particular during the passage of the *Further and Higher Education Act 1992* (the Act)
- the challenge and opportunity presented by that new legislation
- the new national remit of the Council, in place of over 100 local education authorities
- specific statutory duties upon the Council to 'have regard' to the requirements of students with learning difficulties and/or disabilities and guidance from the-then secretary of state that the Council should seek expert advice where necessary
- the paucity of robust information about the number of students taking part and the nature of their learning experiences.

1.2 The committee's brief was designed to help the Council respond to those concerns and take advantage, on behalf of the students and colleges, of the changes introduced by the Act. The committee's terms of reference were:

> *Having regard to the Council's responsibilities towards students with learning difficulties and/or disabilities, to review the range and type of further education provision available, and to make recommendations as to how, within the resources likely to be available to it, the Further Education Funding Council can, by working with colleges and others, best fulfil its responsibilities towards these students under the Further and Higher Education Act 1992.*

1.3 From the start, the Council has been concerned to ensure that its emerging policies and procedures took proper account of the requirements of students with learning difficulties and/or disabilities. Most of its circulars make reference to these students, as do the inspection framework and funding methodology. However, the Council wanted to take a strategic view, that would look beyond the necessary imperatives of starting up a new organisation with a new sector, to the longer term. This view would need to be based on firm evidence and expert opinion. In setting up the committee, the Council was conscious first that no national examination of further education for students with learning difficulties and/or disabilities had previously been undertaken. Although considerable reference to young people is made in the Warnock Report ('the education of etc.'), this report was produced in 1978,

1

and focused on schools. The legislation which followed did not include further education within its provisions. Secondly, the Council was conscious that there was no systematic, comprehensive evidence about the number of participants or the extent of their participation on which its emerging policies could be based.

1.4 To support the Council's wish to be able to take a strategic view, the committee put in place a comprehensive evidence base. The committee was able to draw not only on the evidence collected by or on behalf of the committee itself, but also on the Council's data collections. Here, the committee was particularly fortunate in being able to draw upon the first-ever national data about participation and the first-ever information derived from a national programme of inspections of the quality of teaching and learning in further education, drawn from a single, comprehensive and public inspection framework. In putting together its evidence base, the committee was particularly committed to ensuring that students with learning difficulties and/or disabilities could express their views and describe their experiences. The committee's evidence base included:

- over 1,000 responses to its *Call for Evidence*[1] from students, parents, advocates, colleges, local and national organisations
- a published report of a workshop series[2] for students, in which nearly 300 took part across the country
- presentations from Council staff on aspects of the Council's arrangements, including its inspection framework, funding methodology and regional committees
- evidence drawn from some 200 inspection reports by the Council's inspectorate of the quality of provision in sector colleges and specialist colleges outside the sector
- formal evidence from government agencies, national organisations and colleges, including the Office for Standards in Education (OFSTED), the Department for Education and Employment (DfEE), the National Institute for Adult Continuing Education (NIACE), the Association of National Specialist Colleges (NATSPEC), the Further Education Unit (FEU) and Rathbone C.I.
- a review of the literature and research commissioned from the National Foundation for Educational Research and published in November 1994[3]
- a review of the relevant legal duties and powers, commissioned from the Council's legal advisers[4]
- a map of provision and participation commissioned from the Institute for Employment Studies (IES)[5]
- a project to test the committee's thinking about learning, with a sample of colleges described in chapter 2 and the appendix to annex D to this report
- visits to Scotland, Canada and the USA
- seminars to consider enabling technology, and the perspective of parents and advocacy organisations; and to discuss a focus on learning with practitioners and college managers
- visits to schools, specialist colleges and sector colleges.

OUR MAIN FINDINGS

1.5 The committee found some outstanding examples of good practice. We met many students who are making good progress, gaining relevant and purposeful achievements, and enjoying their work. We talked to committed staff who have relevant experience and who work in well-managed colleges where there is a clear vision for the future of provision for students with learning difficulties and/or disabilities. We found some evidence that the opportunities for these students engaged in further education have increased in recent years, in part because of the arrangements put in place by the Council, but also as a result of sustained efforts by parents, voluntary organisations, advocacy groups, local authorities, teachers and managers in colleges.

1.6 Overall, however, the committee found that, in comparison with their peers:

- the learning opportunities for these students are of poorer quality
- some groups of learners are not yet properly represented in further education.

We say more about each of these below, together with an explanation for our findings.

The quality of learning opportunities is poorer than for other students

1.7 Our first main finding is that, for too many students, the range of programmes does not meet their requirements and does not compare satisfactorily with their peers. Students themselves described some poor learning opportunities. They told us:

> *We are taught as a whole class instead of as individual students, everyone hurrying to catch up or waiting for the rest.*
>
> *I am really confused because all the teachers teach us different ways of doing the same things.*
> *When I have a problem, the teacher says, 'get on, I have taught you how to do that three times already'.*
>
> *The teacher doesn't understand my difficulties in learning. For example, I don't understand plans, diagrams and graphs.*
>
> *We are always given worksheets — some of the words I cannot read or understand. My folder is full of unfinished worksheets and my work is never marked, so I don't know how to make my work better. Nobody cares if you don't finish. The teacher always says my work is 'good' however hard I try.*
>
> *The teacher won't let me do the sums my way — we always have to do it her way.*
>
> *The support assistant doesn't understand why I can't add up, so she just does the sums for me.*
>
> *I learn well in some lessons, but the teachers do not tell each other how I learn best, so in some lessons I do not learn at all.*

Some groups of learners with learning difficulties and/or disabilities are not yet properly represented in further education

1.8 We found that, in total, the volume of learning opportunities in further education is broadly enough for those students with learning difficulties and/or disabilities who apply for a college place. The overall pattern of provision is encouraging and has expanded although there can be significant local variation.[6] In 1995, colleges estimated that some 126,500 students with learning difficulties and/or disabilities were enrolled. This averaged about 300 students per college and about 5.3% of all students enrolled in sector colleges.[7] We think this is about three times the number of students identified in 1985, when a count was last made, although it is difficult to draw valid comparisons because of changes in the composition of the colleges being counted.

1.9 Our second main finding, however, is that some groups of learners are not yet properly represented in further education. These are:

- young people with emotional and behavioural difficulties, some of whom will have been excluded from school or who will have excluded themselves from school
- adults with mental health difficulties, some of whom will come within the scope of care in the community

provisions and may be seeking formal education for the first time in their adult lives

- people with profound and multiple learning difficulties. For these students, expectations are now higher, particularly since they have benefited from the introduction of the national curriculum. In addition, technological advances as well as the growing skills of teachers increasingly make further education a realistic possibility.

EXPLAINING OUR FINDINGS

1.10 We were told that, until recently, there has been a tradition in this area of work for it to be regarded as satisfactory for students with learning difficulties and disabilities simply to attend college and to be grateful for the opportunity. Few checks were made on the quality of the courses. Teachers were rarely asked to account for what they did. The work seldom featured in college-wide procedures and systems of strategic planning, quality assurance, data collection and analysis. Data about students' achievement rates and destinations were hardly ever systematically collected, analysed or used for planning. Few questions were asked about the purpose and relevance of what students with learning difficulties and disabilities were being asked to learn. Managers often lacked awareness and understanding of this work and left staff to get on with their work with no strategic direction and little management of the quality of provision, believing that the staff knew best about what to provide for students. Frequently, no overall goal was set for students' programmes. The standards for the students' work, the quality of teaching and learning and students' achievements were rarely monitored.

1.11 Looking at the evidence we found, we were not surprised that the Council's inspectorate told us that the grades for this area of work were generally lower than in any other. We did find good provision with skilled teachers and knowledgeable managers. Nonetheless, we are greatly concerned with the overall quality of provision nationally.

1.12 We considered how far the serious shortcomings which we found are primarily operational weaknesses, how far they reflect the inevitable evolution of practice or how far they are isolated examples within a further education system which is otherwise working well. We began our work by exploring whether we could effect improvements in the existing arrangements, such as, more guidance to colleges or minor modifications to the Council's arrangements. We make recommendations later about these modifications and improvements in our report.

1.13 However, we concluded that any such improvements would be marginal, short term and would not bring about the fundamental improvement necessary in the quality or quantity of student learning opportunities. Those necessary improvements can be effected only, in our view, if there is first a fundamental exploration of teaching and learning. This is because, without such an exploration, any operational changes would have no obvious purpose or direction. As such, these changes will inevitably fail to address the weaknesses which we found.

1.14 We reached this view by thinking carefully about the reasons for the weaknesses we found in the further education provision and the history of the provision we were asked to review. We describe that history in annex E. The most significant feature of that history is that many colleges have come to and still today organise and deliver their provision for students with learning difficulties and/or disabilities in the intellectual, social and educational climate established by the Warnock Report. The Warnock Report revolutionised thinking about education for young people and undoubtedly led to significant improvements in the opportunities available to young people with learning difficulties and/or disabilities. It paved the way for landmark legislation by introducing the concept of 'special educational needs'. We noted two particular features of the Warnock Report. These are, first, that it sought to shift the definitions of those with learning difficulties and/or disabilities away from a medically-derived set of categories which then almost automatically determined the education that was to be offered. Secondly, the report focused on removing barriers to education. The report noted:

> *Broadly, our task has been to consider how teaching and learning can best be brought about wherever there are children who have particular obstacles to overcome, whether these are primarily physical, sensory, intellectual or emotional.*[8]

1.15 Rather than regarding children in pre-defined categories against which their education would then be delivered, the report referred to 'additional help':

> *Our concept of special education is thus broader than the traditional one of education by special methods appropriate for particular categories of children. It extends beyond the idea of education provided in special schools, special classes or units for children with particular types of disability, and embraces the notion of any form of additional help, wherever it is provided and whenever it is provided, from birth to maturity, to overcome educational difficulty. It also embodies the idea that, although the difficulties which some children encounter may dictate WHAT they have to be taught and the disabilities of some HOW they have to be taught, the point of their education is the same.*[9]

1.16 The revolution in thinking encapsulated in the report and enshrined in the *Education Act 1981* was fundamental. Without a doubt, the report and legislation have improved the range and quality of learning opportunities for those with 'special educational needs'. Many of the children who first gained from the implementation of the report are now in further education.

1.17 The prevailing philosophy of the Warnock Report continues to be reflected in legislation. The *Further and Higher Education Act 1992* requires the Council to 'have regard' to the requirements of students who have a 'significantly greater difficulty in learning than the majority of persons of [their] age' or for whom the facilities usually provided are not accessible. This kind of thinking was reflected, too, in the letter of guidance from the secretary of state to the Council in 1992, in which he asked the Council to ensure that learning difficulties would be 'no bar to access' to further education. Most of the Council's — and colleges' — energies have rightly been devoted to removing the barriers in order to make further education more effective for these students and the system more efficient.

1.18 The Warnock Report and subsequent legislation succeeded in redefining those who needed different provision or extra help with their education. However, the educational philosophy and practices which were established by the report and legislation remained based on identifying the differences between students. This philosophy and practice required distinctions to be made between the relative ease which individuals have in their learning. In practice, this led to a concentration of effort by schools and colleges on removing barriers to learning. Although the evidence presented to us suggested strongly that it was essential to remove these barriers, this work has not led to the quality or quantity of opportunities that are needed today.

1.19 These opportunities are no longer good enough. We concluded that, no matter how much effort is directed at removing barriers, whether these barriers are physical, or to do with the curriculum or teacher understanding, these efforts will not be sufficient. What is required is a fundamental re-examination of *learning.* This must replace an emphasis on understanding and remediating learning *difficulties.* Instead of looking at the difficulties facing an individual, therefore, we decided we needed to examine the environment in which learning could best take place.

THE COMMITTEE'S RATIONALE

FOCUSING ON LEARNING AND THE LEARNING ENVIRONMENT

1.20 We thought carefully about the nature of learning and the environment within which it takes place. We tried to:

- identify how individual students learn best
- identify the individual environment in which a student can learn best.

1.21 The evidence we collected from students, their advocates, colleges, voluntary organisations, agencies and the Council's own inspectorate indicated that much of the poorer provision for students with learning difficulties and/or disabilities is disorganised and fragmented. Too often it is planned in isolation from other further education. Different expectations are too often held of the students, and different standards are used to assess their achievements. Frequently the college has not taken a college-wide approach to the management of students' learning. These factors result in poor-quality learning experiences which are often ineffective for students; which make poor use of human and physical resources; and which do not rest firmly on what students already know, understand and can do.

1.22 In order to build on the strengths of the best provision and to address the weaknesses, we consider that learning opportunities for students with learning difficulties and/or disabilities must in future be characterised by:

- systematic planning and organisation, which includes provision for these students as part of the college's everyday activities and as part of the college's overall management and delivery of learning
- expectations, standards and the quality of learning experiences which are the same for all students.

1.23 We believe that learning can only be fully effective if it is inclusive. We explain what we mean by this term in chapter 2. In the remainder of the report, we explore the changes that are necessary within colleges to the Council's arrangements on the part of other agencies to ensure that learning can be inclusive. We also explore the safeguards which the Council and colleges need to strengthen or put in place to protect the particular interests of students with learning difficulties and/or disabilities.

BENEFITS OF LEARNING WHICH IS INCLUSIVE

1.24 We are convinced that focusing on learning in the way we describe will achieve essential benefits for individuals and the national economy. The further education sector is the main provider of vocational education and training. A succession of white papers on the nation's competitive position as well as the national training and education targets and the recent skills audit[10] demonstrate the importance of investing in peoples' skills. This investment generates economic prosperity both for the individual and for society.

1.25 The need for and benefits from this investment are no different for people with learning difficulties and/or disabilities. The Organisation for Economic Cooperation and Development (OECD) has examined the main indicators of adult status, by which it means the attributes and abilities necessary to live with some independence as an adult. The OECD has argued for many years that the legitimate aspirations of people with learning difficulties and/or disabilities can only be realised if they can achieve some or all of the attributes of adult status. These include personal autonomy, social and community interaction, appropriate family roles and a productive working life leading to economic self-sufficiency.[11]

1.26 For people with learning difficulties and/or disabilities, the importance of learning and qualifications which extend and build on their abilities is particularly high. We found that people with disabilities are more likely to be unemployed than others.[12] They are therefore less likely to attain or maintain the attributes of adult status. They are less likely than other people to have educational qualifications, but those people with disabilities who are in work are more likely to have such qualifications. This suggests that, for people with learning difficulties and/or disabilities, obtaining a qualification is even more significant to their chances of gaining productive employment than it is for the rest of the population. In addition, we found that the costs of the dependency to the nation, setting aside the costs to the individual, of those people with learning difficulties and/or disabilities, are higher than of those without. The costs of dependency to the nation includes benefits and allowances as well as foregone taxation. Ensuring that there are as many opportunities to learn and to achieve as possible is therefore an essential investment for the nation.

1.27 The challenges to prevailing theory and the corresponding changes which are necessary to prevailing practice which we set out in the remainder of this report are immense. Some colleges are already tackling these challenges. Evidence of the beneficial impact of the changes we advocate upon the quality of students' learning and achievements already exists. We saw for ourselves the contrast between effective learning experiences and those experiences where little or no learning is taking place. We illustrate this contrast in chapter 2. The colleges which took part in our exercise to test our thinking were keen to do more. Importantly, they believed that they could do more to ensure effective learning for these students. The financial and management challenges facing the further education sector are considerable and we do not wish to underestimate them. Nevertheless, we hold both to the evidence about the impact on the quality and quantity of learning which could be achieved if the thinking in this report is put into effect and to the unacceptable long-term consequences of not so doing.

STRUCTURE OF THE REPORT

1.28 The report offers a presentation of our thinking about inclusive learning and a presentation of evidence, practical ideas and recommendations to improve the quantity and quality of opportunities for effective learning. In chapter 2, we set out our thinking about learning in more detail. Chapter 3 describes the legal context for the application of this thinking, since we needed first to be sure about the minimum standards to be met by further education and the Council; and secondly, how far we could seek to extend those standards within the framework established by the *Further and Higher Education Act 1992*.

1.29 Each of the remaining chapters 4 to 12 includes:

- the issues
- the committee's principles
- evidence which might indicate the adoption of those principles
- examples of good and bad practice
- summary of main findings
- addressing weaknesses and building on strengths
- recommendations.

1.30 We hope that the analysis that follows will be persuasive. It is based on evidence, much of which has been collected for the first time by the committee. We hope that the evidence, and perhaps particularly the voices of students with whom this chapter started, will convince readers of the report of the case for change.

References

1 FEFC *Disability and Learning Difficulties and Further Education: Call for Evidence from the FEFC Committee*, Coventry, FEFC, 1994

2 SCPR *Student Voices: The Views of Further Education Students with Learning Difficulties and/or Disabilities: Findings From a Series of Student Workshops Commissioned by the Learning Difficulties and/or Disabilities Committee,* London, Skill: National Bureau for Students with Disabilities, 1996

3 J. Bradley, L. Dee and F. Wilenius *Students with Disabilities and/or Learning Difficulties in Further Education; A Review of Research Carried out by the National Foundation for Educational Research*, Slough, NFER, 1994

4 Beachcroft Stanleys *Duties and Powers: The Law Governing the Provision of Further Education to Students with Learning Difficulties and/or Disabilities: A Report to the Learning Difficulties and/or Disabilities Committee*, London, HMSO, 1996

5 Meager, Nigel, Ceri Evans and Sally Dench (of The Institute for Employment Studies) *Mapping Provision: The Provision of and Participation in Further Education by Students with Learning Difficulties and/or Disabilities: A Report to the Learning Difficulties and/or Disabilities Committee*, London, HMSO, 1996

6 Stowell, Richard *Catching Up? Provision for Students with Special Educational Needs in Further and Higher Education*, London, NBHS/DES, 1987

7 Figures taken from the data returned to IES and then calculated for whole sector. Includes some specially designated colleges. The IES study used November 1995 college figures and estimated between 5.3 and 5.7%. The Council's analysis of data from the November 1995 ISR return estimated a student population in colleges of 2,389,700, making the 126,500 IES estimate of students with disabilities/learning difficulties some 5.29% of the total.

8 *Special Educational Needs. Report of the Committee of Enquiry into the Education of Handicapped Children and Young People* (the Warnock Report), London, HMSO, 1978

9 *Ibid.*

10 *Competitiveness: Forging Ahead,* London, HMSO, May 1995; *Competitiveness: Helping Business to Win,* London, HMSO, May 1994; *Competitiveness: Creating the Enterprise Centre of Europe,* London, HMSO, 1996

11 *Disabled Youth: The Right to Status,* OECD-CERI, Paris, 1988

12 *Equality in Employment Targets: A Consultation Paper,* TEC National Council, London, 1994

Chapter 2: Inclusive Learning

In this chapter, the committee describes its thinking about inclusive learning, and looks at how a focus on inclusive learning will improve the quality of learning for students with learning difficulties and/or disabilities. There is also discussion of how this focus will make participation in further education more inclusive, and what the implications of the committee's thinking are for colleges, teachers, learners, and the Council. Finally, the committee looks at how to combine inclusive learning with the continued need to allocate resources for students with learning difficulties and/or disabilities and to monitor the level and quality of their participation in further education.

MEANING OF 'INCLUSIVE LEARNING'

2.1 We argued in chapter 1 that the necessary improvement to the quantity and quality of learning opportunities for students with learning difficulties and/or disabilities can only be brought about through a new focus on learning. Considerable attention has been given by committed teachers, by the Council and by others, to understand and remove the difficulties and impediments to learning experienced by some 20% of learners. Despite this attention, there has not been a corresponding improvement in the quality of learning by these students. Rather than focusing again on the 20% of students who might, at any one time, have learning difficulties and/or disabilities, and yet again on what makes them 'different' from, or more 'special' than, other learners, we looked more closely at taken-for-granted assumptions about how *all* learners learn. This examination is not intended to deny the likely implications of a disability or learning difficulty for a person's learning. But focusing solely on these implications has not worked. We want to challenge the idea of the 'average learner'. The growing number of so-called 'non-traditional' students in colleges, including those with learning difficulties and/or disabilities, require non-traditional, new responses. These responses must include not only changes to structures and procedures, but also a shift in the relationship between teacher and learner.

2.2 Colleges, teachers and others need a greater understanding of how individuals learn and how pedagogy can best match an individual's particular approach to learning. We consider that this understanding can be achieved best by a focus on the learner, and on their learning goals, in a learning environment. If this understanding permeates the classroom, college and further education as a whole, then we believe that learning opportunities will themselves become more inclusive.

2.3 Inclusive learning is a way of thinking about further education that uses a revitalised understanding of learning and the learner's requirements as its starting-point. What the teacher does, what the college does, and what the sector does should be informed and shaped by this understanding. The aim is not for students simply to 'take part' in further education but to be actively included and fully engaged in their learning. At the heart of our thinking lies the idea of 'match' or 'fit' between how the learner learns best, what they need and want to learn, and what is required from the sector, a college and teachers for successful learning to take place. By 'inclusive learning' therefore, we mean the greatest degree of match or fit between the individual learner's requirements and the provision that is made for them.

COMPONENTS OF INCLUSIVE LEARNING

Learners and their requirements

2.4 A learner is someone who is engaged in planned activities which enable them to acquire and develop knowledge, skills and understanding. The extent to which the learner acquires knowledge, skills and understanding is measured by their performance in these activities. In further education, these activities relate to a wide range of provision, including vocational courses, general education, basic skills such as numeracy and literacy, and recreational and leisure courses.

2.5 Educational theorists have described the different ways in which individuals make sense of the world which lead each of us to approach learning differently.[1] This is not to say that the physical or chemical processes of learning differ from person to person. Each individual uses the same processes even when these may function differently, for example, short- and long-term memory, spatial and temporal awareness or the capacity to concentrate. But these theorists argue that each individual has a tendency to learn best in a certain way, using a particular set of tools or processes. The most effective learning takes place when teaching activities and stimuli take account of and lead to the further development of the individual's understanding of the world. Different ways of engaging the learner; different modes of repetition and reinforcement, different styles of teaching and different strategies for providing support for learning can assist the acceptance, retention and retrieval of information by learners with different kinds of intellectual and physical skills. The teacher has the key responsibility of deciding which learning and teaching methods best fit the student's learning requirements.

Learning goals

2.6 Further education colleges are places where people learn. Teachers should find out all they can about the variety of approaches to learning deployed by their students and about these students' prior experiences of learning. This applies regardless of whether the students have a learning difficulty and/or disability. Teachers need to ascertain what the student already knows, understands and can do. They then need to identify new learning goals which would be discussed and agreed with the learner. These goals would vary in their scope and timescale according to the learner's requirements. Some might be reached over a year; others might be achieved in a few weeks. Learning goals would depend on what an individual needed and wanted to learn at that particular point in their lives. We discuss how colleges can assess students' requirements in chapter 5.

Learning environment

2.7 Once the learner's individual style of learning is understood, learning goals agreed and the new learning goals identified, then the next stage can begin. This is the construction of a learning environment that matches or fits the student's learning requirements as closely as possible. The components of the learning environment make up an individually-tailored package of processes, equipment, teaching, the physical environment and so on, which enable the learner to engage actively in their learning. We needed a term which would describe the components essential to a good-quality experience of learning. It needed to refer to the physical components such as learning technology, wheelchair access, library and private study areas, the human components such as classroom assistants, support workers and the curriculum, teaching methods and assessment and accreditation procedures. Most of all, the term should encompass the training and insight of teachers. Although 'learning experiences' is a commonly used term, it seemed to take too much for granted and focus only on the student's capacity to receive what was offered. We use the term 'learning environment' because it comes nearest, in ordinary language, to the idea of a 'learning eco-system'. An individual learning environment would have the following components:

- an individual learning programme
- a curriculum which promotes progress in learning
- effective teaching
- entry and exit procedures, for example counselling and guidance and initial assessment
- opportunities for students to discuss and manage their own learning
- support for learning
- learner support, for example creche facilities
- procedures for assessing, recording and accrediting achievement
- learning materials and resources
- technical aids and equipment
- learning technology
- trained staff
- physical surroundings, for example teaching rooms, canteen, library.

2.8 Support for learning remains an essential component of the learning environment. We say more about this and other aspects of the learning environment in the rest of the report.

The match

2.9 The concept of inclusive learning moves beyond thinking about each of the components of a learning environment as being more or less 'appropriate' to the learner's requirements or about trying to overcome particular barriers to learning. Instead, it concentrates on the idea of 'the match', that is, the degree of fit or correspondence between the learner's individual requirements and the components of the learning environment. In order to bring the match about, some learners might have more time or resources allocated to certain components than other learners.

2.10 It would be possible to decide if each individual component of the learning environment contributed to the match to the individual's requirements. It would also be possible to assess how well each of the components fitted together to form a learning environment that matched the learner's requirements.

2.11 For learners' requirements to be met cost effectively and efficiently, there must be a match at three levels:

- *between the teacher and learner;* by using pedagogy and materials to match the individual's approach to learning and enable them to achieve their learning goals
- *between the college and the learner;* by providing individual learning environments which match the requirements of a wide variety of learners
- *between further education as a whole and the learner;* by providing adequate and sufficient provision which matches the number and individual requirements of those who might participate in further education.

It is not sufficient for the match to be provided at one level; the whole of the system must work toward this goal.

2

2.12 We illustrate what we mean by a good match in the following descriptions of Sarah and Sanjit and their individual learning environments. We illustrate a poor match in the description of Tom and his learning environment. Where Tom is concerned:

- the sector failed to provide effective arrangements to support his transition from school to college
- insufficient information about his learning requirements was passed from his school to the college
- the college did not assess how Tom learnt best and did not assist him to identify realistic learning goals.

As a consequence:

- Tom is asked to undertake inappropriate theoretical work
- his skills to work independently have not been developed
- Tom's teachers have identified his difficulties but they have not developed strategies which enable him to tackle them.

Where Sarah and Sanjit are concerned:

- the sector has provided flexible funding arrangements for the provision of the right learning environment
- the college matched the pace and scope of its assessment to the pace and nature of Sarah's and Sanjit's learning
- the college involves Sarah's parents in reinforcing her learning
- Sarah's teachers use the outcomes of careful observation to understand how she learns best
- her teachers use this understanding to adapt their teaching methods and materials
- the college takes Sanjit's views about the support available seriously
- his college uses his experience to improve the organisation of learning support.

Sanjit

Sanjit is 19 and completing the first year of a GCE A level Art and Design course after achieving high grades in eight GCSEs. He wants to be a commercial designer. A work experience placement in a commercial studio during his last year at school helped Sanjit to understand different customer requirements. Sanjit is almost totally deaf as a consequence of meningitis when he was four years old. He has some residual hearing in the higher registers. Sanjit's speech can be difficult to understand and he finds it easier and less tiring to use British Sign Language (BSL) to communicate. He enjoys using BSL with great speed and wit. For the last two years of his schooling, Sanjit attended a unit for pupils with hearing impairment based in a local comprehensive school. He improved his lip-reading there and spent some time each week working alongside hearing pupils. However, he finds it tiring to lip-read for too long and too much noise or movement distracts him. Sanjit often encounters new concepts and vocabulary for the first time in writing. This sometimes means that he uses words inappropriately when he speaks or has difficulty understanding their meaning in written work unless they are explained to him. Sanjit often mis-spells the endings of words or uses the wrong tense of a verb when he is writing. Sanjit belongs to a local group of young deaf people and enjoys spending his leisure time with other deaf students.

A learning environment that matches Sanjit's requirements

The college has a tradition of working successfully with students who are deaf and has a deaf vice-principal. There is a trained teacher of the deaf and two trained interpreters on the staff. In his last year at school, Sanjit took part in a short bridging course run jointly by the college and the unit for pupils with hearing impairment. During this, he was assessed in order to find out what support he would require for his A level course. Sanjit has a support plan which is reviewed twice a term. He asked for some help in making the transition to a large college. At present, he has two tutorial sessions each week with an interpreter who is a trained counsellor specialising in working with deaf people. In addition, Sanjit and other students who are deaf attend communication skills classes given by the teacher of the deaf. They provide opportunities for Sanjit to practice his lip-reading and to develop new strategies for getting to grips with a hearing environment. Sanjit is encouraged to give his views about his support arrangements and has recently decided that he did not require an interpreter for practical art lessons. This is because the teacher is learning BSL and the calm working environment and good lighting make lip-reading easy. For theoretical lessons, Sanjit shares an interpreter with two other deaf students. This works well because the interpreter is following the same course in order to understand the main concepts and so be able to explain them. Teachers prepare written notes a week in advance and Sanjit uses some of his additional support time to go through any new vocabulary with his interpreter. He uses a computer for most of his written work and checks tenses and endings of words with the interpreter. Last term, Sanjit prepared a training video with a group of other deaf students as part of a practical assignment. The video uses humorous examples to explain how teachers can best take account of deaf students' requirements. It has already been used in the college's induction programme for new staff. Sanjit is an enthusiastic member of the college football team. The team has worked out a system of hand-signals and touch to communicate whilst they are on the pitch. Two or three members have started to learn BSL.

EXAMPLES

Sarah

Sarah is 18 years old and recently left the special care unit of the school she attended since she was five. She established good relationships with her teachers and grew particularly close to one of the classroom assistants. Sarah is a much-loved sister to two younger brothers and plays a central part in the life of her family. She particularly enjoys visits to her grandmother who lives by the sea. Until she left school, Sarah lived at home. Sarah has a progressive neurological disorder which has resulted in profound intellectual impairment and severe physical disabilities. She has learnt to express most of her needs, dislikes and likes through facial expressions and head movements. In addition, she has a spoken vocabulary of six or seven words, including her own name and those of her brothers. Sarah has a progressive visual impairment. She tires easily and has a short attention span. Sarah relies on other people for all her everyday requirements and has received regular physiotherapy, hydrotherapy and speech therapy at school. She uses a wheelchair to move around, with the support of an assistant. Sarah has learnt to use an adapted computer and can activate equipment in the college's sensory room by using a sensitive switch device.

A learning environment that matches Sarah's requirements

Sarah is at the end of her first term at a specialist residential college which provides the learning environment she requires. During the first three months, her cognitive, communication, emotional and physical development and social behaviour has been assessed and an individual programme devised and agreed with her parents. The longer-term aims of her further education have also been agreed though the staff know that these may well change as Sarah's condition progresses. Each member of the staff team understands the role they must play to help Sarah achieve learning goals which are set on a six-weekly basis. Sarah's key worker convenes regular meetings where her progress is reviewed and new goals agreed. Her parents are welcome to attend the meetings and they report on Sarah's progress during weekends and holidays when they find opportunities to reinforce her new learning during domestic and family activities. Sarah's teachers have devised a learning programme which concentrates on extending Sarah's ability to communicate her wishes, likes and dislikes in a number of new situations. Sarah aims to learn the names of her class teacher and key worker. She will also work on her capacity to distinguish objects through touch and smell, using equipment in the sensory room to assist her. Music and aromatherapy are used to help Sarah to relax, thereby increasing her capacity to concentrate and learn. Teaching staff work with Sarah in short, intensive and frequent bursts of activity and her day is structured so that these take place in the morning when she is least tired. Occupational therapists, physiotherapists and care workers reinforce Sarah's new learning by, for example, encouraging her to express her wishes during therapy or personal care sessions. All staff talk to Sarah whilst they are with her, using her name frequently. They take care to ensure a calm, quiet environment which makes it possible for trained staff to interpret Sarah's different methods of communicating. Sarah's progress is recorded after each session. The teaching staff use carefully designed record sheets which describe Sarah's overall learning goals for a six-week period, their breakdown into small units of learning and the activities which will be used to teach each unit. Successful activities and any blocks to learning are identified. For example, staff recently found out that Sarah becomes sleepy and loses concentration if she is cold. Care is now taken to ensure that she sits away from draughty windows or doors. Sarah uses a national record of achievement to record significant successes, for example a first journey on a train earlier in the term was recorded with large photographs and an audio-tape of the noise made by the train. Sarah brought the record of achievement with her from school, together with a folder describing the meaning of each of the signs she uses to communicate. The folder is in a bag attached to Sarah's wheelchair and goes everywhere with her.

Tom

Tom is 20 and has just left the special school he has attended since the age of two. His ambition is to work in a restaurant and he has come to college to achieve a catering qualification. A Saturday job in his uncle's cafe has given him useful experience in serving customers and assisting in the kitchen. His uncle has trained Tom to use the till and he handles money with confidence. Customers and other staff value him for his cheerfulness and his willingness to try new tasks. Tom has Down's Syndrome. He can read five or six words and write his name and manage simple additions and subtractions using counters. He is able to tell the time and can estimate accurately the amount of time it will take to do something. The concepts of weight and measurement are difficult for him to understand and he has not learnt yet how to use a ruler or scales. If tasks are broken down into small steps and carefully explained to him, Tom is able to work independently. Sometimes, his slight speech impediment makes it difficult for him to get his point of view across in discussion. This is frustrating for him, and he prefers to talk to one or two people at a time. Tom tires easily and finds it difficult to concentrate for long periods. Tom has not travelled on a bus alone. Tom does not have a girlfriend but thinks college might be the place where he can meet new people and perhaps start a relationship.

A learning environment that fails to match Tom's requirements

Tom visited college for an afternoon during his last term at school. He decided to join an NVQ level 1 catering course and the college has provided two or three hours a week of additional literacy support. Tom is the only student with severe learning difficulties in his group. He is popular with the other students because he is always willing to do what they want to do. The catering tutor produces a weekly checklist of the practical kitchen activities Tom must complete and carefully directs Tom from task to task. Tom does not begin a new activity until he receives an instruction. Tom copies from the board a description of each activity into his own record book. Tom always stands next to the teacher for practical activities and copies what she does. When she moves around the room he waits quietly for her to return and tell him what to do. Other students help him to weigh and measure ingredients. During a recent review of Tom's progress, his numeracy teacher identified his continuing difficulty with weighing and measuring. Theoretical work often consists of question and answer sessions which involve all members of the group. Tom is generally silent during these. His teacher believes that he is shy and rather slower than the others. She thinks he is not ready yet for a work experience placement. Overall, she believes that Tom may be on the wrong course. Tom is losing some of the improvement he gained in his speech at school where he had regular speech therapy. Tom attends a literacy workshop for a two-hour session each week where he uses the same materials as adults with literacy and numeracy difficulties. A recent assessment indicated that Tom was losing interest in improving his literacy skills. He also forgot any new learning in the time between sessions. Tom is brought to college by his mother and collected by his father. A travel training programme had been organised for Tom but his parents refused permission for him to take part when they realised that, in the first session, Tom was to travel to the city by train on his own. Instead, Tom has classroom sessions which concentrate on the use of maps. Tom has difficulty in understanding the symbolic representation of places and their relationships that maps represent. Sex education for Tom's group is provided by a worker from a local youth organisation. After five or six sessions, the worker discovered that Tom is unsure of the names and location of parts of the body.

2

2.13 As these examples illustrate, inclusive learning means that students are actively engaged in their learning, rather than being the passive recipients of information. Inclusive learning places a new responsibility on the teacher for close observation, skilled assessment and active intervention, resulting in a fundamental analysis of how individuals learn and how teachers should respond. This analysis includes:

- understanding the effects of an individual's cultural, social and personal experiences, including any disability or learning difficulty, on what and how they learn
- observing and analysing the strategies that individuals use to approach learning tasks
- assisting learners to evaluate their strategies and to select effective ones
- choosing tasks which help learners to expand their range of learning strategies
- managing learning in ways which allow a choice of learning strategies and which enable learners to make constructive use of errors
- understanding and taking account of learners' longer-term goals and aspirations when choosing learning tasks
- evaluating the match between a student's changing requirements and the learning environment that is provided
- adjusting the components of the learning environment so that the match is more effective
- observing, assessing and recording progress and achievement including the small steps of progress and achievement made by some learners.

2.14 Inclusive learning differs from student-centred learning although it builds upon some of the strengths of this philosophy, in that it requires a close attention to the individual learner. Student-centred learning concentrates on learning by experience and uses the teacher's understanding of the student's cultural, social and personal background as a starting-point for the provision of new but associated experiences. Although this kind of learning confirms the importance of understanding the student's level of cognitive development, it stresses non-interference by the teacher and a view of teaching as a process of 'drawing out' knowledge, skills and understanding from the learner.[2]

2.15 The committee does not consider inclusive learning to be the same thing as 'integration' or 'including students'. The thinking represented by the term 'integration' is sometimes insufficiently concerned with the quality of a student's learning; concentrating instead on the location and social aspects of a student's educational experience. The thinking represented by the term 'including students' can sometimes assume that students should accommodate themselves to the existing structures, processes, procedures and methods of the sector, individual colleges and teachers. By contrast, the concept of inclusive learning places the greatest importance on the quality of a student's learning. The concept also shifts responsibility from the student to the sector, colleges and teachers. It is they that must fit or match themselves to students rather than the other way around. This match or fit can best be brought about by understanding more about how students learn. This understanding would then be used to determine how the sector, colleges and teachers must change in order to match students' requirements.

2.16 Inclusive learning rejects a number of preconceptions which, in our view, have dogged much of the provision for students with learning difficulties and/or disabilities and have contributed to some of the weaknesses we found during our work. These include the beliefs:

- that these students are different from all other students in the way they learn or in the amount they are capable of learning

- that these students are distinguished by experiencing greater difficulty in learning than all other students.

2.17 We found that students with learning difficulties and/or disabilities have more, rather than less, in common with other students in that all students need an individual learning environment which matches their requirements. They each use the same repertoire of processes for learning. They each bring different experiences of success or failure to the learning task and as a consequence, have developed strategies which may assist or get in the way of new learning.

2.18 Not all students with disabilities experience difficulties in learning. Many of them progress at a rate comparable, or faster, than that of their non-disabled peers. Some students, however, told us of the barriers to learning which they experienced.[3] Their perceptions were strongly supported by evidence from the Council's inspectorate, HMI, OFSTED, colleges and others. We concluded that a significant proportion of students with learning difficulties and/or disabilities do experience difficulty in their learning and that they come to further education with the expectation that learning will not be easy or successful. This is not because they learn in a 'worse' or inferior way to other students, or because of some deficiencies in the students themselves. Rather, we concluded on the basis of the evidence we received, that some students with learning difficulties and/or disabilities experience greater difficulty in learning and achieve less because there has been an insufficient match between how and what they need and want to learn and what is actually provided. Opportunities for participation, types of provision, curriculum content and delivery, assessment, accreditation and learning support do not match what these students require.

IMPLICATIONS OF INCLUSIVE LEARNING

2.19 Most of the rest of this report explores the implications for further education, colleges, students and the Council of adopting our thinking about inclusive learning. We outline some of them here.

Implications for teachers and other educators

2.20 The learner/teacher relationship is probably the most important factor in determining whether successful learning takes place. The teacher is central to the learning process. It follows that teachers' understanding of learning and their capacity to use a variety of pedagogic approaches are crucial. Teachers mediate learning in a number of ways, by undertaking initial assessment, planning a learning programme, devising learning materials and providing resources, and assessing and recording students' achievements. We found that:

- some teachers know little about the variety of ways in which people learn
- teachers' expectations of learners are significant in determining how successful learning will be.

2.21 Given the importance of the relationship between the teacher and the learner, and our concerns about some current practices, a considerable programme of staff training and development is required if inclusive learning is to be achieved.

2.22 In addition to teachers, there are many others, for example, occupational therapists, nurses, care workers, parents, workmates or work supervisors, who work with and help to educate students with learning difficulties and/or disabilities. In particular, learning programmes for people with severe learning difficulties and profound and multiple learning difficulties are often planned and implemented by a variety of people working in different settings. Students also learn from and with each other. Colleges need to work with other educators, to promote the match for the learner. We say more about the role of teachers in chapter 6.

Implications for colleges

2.23 If the committee's ideas on learning are adopted, all colleges will need to pursue a corporate approach to learning. The lead must come from senior managers in colleges. They are responsible for allocating resources, for quality assurance, and staff training and development in order to achieve good practice in teaching and learning.

2.24 There will still be a few students whose particular learning approaches and goals cannot be met within the variety of learning environments usually provided by a general college. For example, students wishing to pursue land-based studies would require the particular learning environments provided by an agricultural college. Students requiring art and design environments may need those to be provided in a specialist college. A student who requires opportunities for learning in a residential setting may have their requirements met in another type of specialist college.

2.25 Sometimes, a learning environment might cost more than can be afforded by a local college, perhaps because scarce expertise or intensive support is required or because a student requires an extended curriculum, (that is, a curriculum which provides opportunities for students to develop independence and other skills for adult life in a residential setting). Then the college has a choice. It either seeks and obtains the funds it needs to provide the right learning environment or funds are allocated for a place at a specialist college already skilled in offering this type of environment and where many of the components are already in place.

2.26 The challenge for colleges is to develop their capacity to respond to different approaches to learning and to identify individual learning goals. If colleges are to meet this challenge successfully, then teachers will need to have the ability to undertake individual assessments for all learners. From these assessments, they should be capable of devising learning environments which would match learners' requirements. Some learners will require broadly similar learning environments and may benefit from working in groups for at least some of the time.

Implications for the Council

2.27 Considerable energy has been expended within the Council and by other national and local organisations, and by parents, professionals and students themselves in ensuring that additional resources are allocated to those students with learning difficulties and/or disabilities who need them. We wish the Council to retain its important focus on these students in any review of its funding arrangements or of its other activities. Much work has gone also into ensuring that colleges provide for an increasing number of people with learning difficulties and/or disabilities. The committee debated long and hard over whether its focus on inclusive learning would be strong enough in itself to ensure that the gains made so far would be sustained. We also considered what further changes would be required to the funding methodology and other mechanisms now in place in colleges and the Council.

2.28 The main implication for the Council is how to adopt and promote a focus on inclusive learning whilst also being able to demonstrate unequivocally that it is fulfilling its legal duties to a group of students specifically identified in the *Further and Higher Education Act 1992*. If learning is genuinely inclusive, these students should be unrecognisable from other students in the way in which their learning is managed by colleges. The dilemma we faced was that unless these students were identified in some way, then it would not be possible to target resources or to monitor their participation and the quality of provision made for them. We concluded that this emphasis on inclusive learning would not in itself be enough to provide the safeguards that all the evidence indicates are still required.

2.29 The implications of promoting inclusive learning require simultaneously that the necessary safeguards are strengthened. This will ensure that students with learning difficulties and/or disabilities are treated in the same way as other students where their learning is concerned, but differently where their support requirements, participation and funding are concerned. This takes into account our own views and, more importantly, the wishes of students, colleges and others.

Implications for learners

2.30 All students will gain from the focus on inclusive learning. It offers the following benefits for learners:

- a closer match between their individual learning styles and teaching approaches
- more success in learning
- fewer experiences of failure
- greater confidence and motivation
- willingness to study more
- increased levels of achievement.

2.31 However, students with learning difficulties and/or disabilities would probably gain more benefits from inclusive learning than other students because the provision for them tends, with some exceptions, to be of poorer quality and to provide a weaker match between their requirements, goals and learning environment. That is, their individual requirements would be recognised and matched and they would be treated in the same way as other students as far as their learning was concerned. All the learners in a college would have their individual requirements identified and matched. Meeting the particular requirements of students with learning difficulties and/or disabilities would be part of the college's usual arrangements rather than an additional or different activity. The college would be expected to demonstrate that the learning it provides is inclusive rather than such students making a case for the right to learn alongside other learners.

A SHARED VISION

2.32 We recognise that our thinking about inclusive learning owes much to the pioneering work already under way in some colleges and in other services. Those colleges involved in the exercise to test the idea (see appendix to annex D) described how they were attempting to put in place or had already established some of the elements of inclusive learning. One college told us how it had re-thought its provision for students with learning difficulties and/or disabilities in order to be more inclusive. Another college said that inclusion was an important part of its corporate mission. Other colleges were trying to achieve inclusive learning and looked eagerly to the committee's report to confirm their vision of further education for students with learning difficulties and/or disabilities. Colleges understood readily that the concept of inclusive learning was the logical next step in the evolution of further education provision for these students.

2.33 The concept of inclusion is used increasingly both here and in the USA by other services working with people with learning difficulties. These services often share the committee's vision of 'bringing about a pluralistic society, inclusive of all people'.[4] Health and social services and voluntary organisations face the same challenge as further education; that is, how to individualise the planning of housing, employment, supported living and training services in order to provide tailor-made personal services. The aim of all provision must be 'inclusion in our communities'.[5]

2.34 In England, one higher education establishment has established a post in 'inclusive education' and in another establishment, staff have lectured and written about inclusiveness for many years. A well-known distance-learning pack for professionals working with (and parents of) people with learning difficulties produced by a higher education establishment uses the concept throughout its materials. The concept of inclusion, meaning full and active participation in society, is part of academic and legal debate on issues of gender and race.

2.35 We have used the term 'inclusive learning' to signal a change in thinking about further education students with learning difficulties and/or disabilities. As this new thinking is refined and developed by colleges and others, we expect that the language used to describe it will also develop.

INCLUSIVE LEARNING AS A PROCESS

2.36 Inclusive learning is a goal to be aimed for rather than a fixed state to be achieved once and for all by the sector, a college or teacher. The sector's capacity to achieve this goal will shift as sources of funding change, as the extent and nature of its collaboration with other providers shifts and as colleges themselves change. Colleges will offer more or less participation as their individual circumstances alter. These might include a shift in managerial commitment and priorities, the gain or loss of staff with particular expertise, funding contingencies, changes in the local community, the identification of new student groups, and the nature of collaborative arrangements with other agencies. This will be true for sector and specialist colleges. Teachers will achieve the kind of direct engagement with the learner that we have in mind with different degrees of success, depending upon their skills and confidence. Whatever the circumstance of change may be, we would expect the sector, individual colleges and teachers to maintain a commitment to inclusive learning.

A VARIETY OF SETTINGS

2.37 Learning takes place in a variety of settings. When we refer to further education in this report we mean:

- general further education and sixth form college
- specialist colleges such as agriculture and horticulture colleges
- independent specialist colleges for student with learning difficulties and/or disabilities
- adult education services
- education provision for over-16s in hospitals, day-centres, secure units, residential homes and other community settings.

2.38 In the rest of the report, we examine some of the implications of inclusive learning in more detail.

References

1 Hazel Francis *Individuality in Learning,* London, FEU/University of London, 1991; D. Kolb *Experimental Learning*, New York, Prentice-Hall Inc., 1984; L. Vygotsky *Thought and Language*, Cambridge, Mass., MIT Press, 1988

2 R. S. Peters *Ethics and Education,* London, Unwin, 1972

3 SCPR *Student Voices: The Views of Further Education Students with Learning Difficulties and/or Disabilities: Findings From a Series of Student Workshops Commissioned by the Learning Difficulties and/or Disabilities Committee,* London, Skill: National Bureau for Students with Disabilities, 1996

4 Julie Ann Racino *et al.* (ed.) *Housing Support and Community: Choices and Strategies for Adults with Disabilities* Baltimore, P H Brookes Publishing, 1993

5 Derek Thomas, Director, National Development Team, *Keynote Speech*, British Institute of Learning Difficulties, International Conference, Oxford, 1995, (unpublished)

Chapter 3: The Council's Legal Duties

In this chapter, the committee explores the Council's legal duties towards students with learning difficulties and/or disabilities, as required in its terms of reference; and in particular assesses how the Council can best interpret and act upon its legal duties in order to promote inclusive learning across the sector as a whole.

THE ISSUES

1. identifying the students with learning difficulties and/or disabilities for whom the Council has a duty
2. deciding how much further education the Council should fund
3. defining the kind of further education the Council should fund
4. whether there are significant legal duties upon other agencies which affect learning and participation in further education.

INTERPRETING LEGAL DUTIES

3.1 The Council asked the committee to advise it on how best it can, within the resources likely to be available to it, fulfil its responsibilities towards students with learning difficulties and/or disabilities. Legal duties towards students with learning difficulties and/or disabilities are important because they:

- represent society's aspirations, as represented by parliament. The framework of the legal duties and how the Council operates within it tells us something about prevailing attitudes towards students with learning difficulties and/or disabilities, and something of what is expected of and for them
- they directly affect the experiences of students at college. For some students, they may determine whether or not they are able to participate in further education
- the costs to students, colleges and the Council if those legal duties are not discharged properly would be high. They would include lost opportunities and frustration for individuals; administrative and legal fees for the Council and for colleges; and loss of public confidence and esteem in further education.

Legal duties of the Council

3.2 The Council's legal duties arise from the *Further and Higher Education Act 1992* and the *Disability Discrimination Act 1995*. The first Act requires the Council to:

- fund sufficient and adequate facilities for further education
- have regard to the requirements of students with learning difficulties and/or disabilities when so doing
- avoid disproportionate expenditure
- assess the quality of provision it funds.

3.3 The second Act requires the Council to make an annual report to the secretary of state on its activities and those of colleges towards students with disabilities; and to require each sector college, as a condition of receiving funds from the Council, to produce a disability statement for students. This Act refers to 'disability', rather than to 'learning difficulty and/or disability', because it has its origins in employment rather than education law.

3.4 In addition to the duties upon the Council, colleges and other agencies such as the health service, social services and local education authorities also have legal duties towards students. These are explored in later chapters of this report, particularly in chapter 8, and in the companion volume (see paragraph 3.11).

3.5 The-then secretary of state followed up the *Further and Higher Education Act 1992* with a letter of guidance to the Council. This offered further information about how the Council might interpret its duties in the light of concerns raised during the passage of the Act through parliament. The letter of guidance strongly enjoined the Council to ensure that students' needs were assessed; to ensure that learning difficulties and/or disabilities were not a bar to access to further education; and to work collaboratively with other agencies in the interests of students. Whilst these injunctions do not have the force of law, they help to set some further parameters for the Council in discharging its legal duties.

3.6 We recognise that the Council must keep within the spirit and the letter of the law to meet its legal duties. Whilst the Council has no choice but to accept them, it has a wide choice about how to meet them. Often, however, it has to balance duties against one another, particularly the duty to make provision without incurring disproportionate expenditure. The Council could, of course, be challenged in the courts if it was thought that it was not meeting its legal duties or was not doing so in an appropriate way.

3.7 One of the most frequent messages we heard during our work was that these students are the only group to whom specific reference is made in the *Further and Higher Education Act 1992*. This message reflects the importance which has been attached to the legislative reference by colleges and others who work with students. It not only places these students fully within the scope of further education, which is in itself a powerful message, but signifies the importance attached to provision for these students by the government and parliament when the legislation was introduced.

Legal duties of other agencies

3.8 As well as investigating the Council's legal duties, our terms of reference invited us to consider the duties of other agencies, since it is only by understanding those that we could advise the Council on how it can best work with colleges and others.

THE COMMITTEE'S PRINCIPLES

3.9 How these legal duties should properly be interpreted and delivered is crucial for students, colleges and the Council. We wanted to be sure we understood the legal framework properly. The reference to these students in the Act, whilst a potentially powerful message, actually tells us relatively little about what should be done by the

Council, or indeed by colleges and others. In particular, we wanted to explore the extent to which the legislation supports the delivery of the inclusive learning which we advocate. In this report we also wanted to make sure that the adoption of this new focus on inclusive learning would be consistent with the Council's legal duties and how it could best be accompanied by any necessary safeguards for the students.

3.10 The committee adopted two principles which informed its analysis and guided its recommendations, that:

- the committee should aim to understand fully the Council's legal duties; to explore the full extent of its powers; and to help others to understand those duties and powers
- wherever possible, the committee should encourage the Council to take a broad and proactive view of its duties.

3.11 A report was commissioned to help us understand the nature and scope of the Council's duties and powers and to review and analyse relevant legislation. This report drew not just on education legislation, but also on legislation in the fields of health and welfare where this is relevant to students, colleges or the Council.[1]

WHAT WE FOUND ABOUT THE COUNCIL'S LEGAL DUTIES

Identifying the students with learning difficulties and/or disabilities for whom the Council has a duty

3.12 Knowing for whom the Council should 'have regard' when it funds further education is central to forming a view about the scope of the Council's duties and whether or not it is discharging them. How to define these students was a major concern to over 100 of the respondents to the committee's call for evidence. These respondents understood the relationship between how students are defined and the extent of their learning opportunities; that definitions act both as boundaries between students and as the admission to extra help; and the differences between definitions used in educational and other legislation. The definition of those students to whom the Council must 'have regard' is set out in section 4 of the Act. This states that a person has a learning difficulty if:

> *he has a significantly greater difficulty in learning than the majority of persons of his age or he has a disability which either prevents or hinders him from making use of facilities of a kind generally provided by institutions within the further education sector for persons of his age.*[2]

3.13 This is a twin formulation, applying to those with intellectual and physical difficulties where these affect their learning. It has led the Council to adopt the description 'students with learning difficulties and/or disabilities'. Neither the Act nor the Council offer a precise specification to define what is meant by 'significantly greater difficulty in learning' or 'facilities generally available'.

3.14 There are two important features of the legal definition of students with learning difficulties and/or disabilities:

- it refers to difficulties in learning, not to difficulties or disabilities as such. Thus, students with a physical disability may not have a difficulty in learning if their college is fully accessible. In our terms, these students have a learning environment which matches their requirements
- its interpretation requires judgements to be made about the needs of one student relative to another. The definition is not an absolute one. Students' learning difficulties are to be seen relative to the ease with which their peers learn.

3

3.15 The definition in the *Further and Higher Education Act 1992* is the same as for schools. It reflects a long period of refinement in thinking about these matters. Until the Warnock Report was published in 1978, children and young people were defined by reference to a label which purported to describe them using a medically-derived set of categories.[3] The then revolutionary thinking in the Warnock Report, which was formalised in the *Education Act 1981*[4], was that these labels told educationalists nothing about the educational needs of the individual. Children with the same label could have very different needs for their teaching and learning. The labels were regarded as irrelevant and, in many cases, harmful because they carried with them a set of inappropriate assumptions which could stigmatise the individual and which did nothing to ensure effective teaching and learning.

2 Deciding how much further education the Council should fund

3.16 We were advised by the authors of the legal report, Beachcroft Stanleys, that the Act does not offer a precise definition of 'sufficiency' or 'adequacy'. No particular number of places or rate of participation has ever been laid down. There is no case law that establishes whether or not an individual has a legal right to a place on the course or at the college of their choice. There is no other case law to help define these terms. However, the Act does contain some pointers. It states that the Council:

should discharge that duty so as:

a. to secure that the facilities are provided at such places, are of such character and are so equipped as to be sufficient to meet the reasonable needs of all persons to whom the duty extends, and

b. to take account of the different abilities and aptitudes of such persons.[5]

3.17 We concluded that the Act implies that further education should meet the reasonable expectations including the reasonable expectations of students with learning difficulties and/or disabilities.

3.18 The Council does not have an overall view about how many places are required nationally or locally in any particular subject area or qualification level for any students. Indeed, for students with learning difficulties and/or disabilities, there has been no data about provision or demand that would have helped with forming such a view. The Council's approach has had three main components:

- allocating funds to colleges in order to promote growth in provision to meet the government's assumptions about growth. To achieve this, it has used its funding methodology to offer incentives to colleges to grow. Additional funds are provided where students, especially those with learning difficulties and/or disabilities, need support which costs more than that for other students. There is therefore no disincentive to colleges to include these students in their expansion plans
- basing the funds it allocates to colleges on applications which reflect their strategic plans. Those strategic plans are expected to match and respond to local needs, based in turn on a thorough analysis by the college of the needs of the local population and employers. Colleges have been specifically encouraged to make reference to students with learning difficulties and/or disabilities in their needs analyses
- setting as a condition of funding, the requirement that each sector college delivers at least the same proportion of provision for students with learning difficulties and/or disabilities as the previous year. In the context of overall growth, this is a powerful lever for increased provision for these students.

3.19 We found some evidence that colleges need — and indeed would welcome — help to improve their analyses of local needs in order to ensure that their provision fully meets all the needs of students with learning difficulties and/or disabilities in their locality. As we mentioned in chapter 1, we also found some evidence that some groups of learners are not yet properly represented in further education. We discuss these concerns and what can be done about them in more detail in chapter 4 on participation.

3.20 During the course of our work, the *Disability Discrimination Act 1995* became law. The Act makes discrimination against people with disabilities illegal in certain circumstances. The anti-discrimination provisions do not include further education, other than as an employer or when providing a service which is not education funded by the Council. This Act does not use the same definition of 'disabled' as the *Further and Higher Education Act 1992*. It is too early to know the impact of this legislation or its omission of education from the anti-discrimination provisions. The *Further and Higher Education Act 1992* creates a strong legal framework and the new Act creates a right to complain where a college fails to live up to the commitments in its disability statement. But these Acts do not explicitly establish rights or outlaw discrimination. We consider that the Council and Department for Education and Employment should keep under review the impact of the new legislation and the way the two Acts are implemented by the Council and by colleges, particularly so that students are aware of their entitlement to complain and to seek redress.

3 Defining the kind of further education the Council should fund

3.21 For students studying full time between the ages of 16 and 19, the duty of sufficiency applies to courses of any kind. For students studying part time, and those over the age of 19 studying full time, the duty of adequacy applies only to courses which fall within the scope of schedule 2 to the *Further and Higher Education Act 1992*. Parts of the schedule are managed by lists issued by the secretary of state. For other courses in the schedule, the Act does not specify by whom or how they are to be interpreted. With the exception of schedule 2(j), the courses apply equally to students with learning difficulties and/or disabilities as to other students. Schedule 2(j) refers to 'a course to teach independent living and communication skills to persons having learning difficulties which prepares them for entry to another course falling within paragraphs (d) to (h) above.'[6]

3.22 For schedule 2(j) courses, the Council has offered guidance in the form of criteria by which judgements can be made as to whether a course falls within the scope of the schedule and therefore can be funded by the Council. Courses which fall outside the schedule cannot be funded by the Council. The Council's criteria currently state that:

i. primary course objective is progression to a course which prepares students for entry to courses listed in sections (d) to (g) above; and

ii. course includes college accreditation which enables the student to progress to courses (d) to (g); or

iii. evidence of progression to courses (d) to (g) can be provided to the Council.[7]

3.23 We found some evidence of uncertainty about the criteria.[8] In some cases, we found that the criteria and their application do not meet the aspirations we have set out. We consider this in greater detail in chapters 4 (on participation) and 5 (on assessing students' requirements). In particular, we found that students' ability to participate and achieve is adversely affected by:

- the current interpretation of the criteria for schedule 2(j) courses
- the availability of suitable courses and accreditation

- the inability or unwillingness of some local education authorities to fund non-schedule 2(j) programmes
- the prevailing understanding of what constitutes progress in learning by students with learning difficulties and/or disabilities.

Whether there are significant legal duties upon other agencies which affect learning and participation in further education

3.24 Many students with learning difficulties and/or disabilities will have contact with and receive services from other agencies as well as their college whilst they study. The letter of guidance to the Council from the-then secretary of state explicitly recognises the impact that this can have. It enjoins the Council to:

> *take account of the role of the careers service, LEAs, health authorities, social services departments and voluntary organisations, all of which may be involved in providing advice or support for individual students. The Council should encourage inter-agency collaboration in order to ensure the best possible response to students' needs.*[9]

We explore some of the practical ways in which collaboration can be promoted in chapter 8.

3.25 The legal report commissioned for us included a summary of the main duties and powers of these other agencies. We found two main weaknesses:

- many people remain unclear about this pattern of duties and powers and how they might fit together to promote participation and high-quality learning
- the duties on other agencies naturally stem from those agencies' responsibilities. They often use different definitions of their clients and their needs. Either they can be couched in different terms from the duties upon the Council, or, when taken together with these duties, they do not form a coherent system.

3.26 Different definitions of their client groups by other agencies can have considerable impact on individuals. Several respondents to our call for evidence wanted clarification about funding responsibilities. For example, they pointed to the differences they saw between the Council and TECs when considering which students should receive additional funding. One voluntary organisation argued that:

> *we have seen over the years in the education service the arguments that have taken place between education, social and health services regarding elements of funding for any one individual. It would be a sad reflection on the development of FE if we were to allow these arguments to continue.*[10]

Many focused on transport. As we show in chapter 4, the availability of publicly-funded transport directly affects students' ability to participate, yet the responsibility for funding transport is not fully understood. Because it is part of a larger set of duties on local education authorities for discretionary awards, or on social services departments, it is not organised primarily to ensure students' ability to participate in further education.

SUMMARY OF MAIN FINDINGS

3.27 One inescapable conclusion from our research is how poor much of the understanding about legal duties towards these students can be. This applies to colleges, parents, voluntary organisations and other agencies. Much of this is explicable given the new nature of the sector and the complexity of the issues. It can seriously hamper the extent to which learning and participation can be inclusive.

3.28 Having looked at whether the law is understood, we looked at whether it is honoured. We used the evidence we collected and which we present in the rest of this report, to derive conclusions first about whether or not the Council is currently discharging its legal duties and secondly about whether it is doing so in a way which ensures inclusive learning across the sector as a whole. We concluded that the Council is working in a way which fully discharges the current interpretation of its legal duties in the light of current knowledge and understanding. We reached this conclusion even though, as we have indicated in chapter 1, there are serious shortcomings in the availability of provision for some people and in much of its quality.

3.29 This conclusion may therefore seem paradoxical. It is not, because what we are urging, and therefore the expectations against which we reached our main findings, require these changes:

- a new way of interpreting the legal duties themselves
- that the expectations by which the adequacy and sufficiency of further education should be judged must evolve and change over time
- that the extent to which each college plays its part should be increased, with an increase in consistency between colleges.

3.30 The fact that we found some groups of people who are not yet properly represented in further education, or some colleges doing less than others, does not, in our view, imply that current provision is insufficient or inadequate. Reasonable expectations about levels of provision and expectations on individual colleges change over time. It does indicate that changes in individual aspirations; in learning technology and pedagogy; in how far people can be encouraged to seek out further education; and in what the Council can demand from each college all enable and require colleges to widen the range of the learning requirements which they can meet. So, whilst we found evidence of shortcomings, we did so by judging the present quality and quantity of further education against more challenging expectations.

3.31 In the rest of the report, therefore, we have judged what we found in current practice against more challenging expectations. In the rest of this chapter, we review the Council's legal duties and how we want to see it discharge them in that light.

ADDRESSING WEAKNESSES AND BUILDING ON STRENGTHS

Identifying the students with learning difficulties and/or disabilities for whom the Council has a duty

3.32 In advocating a focus on learning rather than on learning difficulty or disability we still need to monitor the quantity and quality of further education for some students and not others, as implied by the Act. Otherwise, the Council will not be able to demonstrate that it is indeed 'having regard' to their requirements.

3.33 In replacing the old and often medically-derived categories with a definition more suited to education, the *Further and Higher Education Act 1992* gives us something inherently difficult to define because it is about learning and because it is relative. This has a number of implications:

- it demands of teachers and those who allocate funds to colleges more sophisticated approaches which rest on a student's individual requirements rather than needs ascribed to the student as a result of having been categorised as having learning difficulties and/or disabilities

- it makes it difficult to count students with learning difficulties and/or disabilities, because their requirements may change over time, or the relative nature of the description means that counting practices by colleges is likely to differ, or because developments in provision will influence the extent to which students have difficulties in learning or in gaining access to the facilities available
- if the numbers of students with learning difficulties and/or disabilities in further education cannot be counted on a reasonably consistent basis, then it is difficult to know whether their participation is changing over time
- it is difficult to be confident that participation rates are appropriate because it is difficult to compare the number of those with learning difficulties and/or disabilities in further education with the number of such people in the population at large.

3.34 Our views about interpreting the educational aspects of this definition and the proposed focus on inclusive learning reflect the views of many of the students who took part in the workshop series. One told us, 'We don't need labels. Even if you have got a label, people do not understand you', and another said, 'These words don't describe me; my problems. I need something that will tell people what's my problem.'[11]

3.35 We do not consider that abandoning such labels in order to offer inclusive learning means that the Council and colleges must abandon them for statistical purposes. We received strong encouragement, from many voluntary groups in particular, that the Council should be able to count students with learning difficulties and/or disabilities and to check the change in their participation over time. Counting people is important when allocating resources and ensuring that those who need legal protection receive it. As another participant in the workshops told us, 'Having the label "learning difficulty" helps me get the things I need'.[12] The Council needs to be able to count students in order to be able to demonstrate that it is meeting its legal requirements. We consider that there need be no conflict between having one set of definitions for the purposes of monitoring and another for delivering teaching and learning. We explore this in more detail and offer specific recommendations on the definitions for counting students in chapter 4 on participation.

2 Deciding how much further education the Council should fund

3.36 In advocating inclusive learning, we argued in chapter 2 that learning must become inclusive across the sector as a whole, to match the number and individual requirements of those who might participate. We had to reconcile the more proactive interpretation of the duty to have regard with the duty to avoid incurring disproportionate expenditure. We considered first whether the legal duty to 'have regard' to these students, which currently rests only with the Council, should be shared with colleges. We noted that in Scotland, where there is no funding council, this duty rests with the secretary of state and colleges.[13] A formal extension of the legal duty in England would require primary legislation and therefore the instigation of the Department for Education and Employment. This option would be the most powerful legal lever for expanding the range of provision offered by some colleges. It would also correct something of an anomaly in the current legal framework, which seems to us to give the Council a demanding set of legal duties with relatively few statutory levers to discharge them. We consider that the legislation might usefully be amended. Meanwhile, we propose that the Council invite colleges to share with it the role of 'having regard'.

3.37 The Council's current approach involves encouraging colleges to identify and respond to local needs. The Council does not itself set targets. We consider that this is broadly the right approach. However, in our view it does need to be strengthened, even though much has already been done with the training and enterprise councils (TECs) and others. We discuss these ideas in more detail in chapter 4, but, in summary, the Council needs to:

- give colleges more guidance about how to identify local needs
- tighten its requirements upon colleges to do so
- take decisive action when its expectations are not met.

3 Defining the kind of further education the Council should fund

3.38 The evidence presented to us demonstrated that the interpretation of schedule 2(j) is central to whether or not a course can or should be funded by the Council. Here again we need to balance our aspiration that further education should be accessible to more students with the need to avoid disproportionate expenditure. Courses outside the schedule are the responsibility of local education authorities (LEAs). Some provision is funded by social services departments or by student fees. In principle, therefore, a course which falls outside the schedule can still be offered by colleges, funded from other sources. However, we received much evidence about the funding constraints on LEAs and social services departments. We were told that such constraints made them reluctant to offer funding to colleges for non-schedule 2 courses and that the position has worsened in the years since the Act. Some of this evidence suggested that without Council funding, these courses would not run at all. Other evidence suggested that there is confusion and inconsistency in how schedule 2 is interpreted around the country.[14] We discuss this in more detail in chapters 4 and 5.

3.39 Much of this evidence focused on schedule 2(j), because, according to the wording of the schedule, these are courses specifically for students with learning difficulties and/or disabilities. In addition, because the description of courses requires them to prepare students for entry to another course elsewhere in the schedule in order to count as a 2(j) course, there are sensitive debates about how this could and should be demonstrated. Much of our thinking on this is set out in chapter 5.

3.40 We reviewed the prevailing interpretation of schedule 2(j) in the light of changes in expectations of and by students with learning difficulties and changes in technology. These changes:

- have challenged some conventional thinking about how further education should be defined
- mean more opportunities for learning are now available to more individuals than ever before, some of whom are able to learn, to demonstrate their learning and thereby to be recognised as able to benefit from further education only by very recent technological advances or by changes in teaching practice and skills
- demonstrate that these matters change over time and that a rigid view would be unhelpful and indeed, unsustainable.

3.41 We looked at these changes in the context of parliament's intentions. We did not want to embrace every post-16 activity that may happen to take place in colleges (or indeed elsewhere) within the scope of schedule 2. This is because:

- we must acknowledge the government's intentions that there should be a split in the funding responsibilities between the Council and local authorities
- the Council must not have passed to it responsibilities which properly rest elsewhere or for which it has no funds

- we do not want to devalue or distort other valuable post-16 activities which best meet the needs of many individuals, such as social care or therapy, by imposing an educational framework upon them which might not be appropriate
- we wanted to strike the right balance between spreading the Council's funds widely, consistent with its duties, and not over-extending them with the result that the rest of the provision might be weakened.

3.42 Our detailed recommendations about how to do this are set out in chapter 5 on assessing students' requirements. We believe that these recommendations are consistent with parliament's broader intentions in establishing schedule 2 and that they will enable learning in further education to become more inclusive whilst making the most effective use of the available resources.

Whether there are significant legal duties upon other agencies which affect learning and participation in further education

3.43 It is essential that more individuals and agencies involved with students are clear about the law. If they are not, opportunities for collaboration and participation are lost. We think it is therefore vital that, as well as continuing to attend vigorously to its own legal duties, the Council does what it can to ensure greater clarity and understanding between agencies and of those agencies by students and those who work with them. To that end, we have included the legal report as a companion volume to this report. We would also urge the Council to discuss its respective duties with those other agencies at national level in order to promote understanding and agreement. We say more about this in chapters 8 (on collaboration) and 11 (on funding).

References

1 Beachcroft Stanleys (1996) *Duties and Powers: The Law Governing the Provision of Further Education to Students with Learning Difficulties and/or Disabilities: A Report to the Learning Difficulties and/or Disabilities Committee*, London, HMSO. The report was commissioned following competitive tender.

2 *Further and Higher Education Act 1992*, Section 4(6)

3 *Special educational Needs: Report of the Committee of Enquiry into the Education of Handicapped Children and Young People* (Warnock Report), London, HMSO, 1978

4 *Education Act 1981*, Ch. 60, London, HMSO, 1981

5 *Further and Higher Education Act 1992*, sections 2(3) and 3(2)

6 *Further and Higher Education Act 1992*, schedule 2

7 FEFC Circular 96/01, *Students with Learning Difficulties and/or Disabilities* Criteria for Schedule 2(j), Coventry, FEFC, January 1996

8 Responses to the call for evidence, (unpublished)

9 FEFC Circular 92/08, *Establishment of the FEFC*, London, FEFC, para. 31

10 Responses to the call for evidence, (unpublished)

11 SCPR *Student Voices: The Views of Further Education Students with Learning Difficulties and/or Disabilities: Findings from a Series of Student Workshops Commissioned by the Learning Difficulties and/or Disablities Committee*, London, Skill: National Bureau for Students with Disabilities, 1996

12 *Ibid.*

13 Committee visit to Scotland, November 1995 (see also annex C)

14 Responses to the call for evidence, (unpublished)

PART TWO

Aspects of an Inclusive Learning Environment

Chapter 4: Participation

In this chapter, the committee considers how further education as a whole can provide adequate and sufficient provision to match the number and individual requirements of those who might participate. The committee concludes that this match has not yet been achieved and therefore that certain groups are significantly under-represented and recommends ways of addressing this.

THE ISSUES

1. whether the further education provision for those with learning difficulties and/or disabilities matches their requirements, through:

   a. identifying who does and does not participate

   b. identifying the factors that influence or determine participation by people with disabilities and/or learning difficulties in further education

2. tackling under-representation by colleges, the Council and other agencies, to ensure that further education is more inclusive

3. monitoring and reporting on participation.

PARTICIPATION AND INCLUSIVE LEARNING

4.1 By participation, we mean the extent to which students with learning difficulties and/or disabilities are able to participate fully and are offered the same range of opportunities as other students.

4.2 There are therefore two dimensions to participation: the quality of provision of those who participate and the extent of participation itself. That is:

- ensuring that those already in colleges are enabled to take part more effectively in a learning experience which matches their individual requirements
- increasing the opportunities for participation by those who are not currently participating in colleges.

This chapter addresses the second aspect.

THE COMMITTEE'S PRINCIPLES

4.3 The committee adopted the following principles:

- everyone who can benefit from further education should be able to participate
- further education provision should match the individual requirements of those who might participate

- the further education sector should work in conjunction with other providers to ensure a pattern of provision which maximises participation.

4.4 Evidence which might indicate that a college has adopted these principles includes:

EVIDENCE

- a mission statement which contains a commitment to meeting the needs of the community
- policies which stress the importance of valuing all students regardless of ability or disability
- a thorough community needs analysis, the outcomes of which are used to set recruitment targets
- a requirement for all staff to accept responsibility for the learning and support of these students, as for any other student
- the availability of support for staff to enable them to understand the best teaching and learning strategies and create the most effective learning environments for each student
- well-developed links in the community including those with employers, other purchasers, planners and providers such as health and social services and voluntary organisations
- relevant programmes designed to give students appropriate skills for employment
- opportunities for supported work experience which is well planned and appropriate as an integral part of students' programmes
- structured progression routes from pre-foundation to advanced programmes
- effective support for students' learning
- flexibility in modes of attendance.

WHAT WE FOUND

4.5 Inspectorate evidence gave us the following examples of good and bad practice in participation:

EXAMPLES

College A

The college's mission statement indicates clearly its commitment to meeting the needs of the community. Staff work hard to fulfil this commitment. The equal opportunities policy stresses the importance of valuing all students whatever their ability or disability. All staff accept responsibility for students with learning difficulties and/or disabilities and welcome them into their classes. Support is available for staff to help them understand the needs of the students and the teaching and learning strategies which will be most successful. Close links have been developed with other agencies to identify potential students and to plan programmes which will meet their needs. Collaboration with social services and the local health authority is enabling the college to respond positively to students who have very complex needs. A joint project has been undertaken with a voluntary organisation to identify the employment opportunities in the area. Staff at the college work closely with employers. Programmes are developed to give students the skills they will need to gain employment. Work experience placements are an integral part of the provision and students are supported on their placements. Programmes are structured to enable students to progress from pre-foundation level to advanced level. Additional support is available for students who need help with basic skills. Flexible patterns of attendance and the opportunity for students to extend their period of study help to ensure that students are able to complete their studies successfully.

College B

A good working relationship has been established between the college of agriculture and horticulture and a number of special schools. Staff at these schools are complimentary about the responsiveness and the flexibility of the college in meeting their requirements. The college provides staff and facilities to support pupils with their learning difficulties and/or disabilities in conjunction with the schools. Close links with the special schools have resulted in the development of a proposal for a two-year full-time course in land-based studies for these students. Consultation with the schools and the careers service indicated a demand for the courses and the availability of possible employment once the students left the college.

College C

Currently there is only one course within the college which is available for students with learning difficulties and/or disabilities. Little information is published about the course, other than the fact that it is for students who need help with literacy and numeracy. The students on the course have moderate learning difficulties. The majority of their time is spent in classrooms working on their basic skills. There is little opportunity for students to undertake vocational training as there are no vocational courses in the college below NVQ level 2. The college's strategic plan indicates an intention to develop provision for students with learning difficulties and/or disabilities, but there has not been a comprehensive analysis of needs within the community to identify the type of provision that is needed. The business plans of the various faculties across the college do not indicate how the objectives within the strategic plan are to be achieved. Staff within the faculties regard students with learning difficulties and/or disabilities as the responsibility of the special needs co-ordinator. The prospectus indicates that there is a learning support workshop which is available for all students who need extra help, particularly with their English or mathematics. The workshop is open on Monday, Wednesday and Friday afternoons only.

Whether the further education provision for those with learning difficulties and/or disabilities matches their requirements

4.6 The Council's policy has been to combine a pursuit of growth with a requirement that colleges conduct needs analyses within their strategic plans, against which allocations are made. On this basis, the regional committees have reported that, as far as can be judged with the data available to them, the provision being made by colleges is sufficient and adequate.[1] The Council does not set out to systematically record need. The committee wanted accurate data about need to be able to advise the Council on whether it was meeting its duties. The Institute for Employment Studies (IES) was commissioned to carry out a mapping survey. We worked closely with the Widening Participation Committee, established by the Council in December 1994, to explore data and factors about participation by people with disabilities and/or learning difficulties, and to share the outcomes of the research we describe here.

4.7 We had to commission a new survey because there was no accurate or comprehensive quantitative data on the participation of people with disabilities and/or learning difficulties in further education and the kind of support and education they receive. This is because as we explained in chapter 3, the definition of the students concerned is inherently difficult because it is a relative definition. For example, some people have disabilities but require no additional help to access or succeed in education. It is about learning and not disability. Hence it is almost impossible to check the overall population in colleges against existing research data on disability in the general population when it is not about learning; or to achieve consistent responses from colleges. As a result, different surveys have used differing definitions of disability and learning difficulty and have received different responses, including some people but not others:

- there is confusion between 'learning difficulty' as used broadly to describe an intellectual impairment, and 'learning difficulty' as used to describe all those who have difficulty in gaining access to or engaging in education (the definition used in the *Further and Higher Education Act 1992*)
- the sector is new and central data collection is still being introduced; the individualised student record (ISR) data were not yet robust enough for our purposes
- the National Foundation for Educational Research (NFER) advised us that existing research was focused on the nature of provision rather than on who is taking part or why.[2]

4.8 Before commissioning the mapping study, we explored with members of the research community the level of data which existed and how best to collect what we needed. We decided to carry out new research to determine the quantity of provision in colleges and to study existing data sets in order to identify what the general level of need might be. We were advised not to carry out a national survey on the incidence of disability and/or learning difficulty in the general population, partly because of the cost and partly because of problems in defining the parameters of the study. Moreover, we regarded such large-scale work as properly the responsibility of government.

4.9 In our research project we wanted to:

- identify existing national data on the prevalence of disability or learning difficulty in the population in England
- gather data from sector colleges on the number of students with disabilities and/or learning difficulties enrolled
- identify any groups who appear to be under-represented, and find out why
- compare data on participation with data on need, to assess whether levels of participation meet people's needs.

4.10 The Council currently records data about provision and participation through the ISR. The ISR does not currently provide the comprehensive data that we wanted because:

- the information collected on 'disability' refers to 'registered' students, and does not correspond to the definition of 'disabilities and/or learning difficulty' used here
- it records students for whom additional support units are being claimed by the college, and does not indicate whether students require learning support, what learning support is required and/or provided.

4.11 We thought we could find out whether participation levels met local or national need by comparing data on participation with data about the incidence of disability in the general population. However, such comparisons cannot be made because the data are incomplete and are not collected on a comparable basis. In addition, many potential students may not apply. These factors mean that a simple calculation of the difference between the general population and the college population would be specious. Instead of trying to produce a formulaic answer, we therefore thought instead about how colleges currently identify and respond to needs in their locality, and how the Council encourages them to do so. Colleges are, on the whole, realistic about the extent of their local knowledge. One told the mapping project researchers:

> *We have close contacts with social services, voluntary agencies and schools and we are generally alerted in advance to those students whose needs are directly related to learning support. However, at present, we have no system of gathering quantitative information on the nature of people with learning difficulties and/or disabilities in the local community.*[3]

4.12 Full details of the methodology and findings of the research, which generated responses from 60% of colleges (274), are described in the companion volume, *Mapping Provision.*[4]

4.13 The mapping study tells us that sector colleges estimate some 126,500 students with disabilities and/or learning difficulties are enrolled, as at November 1995. This averages some 300 students per institution and about 5.3% of all students enrolled in sector colleges.[5] This is about three times the number of students identified in 1985, although it is difficult to draw valid comparisons because there has been a change in the number of colleges and sixth form colleges that are now included in the new sector. There is little difference between type of college in the 'average share' per college of students, except in the case of agriculture and horticulture colleges where the share is higher (8.2%) and specialist designated institutions where it is lower, at 1.4%. Added to these are the 1,800 students funded by the Council to attend specialist colleges outside the sector. Unfortunately, we could not include data about post-16 year olds at school because these data are not collected on a comparable basis.

4.14 The mapping exercise did consider overall demand. Two-thirds of colleges believed they could identify potential, but currently unexpressed, demand for participation in further education from people with disabilities and/or learning difficulties. Some were clear that some potential students do not apply because they think the college cannot meet their needs. Responses from 77 colleges indicated that 23,406 potential students (or 300 per college) existed in their areas. They had obtained this data about unexpressed demand from a variety of sources — schools, careers services, social service and health service data and local contacts and networks. The mapping project researchers advised us that if these estimates are realistic, the number of potential students (those not yet expressing a wish to attend but who might if circumstances were right) would be about the same as the number of students already enrolled.

4.15 These findings compare with data collected in a national survey in 1982. This survey found that only 17% of LEAs guaranteed a place to students with learning difficulties and/or disabilities in education after the age of 16 and that the volume of provision was not adequate to meet the needs of school-leavers.[6] A subsequent survey in 1987 found that there were 38,069 students with learning difficulties and/or disabilities in 374 further education and tertiary colleges in England. If this figure is grossed up, it suggests there may have been 42,344 in a total student population in those colleges of 1.7 million.[7] This research was probably the most substantial and it was carried out in partnership with the-then Department of Education and Science. There is no more recent national evidence, although various reports identify gaps in provision for certain groups of students, including those with profound and complex learning difficulties; those with emotional and behavioural difficulties; those with mental health difficulties, and adults with disabilities and/or learning difficulties.[8]

1a Identifying who does and does not participate

4.16 Key findings about the pattern of participation from the mapping study show some similarities with the general population. For example:

- over half (50.8%) of all students with disabilities and/or learning difficulties were aged 25 and over
- just over half of the students were following a general academic or vocational programme (52.8%), as opposed to courses designed solely or primarily for students with disabilities and/or learning difficulties ('discrete' programmes).

4.17 Some of the findings are very different for students with learning difficulties and/or disabilities:

- students from minority ethnic groups were under-represented compared with the student population as a whole (10.3% as opposed to 27.2%)
- a high proportion of students following courses designed solely or primarily for students with disabilities and/or learning difficulties are part time (71.8%)
- nearly half (48%) of all students with disabilities and/or learning difficulties were following pre-vocational and foundation programmes; only 16% were following programmes at level 3 and above
- female students with learning difficulties and/or disabilities are more likely to be part time than male students and are under-represented compared with the student population as a whole.

4.18 Students have the following characteristics shown in table 1, although it is important to remember that the identification of the characteristics of disability and/or learning difficulty is not an exact science. Any associated research can therefore only be a guide as to who is or is not participating.

Table 1. Characteristics of students with learning difficulties and/or disabilities

Characteristic	*% of total students with learning difficulties and/or disabilities*	*Numbers*
moderate and severe learning difficulties	34.0	25,659
specific learning difficulties (eg, dyslexia, dyscalcula)	9.0	6,787
other medical (eg, epilepsy, asthma)	8.2	6,162
multiple disabilities	6.3	4,757
mental ill health	4.4	3,334
hearing impairment	4.4	3,282
mobility difficulties	4.3	3,253
visual impairment	3.5	2,678
other physical disabilities	3.0	2,232
emotional/behavioural difficulties	1.7	1,269
profound/complex disabilities	1.1	829
other	20.1	15,199
Total	**100.0**	**75,441**

4.19 As well as asking colleges about students taking part, the mapping study asked colleges about any students with disabilities and/or learning difficulties who had applied but could not be enrolled. One hundred and seventy colleges (63.4%) said they could identify potential students who applied but could not be enrolled. Estimates of the number 'turned away' in the previous year averaged only 3.9 per college. Colleges identified a variety of reasons for turning students down:

- lack of appropriate staff expertise and suitable accommodation
- inability to meet the requirements of some students because they were 'non-educational'; for example, students requiring 24-hour or residential care, especially for those with profound and complex learning difficulties. Less than half the colleges felt that these unmet needs were being met by other local providers
- 23 colleges (18% of respondents) reported that people with 'profound/complex/severe learning difficulties and/or disabilities' could not be enrolled. This was proportionally the largest number.

4.20 Many colleges are realistic about those for whom they can and cannot provide properly; and also that for some of those people, alternative provision is available. Three colleges told the mapping project team:

> *Students aged 16 to 19 with severe learning difficulties are accommodated in local schools.*
>
> *The college has physical access to all but a few (general) classrooms, so students who are wheelchair users have access to the whole curriculum. We do not have facilities for mobility training or welfare or medical assistance for students. We do not run courses aimed at students with moderate or severe learning difficulties, the lowest level course we run is foundation GNVQ (in business and in health and social care).*
>
> *The majority of the college's building stock is poorly equipped for disabled access. Although the college is striving to address the issue, the costs involved with some buildings is prohibitive.*[9]

4.21 Responses to the committee's call for evidence also indicate perceived gaps in participation, particularly for those with profound and multiple learning difficulties (51 responses), adults with mental health difficulties (61) and young people with emotional and behavioural difficulties (30).[10]

4.22 Additionally, the committee found that about one third of colleges knew of students who had enrolled but whose learning support requirements could not be fully met. Most of these colleges could estimate the numbers of such students and these averaged 30 per college. Reasons advanced by colleges for not meeting these 'internal' unmet requirements included the nature of the student's learning requirements and the resources available. In particular, some colleges were not able to meet the requirements of students with dyslexia and visual impairment. Colleges also suggested that they were not necessarily able to meet the requirements fully of students with mental health problems, those with emotional and behavioural difficulties, and students with severe learning difficulties. Resource constraints, whether financial, physical or human, were the main reasons given by colleges for not fully meeting the requirements of students already enrolled. Some 48% of colleges identified a lack of trained personnel to support these students.

People with profound and multiple learning difficulties

4.23 People with profound and multiple learning difficulties form the group most often mentioned to us throughout our work as unable to access further education. Many responses to the call for evidence from major national organisations as well as from parents and others indicated considerable concern over what they saw as the absence of further education provision for people with profound and multiple learning difficulties. Other evidence suggests a lack of staff development and general awareness of the potential of further education for these adults[11] although some steps have been taken to address both these issues.[12]

People with mental health difficulties

4.24 We were advised that there are also concerns about participation by people with mental health difficulties. Responsibility for their education can fall between several stools. If health and social services purchasers do not choose to purchase education provision, then the programmes in some day-centres, hospitals and secure units might be at risk. Their importance has been noted by the Mental Health Act Commission[13] and in the government's objectives in *Health of the Nation*[14], which reported that one in four adults will suffer mental health difficulties at some point. Education provision enables individuals to retain and improve their independence and capacity to learn at times of remission or once their illness has ended. Programmes have often been self-financed using specialist staff from nearby colleges and adult education services. These programmes have depended on close links with the education service and a particular perception on the part of providers about the value of education to the student. Some colleges reported particular difficulties in meeting the requirements of adults with mental health problems. Others continue to try hard to respond to these requirements. A northern college told us it is developing a volunteer support scheme but said it was difficult to reconcile this area of work with funding based on achievement. One college in London told us of a project which aims to assist people with mental health problems or learning difficulties to move from sheltered employment into the open job market. The project offers training in specific vocational skills as well as in the generic skills students might need, such as social and personal skills, communication, managing their own travel and time-keeping; work areas are catering, gardening and office skills.[15]

A third college told the mapping project researchers:

> *Through our links with the local community and our network we provide outreach work for a local mental health group; at present in connection with a local mental health residential setting, we are to start two classes a week in the centre to provide a core of their choice.*[16]

Young people with emotional and behavioural difficulties

4.25 Colleges, schools and voluntary organisations told the committee about the lack of good-quality opportunities which specifically aim to support young people with emotional and behavioural difficulties, and that, when provision is made, it is often unsuitable.[17] The figures on school exclusions are pertinent here. Though not all these young people will have emotional and behavioural difficulties, Sir Ron Dearing noted the concern which such data should cause. The numbers being permanently excluded have increased from an estimated 2,910 in 1990-91 to an estimated 11,181 in 1993-94.[18] One college told us it offers courses for pupils at the local referral unit but a more common observation was that colleges could offer more than this:

> *A serious rethink on strategy needs to be done if post-16 colleges are to realise the potential of these students, many of whom are clearly disenchanted with education.*[19]

4.26 Evidence from TECs indicates that many young people are not participating in education and training because they are unable or unwilling to do so; they are unaware of what is available or where to find it; they are unconvinced of its value; or they think they will not get the support they need. Research for the TEC chief executives identified 11 indicators of disaffection, including, 'those subject to mental health or emotional problems; those exhibiting aggressive/disruptive behaviour...those that have had little or no support in growing up ...those that have had bad experiences or have been non-attenders at school'.[20]

4.27 Some colleges have developed strategies for supporting such students, for example, by establishing bridging courses with local schools; by employing an educational psychologist to provide advice and support for staff and students; or developing particular provision for school refusers and school excludees, including the support of an experienced worker from a voluntary organisation.[21]

Older learners with disabilities and/or learning difficulties

4.28 We also heard much evidence that indicated a strong belief that the division of funding responsibilities at incorporation (as described in chapter 3) puts courses for older learners with disabilities and/or learning difficulties at risk.[22] We were told that adults with disabilities and/or learning difficulties experience some barriers to learning in common with other adult learners (that is, lack of awareness of their learning needs, lack of confidence and the absence of access and guidance) but that these can be intensified. Adults with disabilities may have particularly limited experiences, lack confidence and assertiveness, need extra support in terms of transport, equipment and personal care, have little choice or autonomy in their lives, face attitudinal barriers and prejudice and depend on others to access education, such as parents, relatives, day-care or hostel staff.[23] We noted that some older people with learning difficulties may never previously have experienced formal education, which only included those with most severe need after the passing of the *Education (Handicapped Children) Act 1970*.[24]

Identifying the factors that influence or determine participation by people with disabilities and/or learning difficulties in further education

4.29 Part of the mapping project explored the factors which influence or determine participation. Many of the colleges responding to the mapping project gave us their views. We put this research alongside the powerful evidence we received from students, parents and others. During the committee's exercise to test its approach, 20 colleges gave careful consideration to recruiting a wider variety of learners. What constrained them, they said, was:

- staff training, expertise, attitudes, awareness
- suitable staff time and conditions of service
- lack of an inclusive, accredited and valued curriculum
- the college's image and view of itself in the community, its mission and the constraints placed by the governing body and senior managers
- funding the college's cost-effectiveness policy, a lack of resources or budget limits
- poor co-operation from other agencies, or not being seen as a key planning partner
- competition from other providers
- lack of expertise in marketing.[25]

4.30 We discuss the staff development issues in chapter 12; the curriculum in chapter 9; college management in chapter 6; and co-operation between agencies in chapter 8. We found four areas where there are other factors influencing provision for people with disabilities and/or learning difficulties, which we discuss below. These areas are: transport; collaboration and planning; the organisation of provision including physical access; and understanding the requirements of older learners.

Transport

4.31 Transport for those wanting to attend college was a significant concern to 147 respondents to the call for evidence, especially those over the age of 19. Five main points were made to us:

- confusion about funding responsibilities
- poor co-ordination
- time barriers
- transport in rural areas
- cost barriers.

4.32 Many respondents wanted clarification over funding responsibilities. The provision of transport to college for students is governed by the *Education Act 1944*. LEAs have a duty to fund free transport to college where the course being studied is the nearest to the student's home and where the 'transport must be necessary' to facilitate the student's attendance. What makes it 'necessary' could be distance, the age of the student, the ability of the student to take the route, and whether or not the student has learning difficulties, but not the student's finances. We were advised that it is the LEA that decides what constitutes 'necessary' transport.[26] One college told us that their local social services department had identified 28 people wishing to attend college but who were unable to do so because they needed transport. Social services departments tend to use their powers in relation to what they themselves provide, although they have the power to provide transport for their clients. Another college told us:

> *It is a frustrating situation when students attending the same course do not get the same transport service*[27]

4.33 Poor co-ordination was equally frustrating. We heard of one 18 year-old student who enrolled in a college and was then told by her LEA that it would cease funding her transport, halfway through the course, when she was 19.[28] There is little co-ordination between LEAs and social services departments and, as a result, provision sometimes has to move to day-centres instead of bringing day-centre clients to college.

4.34 Respondents told us about barriers of time, where transport to and from college is not arranged to match college starting or finishing times, or where there are few or difficult connections between transport times. One parent in Lancashire commented that her daughter had to give up her course because of a 3 and a half hour journey each day.[29] It is frustrating for students to spend time on travel which could be spent on learning. Students at the workshops told us that the unreliability of public transport was a source of anxiety for them. One said:

> *Sometimes the buses don't turn up or break down. I get worried.*[30]

4.35 Transport costs can also be prohibitive. Students at the workshops told us that even subsidised schemes run by voluntary organisations, such as 'Ring and Ride' required a contribution, which they felt created a barrier to attendance.[31]

Collaboration and planning between further education and LEAs, social and health services and voluntary organisations

4.36 Much of the evidence we received testified to an absence of joint work between social and health services and further education managers. It also indicated that lack of knowledge and expertise in collaboration and joint planning among staff in further education were key factors in the lack of provision.[32] Where joint working does exist, it is often in the early stages of development. We found that some social services authorities omit further education from community care plans for their area and that they are not obliged to consult colleges or LEAs before drawing these up. Few senior managers or co-ordinators in colleges are fully involved in community care planning groups. Few college strategic plans include material from community care plans locally: for 1995-96, only 35% of sector colleges consulted social service departments when conducting their needs analysis.[33] Education provision is seen by some as merely an expensive form of 'day-care' and social services departments do not always find the money to purchase provision at full cost for their day-centre users.[34] These matters are explored further in chapter 8 on collaboration.

4.37 The biggest criticism of further education that we heard from social services, health and voluntary organisations is that colleges are reactive rather than proactive, often confused by funding and legal responsibilities and rarely collaborative in planning and purchasing.[35] One social services department commented that the only significant liaison with further education occurred when FEFC forms on specialist placement had to be completed. Another reported active joint planning between the local health care trust, local authority, further education and local voluntary organisations, parents, carers and users. They said:

> *There is a need for national debate about the contribution of these services [to] meeting the further education needs of people with learning disabilities...[There should be] national advice and guidance of the provision and/or funding of special further education by LEAs, social services and health authorities, stating what is expected of each.*[36]

The organisation of provision and its accessibility

4.38 Many of those who told us of difficulties over participation argued that the way provision is organised and funded can act as a barrier. One senior social services planning officer told us that, prior to incorporation, colleges had 'little or no vision' about the possible links with community care, statements of shared

4

values, joint activities and planning, or the use of contract agreements in the provision of services. Provision and level of support for students with disabilities and/or learning difficulties, she continued, varied according to where students lived and which college they attended, but the introduction of a market economy was likely to cause more variation. She concluded that, 'Colleges do not appear to be wholly informed and clear about the new funding arrangements, or able to explain them to colleagues in other agencies'.[37] The absence of 'vision', of seeing the possibilities of further education for people with disabilities and/or learning difficulties, is a barrier to participation. For example, for adults with mental health difficulties, and young people with emotional and behavioural difficulties, fear and ignorance on the part of those working in the sector about these learners, and lack of recognition of the sector's potential on the part of social services can be powerful factors affecting participation. The inspectorate told us that colleges are not very good yet at planning what they provide and that they lack accurate information about the extent to which certain groups are represented in further education. Some colleges which planned to extend their vocational programmes to such students are doing so without any systematic analysis of either need or demand.

4.39 Several colleges cited the inaccessibility of their accommodation as a key factor in preventing participation. Two said:

> *For students with physical disability, for example, wheelchair [users], our college is almost impossible to access. On each occasion when we have been asked we have provided individual support by employing an assistant. We have also educated successfully partially-sighted students by providing special equipment and individual tuition. Our problem is that students do not apply, probably because they perceive the difficulties themselves. We never turn anybody away.*

> *With respect to open access, the college has inherited, post-incorporation, several buildings which do not lend themselves to open access. This matter is being addressed.*[38]

4.40 The survey of health and safety matters in sector colleges commissioned by the Council identified a list of capital projects in priority order.[39] Whilst a small proportion of this work was required to improve physical access, we found that a survey looking specifically at physical accessibility of state colleges for students with disabilities and learning difficulties is now required. Ninety-four respondents to the call for evidence argued for more attention to be paid to the accessibility of provision in any future surveys of buildings; advocated that colleges report on accessibility or told us of the barriers to participation presented by the physical features of college.[40] We discuss this further in chapter 11.

4.41 Schedule 2 to the Act can be a further barrier, because some existing and valuable educational provision aims to maintain or strengthen the skills these students already have and does not necessarily lead to the learning outcomes covered by the schedule. There is some evidence, too, that some colleges have ceased to offer provision because they feared it would not fall within schedule 2, and would not be approved by the Council for funding purposes.[41] We discuss this further in chapter 9.

Understanding the requirements of older students

4.42 Over 100 respondents offered evidence about adult students and their particular requirements. Their main areas of concern were:

i. *the purpose of education for adults;* a survey of 215 colleges and 65 LEAs in 1995 found a marked skew in the curriculum toward basic skills tuition; cuts in provision affecting people with severe or profound learning difficulties; one in three respondents indicated that the wider use of accreditation was excluding some people with learning difficulties.[42]

ii. *definitions of schedule 2 to the Further and Higher Education Act 1992*; the new distinction between schedule 2 and other courses has resulted in much uncertainty about what makes courses eligible for Council funding. Respondents told us that uncertainty about the need for accreditation or that courses should lead to a vocational or academic outcome had threatened the provision of some lip-reading classes for those losing their hearing, part-time courses for students with mental health problems, and courses for students with profound and multiple learning difficulties.[43]

iii. *progression routes;* these may not exist for some adult learners and some vocational programmes may not meet all their requirements, particularly those programmes for part-time students with severe learning difficulties.

iv. *focus of colleges*; there may be too great a focus on the full-time and younger learner. We were told that not all colleges value adults' previous experience, and that they do not fully understand the episodic nature of their learning, the complexity of their reasons for learning, and the financial difficulties facing those who wish to study.[44]

v. *reduction in non-schedule 2 provision by local education authorities*; this leads to direct pressure on providers to ensure that more and more provision is identified as falling within schedule 2.[45] The analysis of external institutions' three-year strategic objectives reported to the Council in July 1995 shows that 33% identified LEA policies on non-schedule 2 provision as the most serious threat to their achievement of their strategic plans, mentioned most often after 'competition from other colleges'.[46]

SUMMARY OF MAIN FINDINGS

4.43 When we analysed this evidence in the light of our principles and the indicative evidence set out earlier, we found it difficult to draw absolute conclusions about whether the further education participation for those with learning difficulties and/or disabilities matches their requirement. This is because the data do not allow such comparisons to be made easily and because colleges are trying to respond to those who present themselves for further education. Colleges are not, on the whole, trying to stimulate extra demand from those who currently do not, for whatever reason, seek out further education. However, we are clear that there are some important weaknesses in the current pattern of participation:

- emerging evidence of under-participation by those with emotional and behavioural difficulties, mental health difficulties, and profound and multiple learning difficulties
- colleges are often at an early stage in the development of their ability to assess local needs systematically and to know how to stimulate demand within their local populations
- emerging evidence of difficulties confronting adults with learning difficulties and/or disabilities.

4 ADDRESSING WEAKNESSES AND BUILDING ON STRENGTHS

Whether the further education provision for those with learning difficulties and/or disabilities matches their requirements

4.44 At present, the Council expects colleges to undertake a needs analysis to inform their strategic planning. But colleges told us they wanted more help with their needs analysis. We think the position would also improve if the Council required colleges to account for student populations which do not sufficiently reflect the nature of the local population.

4.45 If needs analysis were carried out thoroughly and if their funding were acted upon systematically, the result would be a sector that is more inclusive than it is today. Including more students with these particular needs, through developing effective learning environments, would benefit both the country and the individual in the medium and long term. There are sound economic as well as human reasons for pursuing a more inclusive sector and in particular, encouraging those currently under-represented to take part. Young people with emotional and behavioural difficulties who do not achieve in initial education or participate in further education at the moment, and older people, too, represent a waste of talent and potential. The costs of supporting those with mental health difficulties are high and might be less were there to be effective involvement in further education of people with mental health difficulties. The idea — which we strongly support — that mental health service users might benefit from educational provision is strongly to the fore in other countries, for example, in Australia.[47]

Tackling under-representation by colleges and the Council to ensure that further education is more inclusive

4.46 Part of the mapping project explored areas of provision which colleges feel they cannot make. Specialist colleges will continue to offer opportunities which are crucial to ensuring that some individuals can participate in further education. They can offer both a residential experience and specialist facilities. We found that sector colleges and specialist colleges could do more to share their expertise, for example, through ‘clustering’ to share resources or courses to make it easier for students to move easily between colleges. This kind of joint initiative could be encouraged through funding methods and strategic planning. A start has been made by the Council in making the rules about funding much clearer where sector and specialist colleges work together.[48]

4.47 Colleges would also tackle under-representation more vigorously if the inspectorate’s assessment of the quality of range and responsiveness in a college took account of the range of provision required in an area. The views of other inspectorates such as OFSTED and the social services inspectorate should also be sought. Responsibility for ensuring that there is adequate and sufficient further education provision is split between LEAs and the Council. The committee believes that it is the overall provision in a geographical area which should be assessed for adequacy and sufficiency rather than the responsiveness of the different providers. The Council’s inspectorate might be charged with reporting on the extent to which both the system as a whole and individual colleges are responsive to the requirements of people with disabilities and/or learning difficulties in their community. Joint inspection with social services inspectorate and OFSTED should be increased with this in mind.

4.48 A guide for colleges about how to map their local populations and plan accordingly, using the best practice to be found in the sector, would also help colleges tackle under-representation. This would go some way to addressing those weaknesses in the way provision is organised which we discussed earlier.

4.49 The Council also needs to adopt a more proactive approach regionally and with individual colleges. Colleges told us that the Council should monitor more effectively the make-up of a college's student population and require a profile of the local community, to be included in the college's strategic plan. The Council should also require an explanation from any college where the population in the college does not reflect the nature and characteristics of the local population.

4.50 Colleges need to respond specifically to the indicators of disaffection identified by the TECs. They also need to develop flexible, individually-tailored approaches to these students which recognise their capabilities and also provide them with a secure and safe learning environment. Clear guidelines and training for staff, good assessment and individual support plans, and effective referral and supervision arrangements are essential to good provision.

4.51 Colleges taking part in the committee's exercise to test the focus on inclusive learning told us that this was more likely to be achieved through better focused and promoted programmes and opportunities, increased awareness raising among all staff and a more strategic approach to needs analysis. In the medium term, colleges suggested better outreach work, better links with schools and agencies, the development of more pre-foundation courses, and survey work to compare the student profile with that of the community. In the long term, colleges suggested recruitment targets for specific groups, improvement of the accessibility of accommodation, reviewing and extending ranges of courses, better strategic planning with health and social services, and better marketing to adult groups. These views point to the need for a whole-college approach which draws together these aspects of their activities.[49]

4.52 At regional level, a strategic purpose could be brought to bear on improving participation if the Council set up subcommittees of its regional committees to review, monitor and stimulate collaboration to address participation. We say more about this in chapter 8. The subregional groupings established following the publication of the second competitiveness white paper[50] offer a model. These groups are charged with identifying local employment and industrial needs from the further education sector and considering bids from colleges to mount provision which meets those needs. A relatively small sum of money (about £20 million a year) is allocated on the basis of the subregional groups' views. We consider that subcommittees which included representatives of the relevant agencies as well as colleges could perform a similar function specifically for students with learning difficulties and/or disabilities. They could:

- map the local population and ensure that data are available to colleges
- identify gaps and consider strategies for meeting them, possibly involving a small amount of start-up funding and collaborative working between colleges and other agencies
- make good use of TEC research about the local labour market needs
- include representatives of specialist and sector colleges
- review and set targets for the total pattern of local participation by looking across the usual boundaries between college, local education and social services provision; this target-setting could, perhaps, be informed by more joint inspection activity between OFSTED, the social services inspectorate and the Council's inspectors.

Monitoring and reporting on participation

4.53 The committee considers that there is a case for significant further research into:

- the lack of participation among women with disabilities and/or learning difficulties
- low participation from ethnic minority groups
- the barriers experienced by young people with emotional and behavioural difficulties
- the needs of and barriers faced by adults with mental health difficulties.

4.54 For the Council to be satisfied that it is making adequate and sufficient provision, it needs to monitor and audit participation. Council and colleges need better data on who participates in further education, who does not, and what strategies might be used to improve participation in certain areas. Some of this will rely on research agencies.

4.55 The Council should systematically collect and make available data on local and regional levels of participation of students with disabilities and/or learning difficulties and provide this to the regional subcommittee we have suggested, to assist their own planning and monitoring of colleges' provision for these students. The ISR should be developed to achieve this.

4.56 Three improvements are needed to the ISR to ensure that reliable data on provision and participation will be available annually to the Council and ultimately to colleges. The Council should:

- use a new definition of disability in the ISR to include moderate and severe learning difficulties, specific learning difficulties, emotional and behavioural difficulties and mental health difficulties
- replace the existing disability field with a field for those students identifying themselves as having a learning difficulty and/or disability, which specifies the type(s) of learning difficulty and/or disability they have
- introduce a new field in the ISR which identifies whether the student has been assessed as requiring additional support for learning, irrespective of whether such support is funded through the additional support funding methodology.

4.57 The Council itself could set an example by reporting its progress on implementing the recommendations in this report in its annual report to the secretary of state which is required by the *Disability Discrimination Act 1995*.

RECOMMENDATIONS

4.58 The key recommendations about participation:

Strategic planning

4.59 The Council should provide colleges with more help in planning their provision strategically and should require them to take more systematic account of local needs. It should also promote collaborative planning between colleges and other agencies in a local area. Specifically, the Council should:

- develop and publish the practical guide for colleges which is currently being produced as a result of collaborative work between the committee and the widening participation committee
- require colleges to use that guide in their needs analysis
- require colleges to explain in their strategic plan why the student population does not reflect the local population and comment on this in the published inspection reports, including a grading based on the extent of the match between the two populations
- set up regional subcommittees charged with monitoring the participation of those with learning difficulties and/or disabilities in the region and with encouraging colleges and others to respond collaboratively,

possibly by setting targets and using start-up funding, where there is evidence of gaps in provision

- report on the effectiveness of these arrangements in its annual report to the secretary of state which is required under the *Disability Discrimination Act 1995*
- consider extending to colleges a requirement to 'have regard' to the local needs of these learners in their strategic plans, as a condition of funding.

Data

4.60 The Council should amend its individualised student record (ISR) so that more effective data on the participation of students with disabilities and/or learning difficulties are collected. Specifically the Council should:

- rename the existing 'registered' disability field in the ISR as 'disability and/or learning difficulty'. This field would refer to students identifying themselves as having a disability and/or learning difficulty and would allow them to specify the type(s) of disability and/or learning difficulty they have
- issue broader guidance on the definition of disability to be used in the ISR to include moderate and severe learning difficulties, specific learning difficulties, emotional and behavioural difficulties, and mental health difficulties
- introduce a new field in the ISR which identifies whether the student has been assessed as requiring additional support for learning, irrespective of whether such support is funded through the Council's additional support funding methodology
- retain the field in which Council-funded additional support is recorded.

Disaffected young people

4.61 The Council should encourage the Department for Education and Employment to produce a national strategy by which colleges, schools and others can better address the needs of disaffected young people, as highlighted in the Dearing Review of the 16 to 19 curriculum.

Funding

4.62 The Council should encourage concerted action by colleges and other agencies to promote opportunities for participation particularly by under-represented groups, through their funding. Specifically:

- the Council should encourage local education authorities to transfer management of their discretionary awards and transport budgets to colleges to explore how far a more coherent system of funding can be developed which better matches the learning and learner support needs of students
- the government should consider the advantages of a single post-16 funding agency which includes discretionary awards and funding for schools and external institutions, to ensure that there is greater consistency of participation between areas and so that the choice of provision made by students is not adversely affected by differences in the way courses are funded
- the Council should urge the Department of Health and the Department for Education and Employment to work together to create a joint strategy and provide guidance and advice to purchasers and providers. The guidance should make specific reference to adults with profound and complex learning difficulties; and those with mental health difficulties.

4

References

1 FEFC Circular 96/02 *Analysis of Institutions' Strategic Planning Information for the Period 1995-96 to 1997-98,* Coventry, FEFC, January 1996

2 J. Bradley, L. Dee and F. Wilenius *Students with Disabilities and/or Learning Difficulties in Further Education; A Review of Research Carried out by the National Foundation for Educational Research*, Slough, NFER, 1994, p. 8

3 Responses to the mapping project, (unpublished)

4 Meager, Nigel, Ceri Evans and Sally Dench (of The Institute for Employment Studies) *Mapping Provision: The Provision of and Participation in Further Education by Students with Learning Difficulties and/or Disabilities: A Report to the Learning Difficulties and/or Disabilities Committee*, London, HMSO, 1996. The mapping exercise commissioned by the committee indicated the significant national data sets and analysed each of them to form some general figures relating to incidence of disability within the general population. Much of the data overlapped and it was not possible to deduce the likely need in the general population, a proportion of whom might reasonably be thought to require further education. The second part of the research surveyed the provision made in colleges through a national questionnaire. It involved a pilot survey undertaken in 20 colleges in spring 1995 and a postal questionnaire piloted with a sample of 100 sector colleges in the summer term 1995. The main survey itself was launched in October 1995, covering all sector colleges and a sample of external institutions, and concluded by mid-March 1996. The survey related to all students enrolled on 1 November 1995. There was a response rate of just over 60% (274 colleges). The distribution of responses by type of college and region is statistically representative of the sector as a whole, but higher response rates were achieved from larger institutions.

5 Figures taken from the data returned to the IES and then calculated for the whole sector. This includes some specialist designated colleges. The IES study used November 1995 college figures and estimated between 5.3 and 5.7%. The Council's analysis of data from the November 1995 ISR return estimated a student population in colleges of 2,389,700, making the 126,500 IES estimate of students with disabilities/learning difficulties some 5.29% of the total.

6 NUT survey 1982, quoted in J. Bradley, L. Dee and F. Wilenius *Students with Disabilities and/or Learning Difficulties in Further Education; A Review of Research Carried out by the National Foundation for Educational Research*, Slough, NFER, 1994

7 Richard Stowell *Catching Up? Provision for Students with Special Educational Needs in Further and Higher Education,* London, National Bureau for Handicapped Students, 1987. This survey did not include sixth form colleges, independent colleges, schools, adult education establishments or Hereward College of Further Education. There was a 93% return overall.

8 i. Her Majesty's Inspectorate *'Students with Special Needs in Further Education': Education Observed 9,* London, DES, 1989

ii. Her Majesty's Inspectorate *'Special Needs Issues': Education Observed,* London, DES, 1990

iii. J. Bradley, L. Dee and F. Wilenius *Students with Disabilities and/or Learning Difficulties in Further Education; A Review of Research Carried out by the National Foundation for Educational Research*, Slough, NFER, 1994, p.9

iv. Office for Standards in Education *Adult Education and Youth Work within Local Education Authorities: A Review of the Year 1994/95: A Report from the Office of Her Majesty's Chief Inspector of Schools,* London, OFSTED, 1995 paras 16 – 17

v. Evidence from NIACE presented to the committee (unpublished), drawn from NIACE *Still a Chance to Learn?: A Report on the Impact of the FHE Act 1992 on Education for Adults with*

Learning Difficulties, Leicester, NIACE, 1996 and Veronica McGivney *Staying or Leaving the Course: Non-completion and Retention of Mature Students in Further and Higher Education,* Leicester, NIACE, 1996.

9 Responses to the mapping project, (unpublished)

10 101 respondents offered evidence on perceived gaps in FE provision for those over the age of 19. Responses to the call for evidence analysis, (unpublished)

11 Further Education Unit *'Adult Status for All?' FEU Bulletin,* London, FEU, February 1991

12 Further Education Unit/MENCAP *Learning for Life: A Pack to Support Adults who have Profound Intellectual and Multiple Physical Disabilities,* London, FEU, 1994

13 The importance of providing further education to mental health patients in NHS regional secure units and the problem of who was responsible for funding it was mentioned by the Mental Health Act Commission in their report to parliament in 1989. The Mental Health Act Commission, *3rd Biennial Report 1987-89,* London, HMSO, 1989

14 *Health of the Nation: A Strategy for Health in England,* London, HMSO, 1992, chap. 17

15 Responses to the mapping project, (unpublished)

16 *Ibid.*

17 *Ibid.*

18 Figures supplied by the DfEE.

19 Responses to the call for evidence, (unpublished)

20 *Dissatisfaction and Non-participation in Education, Training and Employment by Individuals aged 18-20: A Research Study Undertaken by Aspire Consultants on Behalf of the TEC Chief Executives Network on Equal Opportunities and Special Training Needs,* London, Department for Education and Employment, 1996.

21 Responses to the call for evidence, (unpublished)

22 By 'adults' or 'older learners' the committee means those over the age of 25. This is the age referred to in the evidence from NIACE.

23 Responses to the call for evidence, (unpublished)

24 *The Education (Handicapped Children) Act 1970*, London, HMSO

25 Unpublished committee papers on testing the committee's approach.

26 Beachcroft Stanleys *Duties and Powers: The Law Governing the Provision of Further Education to Students with Learning Difficulties and/or Disabilities: A Report to the Learning Difficulties and/or Disabilities Committee*, London, HMSO, 1996

27 Responses to the call for evidence, (unpublished)

28 *Ibid.*

29 *Ibid.*

30 SCPR *Student Voices: The Views of Further Education Students with Learning Difficulties and/or Disabilities: Findings from a Series of Student Workshops Commissioned by the Learning Difficulties and/or Disablities Committee*, London, Skill: National Bureau for Students with Disabilities, March 1996

31 *Ibid.*

32 Responses to the call for evidence, (unpublished)

33 FEFC Circular 96/02 *Analysis of Institutions' Strategic Planning Information for the Period 1995-96 to 1997-98,* Coventry, FEFC January 1996

34 Responses to the call for evidence, (unpublished)

35 *Ibid.*

36 *Ibid.*

37 *Ibid.*

38 Responses to the mapping project, (unpublished)

39 Known as the 'Hunter survey'.

40 Responses to the call for evidence, (unpublished)

41 *Ibid.*

42 NIACE *Still a Chance to Learn?: A Report on the Impact of the FHE Act 1992 on Education for Adults with Learning Difficulties,* Leicester, NIACE, 1996

43 Responses to the call for evidence, (unpublished). Lip-reading classes were the subject of 98 responses; 70 respondents referred to mental health provision.

44 Evidence from NIACE presented to the committee, (unpublished)

45 NIACE *Still a Chance to Learn?: A Report on the Impact of the FHE Act 1992 on Education for Adults with Learning Difficulties,* Leicester, NIACE, 1996

46 FEFC Circular 96/02 *Analysis of Institutions' Strategic Planning Information for the Period 1995-96 to 1997-98,* Coventry, FEFC, January 1996

47 *Human Rights and Mental Illness: Report of the National Inquiry into the Human Rights of People with Mental Illness* Australian Government Publishing Service, 1993, chap. 13. This major report specifically identifies the significant potential of education for adults with mental health difficulties.

48 FEFC Circular 96/01 *Students with Learning Difficulties and/or Disabilities,* Coventry, FEFC, 1996, para. 38

49 Unpublished papers from testing the committee's approach

50 *Competitiveness: Helping Business to Win,* London, HMSO, May 1994

Chapter 5: Assessing Students' Requirements

In this chapter, the committee examines how students' requirements should be assessed effectively in order to ensure inclusive learning.

THE ISSUES

1. effective assessment of students' requirements
   - a. obtaining the information colleges need about students and the role of link courses
   - b. assessing the requirements of students seeking funding at specialist colleges
2. funding the assessment of students' requirements
3. providing ongoing assessment for students' learning.

ASSESSING STUDENTS' REQUIREMENTS AND INCLUSIVE LEARNING

5.1 Effective assessment of students' requirements is at the centre of the committee's thinking about inclusive learning. Colleges must be able to identify and meet the requirements of new groups of learners. They will have new responsibilities, particularly in the early stages of a student's learning programme when they must identify how students learn best and their individual learning goals. By assessing requirements, we mean a process designed to identify:

- how an individual learns best — their approach to learning
- what an individual needs and wants to learn — their goals
- what must be done in order to effect the match between these.

5.2 The process of assessing students' requirements should ensure that:

- the student is an active partner; and parents and carers are involved where appropriate
- support for self-advocacy, independent guidance and advice is available
- the student's strengths and potential are recognised
- a realistic timetable for learning goals relevant to the student's life is specified

- the necessary support for learning is costed
- assessment takes place where the student is likely to learn
- information from other assessments is taken into account
- information from the assessment is used by other agencies working with the student
- the roles and responsibilities and action to be taken by different staff, college departments and external services are identified and recorded
- a schedule is set for monitoring and reviewing the student's progress.

THE COMMITTEE'S PRINCIPLES

5.3 The secretary of state's letter of guidance[1] advised the Council 'to ensure that adequate arrangements exist for assessing the needs of students with learning difficulties and/or difficulties and for identifying provision'. The committee wished to know if the existing arrangements for assessing students' requirements were good enough and whether they would enable colleges to provide inclusive learning. The assessment of students' requirements must be continuous and properly funded. It should be inclusive in that it is:

- *guided by the students' wishes;* the assessment process should offer opportunities and support to the individual, or their advocate, to make their views and wishes known and to influence decision-making
- *fair;* the assessment process should be impartial and take into account individual differences, including any effects of the student's ethnicity, gender and age in relation to their disability or learning difficulty
- *transparent;* the purpose, criteria, and outcomes of the assessment process should be understood by the student and, where relevant, their parents, carers or advocates
- *accessible*; the assessment process should be straightforward and uncomplicated so that the students and their parents or advocates may participate more easily and fully.

5.4 Evidence which might indicate that a college has adopted our principles includes:

EVIDENCE

- whole college policy on assessing students' requirements which is based on principles of equal opportunities
- centralised screening and assessment procedures
- established links with schools, the careers service, voluntary organisations, peripatetic services, the LEA
- a variety of instruments and materials for different types of assessment, for example, large text
- a programme of link courses with schools which help the college to assess the requirements of potential students
- arrangements for explaining the assessment process to students, parents and carers and for providing support for advocacy
- an induction programme during which a student's learning style, learning goals and learning environment are identified
- the outcomes of the assessment process are used to devise effective learning programmes
- procedures for collating evidence of students' progress in all aspects of their learning
- regular reviews of the match between the student's learning style, learning goals and learning environment
- procedures for taking account of information in care plans
- arrangements for involving students in assessing and recording their own progress.

5.5 Inspectorate evidence gave us the following examples of good and bad practice in assessing students' requirements:

EXAMPLES

College A

Well-established links with local schools, the careers service, the local authority and voluntary agencies in the community enable staff at the college to obtain detailed information about students prior to their starting college. Many of the students who go straight to college from school have attended link programmes at the college. There are parents' evenings at the end of the link programmes when staff are available to talk about college courses. All students are assessed during a carefully-planned induction week in order to identify their learning styles and learning goals. Learning support requirements are assessed at the same time. Advocacy support and specialist guidance are available for students who need it. Key staff have undergone training in different assessment techniques. The college draws on expertise in the local educational psychology service, Royal National Institute for the Blind (RNIB) support service and a nearby specialist residential college in order to carry out specialist assessments. The college has negotiated a contract with the local careers service which enables students to have good-quality advice and guidance at each stage of their college programme. College staff have attended a number of pupils' 14+ reviews and are familiar with the process of transition planning and the code of practice. Staff use the information in transition and care plans when they devise learning programmes. Subject teachers have found a variety of ways of helping students to assess and record their own progress. Students appreciate the opportunity to be involved and are able to describe their progress and to identify the next stage in their learning. Learning support is carefully linked to the students' main programmes. The college has a policy of involving students in regular reviews of the support they receive. A survey last year indicated that students were very positive about the support they receive and feel it is helping them to succeed. Weekly tutorials are held. Sometimes these are for individual students and sometimes for groups. They are used to review students' progress and to develop their record of achievement.

College B

The college does not have an induction programme and there are no agreed procedures for interviewing students. Departments use a variety of written tests which often bear little relation to the courses which students want to follow. Some of the tests use examples that might be offensive to members of certain ethnic groups. Many of the students are not able to read the information provided by the college about its provision. They rely on teaching staff to explain the different options. Staff complain that students are sometimes guided onto inappropriate courses in order to maintain course numbers. Learning support is provided through a 'drop-in' workshop on the main site. Students receive a leaflet about the workshop but must then arrange their own attendance. Staff in the workshop use a standard literacy and numeracy test to screen students. This does not identify the requirement of students with learning difficulties. They are expected to use the same workshop materials as other students. Class teachers are not aware of the support that is given to students within the workshop. Assessment records are filed in the offices of heads of departments and not seen by teaching staff. Some students have individual learning plans but they do not take into account the outcomes of students' assessments. Students often find themselves tackling work they have done before. The tutorial system is under-developed and students have few opportunities to discuss their progress with staff. Students speak angrily of the negative feedback about their learning they receive from some staff.

Effective assessment of students' requirements

5.6 A substantial number (376) of the responses to the committee's call for evidence indicated that effective assessment of students' requirements is a major issue in the quality and effectiveness of students' learning. The assessment process prior to and upon entry to college was of key importance to many of the students attending the student workshop series. These students told us:

- their learning suffered if their support requirements were assessed too late in their programmes of study; they considered it important to assess their support requirements at the pre-entry or induction stages
- inadequate procedures for assessing students' requirements sometimes resulted in students being placed in an inappropriate class; for example, a student who was deaf might be wrongly placed in a class for students with learning difficulties
- students sometimes felt that they were not fully involved in the assessment process and that their learning goals were decided by others
- good assessment of their requirements provided as part of a carefully-planned induction programme enabled students to say what they wanted and to feel confident that they were enrolling for the programme of study that was appropriate for them.[2]

5.7 The Council has stressed the importance it attaches to effective assessment of students' requirements by publishing the guidance on effective transition which the-then Department for Education presented in evidence to us.[3] A number of colleges described the careful way in which they set out assess students' requirements. One college told the researchers carrying out the mapping project:

> *Previous schools, parents and students are asked for information about learning support needs prior to enrolment. Appropriate assessments...are arranged and support provided where appropriate. During the first term students are encouraged to self-identify learning support needs. Staff are also asked to suggest those with specific support needs. These students are assessed externally using a variety of literacy, numeracy and other tests devised by the British Psychological Society*[4]

5.8 However, the quality of the assessments and procedures used by some colleges are poor and there is a consequent failure to identify students' support requirements. For example, some colleges use literacy and numeracy screening tests as the only form of initial assessment for students with learning difficulties and/or disabilities, even though these tests were not designed to identify learning difficulties nor to identify how an individual learns best.[5] The inspectorate's evidence confirmed that some teachers lack the skills to find out how individuals learn best, to identify their learning goals and to assess their progress. Often this was because teachers have not been given sufficient training.[6]

5.9 We found that:

- some assessment procedures are inadequate for the purpose of identifying strengths and the student's support requirements
- the outcomes of some assessments are not used in the development of individual learning programmes.

5.10 A worrying number of college staff were unaware of the information and guidance from the Council which would enable them to do their job more effectively. In addition, health and social services were unaware of the Council's funding arrangements and therefore less able to fulfil their duty under the *Disabled Persons (Services, Consultation and Representation)*

Act 1986 to provide information about education to people with learning difficulties and/or disabilities.

5.11 Some colleges which offered extensive details of their arrangements for assessing students' requirements also pointed out the difficulty of implementing these arrangements if students do not wish to take part:

> *All prospective students are encouraged to identify learning difficulties and/or disabilities on the enrolment and/or at interview and/or to the learning difficulties and disabilities manager. This would enable assessment to be made and support systems [to be] in place for the start of the course. However, there are still gaps and discrepancies in the system and large numbers of students are not asking for support.*[7]

5.12 The careers service is particularly important in helping young people to make informed choices about their further education. We received much evidence that demonstrated how crucial the careers service can be for young people who need impartial guidance and information about options. Its responsibilities are enshrined in the code of practice which accompanies the *Education Act 1993*. The responsibilities of the careers service are considerable and their client group includes young people with special educational needs until they are settled in their career intention. There is thus no upper age limit for their involvement with these clients.

5.13 However, contracts between individual careers services and government offices are confidential. This makes it difficult to judge whether these contracts give sufficient attention to students with learning difficulties and/or disabilities. The role of sector colleges in shaping the terms of the contract and the service delivered varies considerably. Service level arrangements at local level do not always make specific reference to students with learning difficulties and/or disabilities. In some instances, one specialist officer may have to serve all the special schools in an education authority and the local college or colleges, and may not have enough time to provide the support that many students require. In addition, we heard that not all careers services were able to involve specialists or keep up to date with developments in further education.[8] It is now harder for some careers services to provide the degree of continuity between school and college that students need, partly as a result of the reorganisation of the service.

1a Obtaining the information colleges need about students and the role of link courses

5.14 The value of link courses as an important means of identifying the requirements of school pupils who will go on to the college was stressed to us on many occasions by a substantial number of those giving evidence. Students in the workshop series described how these courses enabled them to find out about the college in easy stages. The inspectorate told us of the valuable opportunities these courses can provide for students' requirements to be assessed over a period of time in the setting in which their learning will take place.[9] OFSTED indicated the importance of link courses in assisting young people to make an easy transition from school to college.[10] Some colleges are heavily involved: one college taking part in the mapping project reported over 150 pupils attending college from local special schools.[11]

5.15 Many courses which had been funded by the local authority disappeared as a result of changes under the *Further and Higher Education Act 1992* and the local management of special schools. However, many colleges and schools are trying hard to offer a range of opportunities for the students and the colleges to get to know each other and to facilitate an effective transition from school to further education. One college told the researchers carrying out the mapping project:

> *Since TVEI funding finished in schools, our college has offered a Links programme to local schools at a reduced rate because we felt this is an area of value to both the schools and the college. We provide these links in a variety of ways, to two mainstream secondary schools...a local special school for pupils with moderate learning difficulties...the local school for pupils with emotional and behavioural difficulties...the local pupil referral unit...this is a growth area since incorporation.*[12]

5.16 Link courses play a vital role in preparing young people for college and in giving both the college and the student a valuable opportunity to get to know one another. They provide opportunities for information about students to be exchanged. These courses are important for those young people who have had difficult or unsuccessful experiences of school. They are more likely to opt out of the education system before school-leaving age. Sir Ron Dearing's review of the 16 to 19 curriculum referred to the growing numbers of pupils who are either excluded from school or exclude themselves[13] and we consider this in chapter 4. Despite this obvious need, we found considerable concern about the future funding of link courses.[14]

1b Assessing the requirements of students seeking funding at specialist colleges

5.17 The committee's call for evidence was issued only 19 months after the Council was established. This meant that responses were received when the Council's procedures for funding placements at specialist colleges, which apply to some 1,800 students a year, were still being put in place. Eighty-six respondents concentrated on these procedures. Many concentrated on what were in effect teething troubles. Other respondents raised important issues relating to the consistency and speed of the Council's decisions.[15] These are tackled in our recommendations.

5.18 Other evidence focused on what was considered by some to be the negative nature of the process to agree funding to attend a specialist college. The *Further and Higher Education Act 1992* requires the Council to fund a placement only where sector provision is not adequate. The Council has interpreted this to mean that a sector college must state that it cannot make provision for a student before funding can be agreed for a placement at a specialist college outside the sector. Some respondents told us that this involved a painful process of rejection by the sector college before funding can be agreed for a student to attend a specialist college. One college told us 'the college is being used to prove we cannot cope with some students with disabilities in order to support residential further education'.[16] Staff in specialist colleges commented that the placement process sometimes did little to bolster the self-esteem of young people who are in the midst of an often-difficult transition. These staff wanted the students to feel able to choose the college as well as the college selecting its students.

5.19 Whilst the main characteristics of assessing of students' requirements effectively are to be found in both sector and specialist colleges, we received evidence which applied particularly to the specialist residential colleges:

- some specialist colleges need to improve their methods of drawing together and assessing and recording progress in different aspects of a student's learning
- some specialist colleges need to take greater account of the ethnicity, culture and home background of students in their assessment processes in order to provide the right kinds of opportunities for students.

2 Funding the assessment of students' requirements

5.20 The Council's funding methodology emphasises the importance of assessment by allocating about 10% of the total units of activity to the 'entry' phase of the learning programme; and by requiring colleges to put together a learning agreement signed between the college and the student, based on that assessment. In addition, colleges can include the extra costs of specialised assessments as part of the additional support component of the methodology. We explore this further in chapter 11.

5.21 In the early days of our work, we found that many respondents were not sufficiently informed about this aspect of the funding methodology. There was a clear need for the Council to provide information and guidance on its activities. The committee was able to provide guidance which the Council sent to colleges in *How to Apply for Funding 1996-97,*[17] clarifying the definition of learning support and describing how the assessment form should be used as part of the assessment cycle.[18]

5.22 Other colleges are concerned that the threshold for the additional support bands (currently set at £170) deters them from undertaking thorough assessments as well as from offering students the necessary learning support. Colleges in the committee's exercise to test its thinking about inclusive learning (see appendix to annex D) indicated that the threshold might deter some colleges from recruiting large numbers of learners who required low-levels of support. This has particular consequences for part-time adult students, some of whom require high levels of specialist support but for a relatively short period. One college told the researchers in the mapping project:

> *The majority of students with learning difficulties at this college have levels of literacy and numeracy which do not attract additional units of support but which nevertheless require additional support if students are to be successful.*[19]

The threshold presented particular difficulties for smaller colleges with a high average level of funding. The committee gave considerable thought to this matter. We wish to see the level of generally available learning support raised and improved in every college. This is vital if colleges are to meet a wider variety of requirements as part of their everyday activities. We consider this issue further in chapter 7 (on support for learning) and in chapter 11 (on funding).

3 Providing ongoing assessment for students' learning

5.23 Students want to be involved in assessing and recording their own progress. One told us:

> *It is important for us to assess our own improvement, not just have someone telling us how well, or otherwise, we have done. Having standards is important — achieving them boosts our confidence.*[20]

5.24 Some students do not have their learning recorded appropriately. Some specialist colleges for students with learning difficulties and/or disabilities find difficulties in assessing and recording the different elements of the students' learning. Students taking part in the workshop series said that they were often not sure if their progress in learning was being monitored, though the majority knew that teachers kept records. They told us that feedback on progress:

- varied in frequency between once every few weeks to twice a year
- was irregular
- was given only sometimes when things were not going well
- sometimes failed to provide advice and guidance.[21]

5 SUMMARY OF MAIN FINDINGS

5.25 When we analysed this evidence in the light of the principles and indicative evidence set out earlier, we found the following main weaknesses:

- college staff do not always understand how to obtain funds for additional support based on a thorough assessment of students' requirements
- colleges do not always get the right balance between using information about a student's previous educational experience and assessing their new requirements
- the feelings of rejection of some students when they seek funding to attend a specialist college
- insufficient collaboration between the college and other services involved with the student.

5.26 If colleges fail to identify students' requirements correctly then:

- the provision of appropriate support may be delayed
- teachers may be unprepared to teach a person with a disability or learning difficulty
- the right equipment and materials are not available at the right time
- buildings and adaptations to accommodation and facilities may not be accessible to all students
- students may repeat work that they have already done
- students may lose motivation, make poor progress and under-achieve.

ADDRESSING WEAKNESSES AND BUILDING ON STRENGTHS

1 Effective assessment of students' requirements

1a Obtaining the information colleges need about students and the role of link courses

5.27 Colleges need accurate and timely information about the student's previous educational experience. At the same time, however, colleges need to let students feel that they are making a fresh start in further education and that their past experiences are behind them.

5.28 It is important that both the college and the school have a clear policy on transition to further education. The importance of easy and effective transition is now enshrined in the code of practice underpinning the *Education Act 1993*. Under the terms of the code, those young people who have had statements of special educational need at school will also have a transition plan prepared with them as they approach the end of their schooling. The code of practice sets out the principles upon which the transition plan is made. The plan identifies how different agencies will support the young person's transition from school. The code of practice sets out the same principles for preparing a transition plan as those we advocate for assessing students' requirements. The young person, and where appropriate, their parents, should be involved in preparing the transition plan. In addition, the plan should:

- focus on the young person's strengths as well as weaknesses
- clearly specify the agencies and individuals who have responsibility for different aspects of the young person's development

- be properly structured and balanced
- indicate how the young person may obtain information, support and guidance
- show how the young person's curriculum, including link courses, will prepare him for transition to further education
- indicate how the young person's record of achievement will be used
- specify the kind of information about the young person that will be given to the college.[22]

5.29 Colleges need to understand the implications of the code of practice and:

- take part, where possible, in the meetings to draw up a young person's transition plan
- take into account the outcomes of the 14+ review when deciding how a student learns best, their learning goals and the learning environment that is required
- take the plan into account at each assessment and review of a student's progress
- establish and ensure effective communication between the college and schools
- provide the student and their family with accessible information about the college and the support it offers
- work with schools to establish link provision, provide 'taster' courses, induction programmes, visits and other activities in order to provide opportunities for assessment, counselling and guidance
- work with schools to ensure that parents or carers are aware of what the college offers.

5.30 Colleges need to ensure that they work with agencies which may be involved with older students. Some have plans drawn up by other services. These may set goals for housing, mobility, physical care, day-care or other aspects of a person's life. The college has a responsibility to ensure that what the student learns contributes to the rest of the student's life. To do this the college should:

- have identified its own role in enabling the individual to fulfil their broader aspirations, and be able to explain this role and its value to other service providers involved with the individual
- be able to cost and guarantee the quality and ensure the timeliness, effectiveness and efficiency of the learning opportunities it provides
- take part in assessments and reviews of students' progress carried out by the other services and invite them to take part in its own.

5.31 Some colleges need to improve and develop their expertise in assessing students' requirements, particularly for students who are under-represented in the sector. Staff in some colleges will need new skills and techniques if they are to assess the requirements of students who are unfamiliar to them.

5.32 We concluded that much could be gained from closer collaboration between the sector and specialist colleges to improve ways in which students' requirements are assessed. Such collaboration could lead to:

- access to specialist resources to help sector colleges to carry out complex diagnostic assessments
- sharing of expertise in the assessment and recording of student progress
- a greater understanding of any particular requirements which students from ethnic minority backgrounds might have in relation to their residential provision.

5.33 Link courses are crucial in helping many students to feel at ease and to be successful in their transition to further education, and for enabling colleges to assess student requirements. These courses are too important to allow them to fall victim of short-term funding disputes or to allow the varied practice that we found across the country to continue.

5.34 It is important for staff to have expertise in assessment. There is an urgent need for materials and guidance to assist teachers in diagnostic assessment and in assessing and recording students' progress. There is a particular need for college staff working with students who are supported by other agencies to train with staff from these agencies, in order to improve their skills in undertaking joint assessments.

5.35 We were impressed by the number of colleges which have adopted a corporate approach to assessing students' requirements. Colleges which have central admission processes carried out by properly-trained staff usually have consistent practices in identifying students' requirements.

1b Assessing the requirements of students seeking funding at specialist colleges

5.36 The growing number of students with complex difficulties who are seeking funding to attend specialist colleges means that:

- it may take longer and cost more to assess their requirements
- finding the right match between a student's preferred way of learning, their learning goals and the best learning environment may take longer
- students with complex or profound disabilities and learning difficulties are more likely to require physical care or therapy as part of their total programme. Their requirements for physical care or therapy should be assessed by different professionals working as a team which has a clear understanding of the student's aspirations. Care or therapy may be funded by different agencies. It may take time to arrange such funding, particularly where it is difficult to distinguish clearly between physical care, rehabilitation, therapy and education
- some specialist colleges are not yet able to identify clear learning goals for their students and then set targets against which their progress and achievement can be measured.

5.37 The Council could assist students and these specialist colleges if it allowed them a longer period in which to identify in more detail the student's learning objectives. Identification could take place once funding has been agreed. It need not necessarily lead to an extension of the student's course overall which would necessitate additional funding.

5.38 The expertise and experience of certain sector colleges in assessing and meeting the requirements of students with learning difficulties and/or disabilities from different ethnic groups and cultural backgrounds could be used to assist some specialist colleges to meet the needs of these students better and to allay the concerns of their parents or carers.

5.39 It is important that assessment to decide whether or not a student should be given a placement in a specialist college should be carried out according to publicly-stated criteria. The Council's annual circular and its leaflet for students have helped to explain how decisions about placements are taken. The circular specifies the criteria. These are that:

- the student's educational needs have been adequately assessed, and that the individual and their advocate have been involved in the process and professional advice has been available to them
- the facilities available in the sector are not adequate to meet the individual's needs
- the recommended placement is in the student's best interests
- appropriate educational provision cannot be secured for the individual either in the sector or through an alternative placement which would represent better value for money.[22]

5.40 We consider that these criteria reflect the principles set out in paragraph 5.3. We also believe that the criteria and their effectiveness should be kept under review. The Council could further improve the way it makes decisions about placements in specialist colleges, and the understanding of the general public of how these decisions are made, if it:

- included in its annual report to the secretary of state, required by the *Disability Discrimination Act 1995*, details of how it is meeting its targets for making decisions on placements speedily
- considered ways of making the process more positive for the students by, for example, requiring a sector college to provide an initial assessment and interview before making a decision about a student
- allowing specialist colleges a longer period in which to assess the requirements of students with the most complex requirements, once a decision to fund their place has been taken.

5.41 Some sector colleges told us that the Council should fund them to carry out assessments even when these lead to a decision that the college cannot meet the requirements identified. We think the Council should review this matter with the relevant representative bodies during its review of the funding methodology.

2 Funding the assessment of students' requirements

5.42 The funding methodology has already encouraged colleges to focus on assessing students' requirements. It does this directly, by including within the tariff about 10% of units for the entry phase of the learning programme, thus recognising that about 10% of a college's costs in relation to any individual student should be involved in assessing their requirements. The methodology also implicitly encourages colleges to carry out effective assessments of students' requirements as a result of the weighting attached to students' successful completion of their courses. This means that the college has a direct interest in ensuring that the student enrols on an appropriate programme with the necessary learning support to enable them to achieve their learning objectives.

5.43 In addition, the Council includes within the additional support bands the costs of specialised assessment. This means that colleges can claim additional units to meet those costs. However, we are conscious that our recommendations place new and additional responsibilities on colleges in relation to the assessment of students' requirements:

- to recruit and meet the requirements of new groups of learners, including those who are likely to require lengthy or specialist assessments of their requirements
- to identify how students learn best, what their learning goals are and their required learning environment
- to ensure college staff understand how the process of assessing students' requirements can be funded.

5.44 Colleges in the committee's testing exercise told us that the costs of these new responsibilities could not be met adequately if the weighting for the entry element remained at its present level. The committee wishes the Council to take these new costs into account by allocating new funding to the entry stage of the learning programme within the current methodology, and by ensuring that the new demands are taken into account in any future review of the methodology.

5.45 The other outstanding issue concerns responsibility for funding link courses, where, in our view, the provision varies too widely across the country. The Council should allow colleges to include within their calculation of additional support that element of their link courses which is genuinely about assessing the requirements of potential students. We recognise that this may be difficult because the individuals concerned will not be enrolled at the college and will, in many cases, be under the age of 16. The Council could seek a transfer of funds from local education authorities to meet the extra costs involved.

3 Providing ongoing assessment for students' learning

5.46 Teachers must be able to break down learning into small components and to assess and record the achievement of each component. They must be able to involve students in assessing and recording their own progress. Opportunities for increasing teachers' skills in assessment and the recording of students' progress are an important part of our proposal for a quality initiative. A student's record must show their:

- preferred way of learning
- learning goals
- learning environment, including learning support
- learning programme
- progress in learning
- achievements
- possible future requirements.

5.47 We attach particular importance to rigorous assessment and recording of progress in the different aspects of a student's learning at a specialist residential college. We have seen examples of good practice in which progress in one area of learning, for example, skills for independent living, is supported by work on complementary skills, such as literacy or numeracy.[23] Common assessment and recording procedures make a student's learning more coherent; and help to avoid the fragmented learning experienced by some students. Some of the specialist colleges and the sector need to increase the attention they pay to recording progress in learning rather than listing tasks undertaken by students.

5.48 Some students' learning does not progress in a straightforward fashion. For example, students with mental health difficulties may experience periods of poor concentration which lead to gaps in their learning. For other students, learning to make use of the college canteen or library represents substantial progress. Teachers need to be sensitive to factors which might influence learning and be ready to identify it wherever and whenever it happens. The national record of achievement should be used more systematically to record students' progress and achievements in a wide range of activities.

5.49 Students need to receive guidance and support throughout their learning programme. For example, a tutorial programme should provide opportunities for them to discuss and review their progress. The match between a student's requirements and their learning environment should be reviewed at regular intervals. The student's views should be taken into account before changes are made. We say more about the mechanism that might hold together the different aspects of a student's further education in chapter 8.

RECOMMENDATIONS

FUNDING THE ASSESSMENT OF STUDENTS' REQUIREMENTS

5.50 The Council should continue to recognise the costs of providing effective individual assessment and should promote a wider understanding of its funding by publishing accessible information on its funding arrangements.

5.51 The Council should consider allocating additional new funds to the entry stage of the learning programme within the tariff, to take account of the new costs of assessment which may arise for all students as a result of the committee's recommendations.

ASSESSMENT FOR PLACEMENT AT A SPECIALIST COLLEGE

5.52 The Council should continue to improve its methods for funding students at specialist colleges. Specifically, in relation to the assessment of students' requirements, it should:

- publish details of its response rate for placement at specialist colleges, preferably as part of its report to the secretary of state
- take account of the importance and complexity of assessing students' requirements by retaining its insistence on an assessment and interview by a sector college before a placement decision is made. The Council should, however, recognise that for some students, the first term's placement might also represent an assessment which should be funded, without necessarily lengthening the overall period of the course
- work with representatives of the careers service, local education authorities and the Department for Education and Employment to ensure that careers officers retain and improve their knowledge of further education in sector and specialist colleges so that they may continue to advise students effectively on their options. They should also be encouraged to maintain their contact with students at specialist colleges as part of their contractual obligations to students with learning difficulties and/or disabilities, until such students are settled in their career or future training intentions.

Students with transition plans

5.53 The Council should further encourage colleges to take account of a student's transition plan by:

- requiring evidence during inspection that the college has in place arrangements for using information in transition plans to contribute to the assessment of students' requirements and to subsequent reviews and assessment of students' progress and achievement.

Students with care plans

5.54 The Council should require evidence during inspection carried out by the Council, or jointly with OFSTED, or the social services inspectorate, that the college and other services participate jointly in assessment and reviews and that the learning opportunities provided by the college are consistent with the overall aims of the student's learning and care plan(s).

ASSESSMENT OF PROGRESS IN THE LEARNING OF STUDENTS AT SPECIALIST RESIDENTIAL COLLEGES

5.55 The Council should promote more effective assessment of progress in the learning of students at specialist residential colleges. Specifically, the Council should require these colleges to:

- develop assessment and recording procedures which draw together different aspects of a student's learning programme by strengthening this aspect of its inspection of specialist colleges and by requiring the colleges to describe their assessment and recording policies when a placement is being considered
- improve the skills of staff in assessing how students with profound and multiple difficulties learn best, what their learning goals are and how their learning environment can best match their requirements.

5

References

1. FEFC Circular 92/08, *Establishment of the FEFC,* London, FEFC, July 1992

2. SCPR *Student Voices: The Views of Further Education Students with Learning Difficulties and/or Disabilities: Findings From a Series of Student Workshops Commissioned by the Learning Difficulties and/or Disabilities Committee,* London, Skill: National Bureau for Students with Disabilities, 1996

3. FEFC Circular 96/01, *Students with Learning Difficulties and/or Disabilities,* Coventry, FEFC, January 1996, annex D; evidence from the DfEE on the code of practice

4. Responses to the mapping project, (unpublished)

5. Responses to the call for evidence, (unpublished)

6. Evidence from the FEFC inspectorate, (unpublished)

7. Responses to the mapping project, (unpublished)

8. Evidence presented to the assessment working group, (unpublished)

9. Evidence from the FEFC inspectorate, (unpublished)

10. Evidence from OFSTED presented to committee, (unpublished)

11. Responses to the mapping project, (unpublished)

12. *Ibid.*

13. Sir Ron Dearing *Review of Qualifications for 16 to 19 Year Olds,* Middlesex, SCAA, 1996

14. Responses to the call for evidence, (unpublished)

15. Analysis of the responses to the call for evidence (unpublished); Evidence from NATSPEC and AMA, (unpublished); Visits to Derwen College, RNIB Vocational College, Portland College and Hinwick Hall College (see also annex F)

16. Responses to the call for evidence, (unpublished)

17. *How to Apply for Funding 1996-97*, Coventry, FEFC, December 1995

18. Guidance produced by the committee's short-life task group, used in *How to Apply for Funding 1996-97*, Coventry, FEFC, December 1995

19. Responses to the mapping project, (unpublished)

20. Responses to the call for evidence, (unpublished)

21. SCPR *Student Voices: The Views of Further Education Students with Learning Difficulties and/or Disabilities: Findings From a Series of Student Workshops Commissioned by the Learning Difficulties and/or Disabilities Committee,* London, Skill: National Bureau for Students with Disabilities, 1996

22. FEFC Circular 96/01, *Students with Learning Difficulties and/or Disabilities,* Coventry, FEFC, January 1996, annex C

23. Visits to specialist colleges by assessment working group (see also annex F)

Chapter 6: Teaching, Learning and Management

In this chapter, the committee examines the factors that contribute to effective teaching and learning, and considers the implications for college management.

THE ISSUES

1. the factors that contribute to effective teaching
2. improving the quality of teaching and learning
3. the factors that contribute to the management of good teaching and learning
4. the role of senior managers in supporting and delivering high-quality learning programmes within an effective learning environment; and the role of the college co-ordinator.

TEACHING, MANAGEMENT AND INCLUSIVE LEARNING

6.1 Much of this report concerns how to make teaching, learning and management more effective in order to ensure inclusive learning for students with learning difficulties and/or disabilities. Here we consider the components of effective teaching and how these can best be measured by colleges.

THE COMMITTEE'S PRINCIPLES

6.2 We have set out our principles for inclusive learning in earlier chapters. These principles informed our thinking about good teaching, learning and management. The committee's principles in this chapter are:

- good teachers take account of how students learn and of their learning goals and help students to progress and achieve success
- good management supports and promotes good teaching and improves learning opportunities.

6.3. Evidence that would indicate the adoption of our principles in teaching and learning includes:

EVIDENCE

- the identification by teachers of students' individual learning styles
- the identification and recording by teachers of students' individual learning goals
- individual learning environments match students' requirements
- the recording of students' progress
- detailed schemes of work
- lessons planned to meet a range of individual students' requirements
- learning tasks which are well structured to enable students to succeed
- evidence that students are learning and that they receive regular feedback on how to improve
- students are actively included in the assessment and the recording of their progress
- evidence that students' achievements are used to enable them to gain accreditation
- well-qualified and experienced staff
- staff who have high expectations of students
- staff who value and make use of the learner's experiences in their teaching
- availability of learning opportunities in real rather than simulated living and work environments
- preparation, monitoring and review of work experience placements
- opportunities for students to learn to work independently
- opportunities for students to practice skills in representing and speaking for themselves (self-advocacy).

6.4 Evidence that would indicate the adoption of our principles for management includes:

EVIDENCE

- the commitment of college governors to monitor the strategic objectives for developing inclusive learning
- college mission, strategic plan and policy documents which embrace inclusive learning
- knowledge and leadership from the senior management team to co-ordinate and develop inclusive learning across all the college
- commitment of co-ordinators to helping faculties develop clear targets for devising and implementing disability statements
- a clear management structure and detailed job specifications
- regular, minuted team meetings involving part-time staff to record and monitor progress towards inclusive learning
- foundation level courses in all departments or faculties
- departmental or faculty operating statements, derived from the colleges' development plan, which identify the process to be used for making learning effective for all students
- systems and procedures for identifying support requirements as part of each student's learning environment
- systems and procedures for collaboration with external agencies
- guidance for teachers on how to manage the match between students' requirements and the development of an individual learning programme
- quality assurance arrangements which monitor the extent and impact of inclusive teaching and management, on participation and standards of achievement.

6.5 Inspectorate evidence gave us the following examples of good and bad practice in teaching, learning and management:

EXAMPLES

College A

The majority of staff are well qualified and experienced in teaching students with learning difficulties and/or disabilities. Schemes of work are detailed and thorough. Teachers work together to ensure that different topics relate to each other, plan programmes together and collaboratively review individual progress. Lessons are meticulously planned to ensure that the requirements of each student can be matched. Staff have a good understanding of cognitive development and the impact that learning difficulties and disabilities can have on this. By cognitive development, we mean the processes by which students acquire knowledge, skills and understanding. These processes include perception, intuition and reasoning. Teachers use their knowledge to break learning down into small steps which match students' activities. Tasks are carefully structured to ensure that students can experience success. Students are encouraged to depend less on learning support assistance and to take more responsibility for their learning. Staff have high expectations of the students and work hard to make lessons interesting and stimulating. Many students have the opportunity to undertake vocational training in the real work environments within the college. Work experience is an integral part of vocational programmes. Careful preparation, monitoring and review help to ensure that the placements are successful. During lessons, lecturers keep a careful check on students' individual understanding and provide regular positive feedback to students. Assessments are thorough, with students contributing to the assessing and recording of their progress. Lecturers are rigorous in demanding evidence of students' understanding and achievements for the purposes of internal and external verification. Recording procedures are exemplary.

College B

In one support session, a student studying at GNVQ advanced level received high-quality individual support for his dyslexia. The student was unable to read or write. The teacher assisted him to plan and draft an essay on epidemiological trends in AIDS, using open-ended questions and prompts to assist in forming the material. A draft was prepared, each sentence being dictated by the student who would then key in the essay, one letter at a time, at home that evening, returning the next day for the teacher to read the work to him. The student was keeping up the same pace of work as other students in his group.

College C

The quality of much of the teaching of students with complex learning difficulties was poor. Sessions offered insufficient challenge and consisted of inappropriate activities, the purpose of which was not clear. Insufficient consideration was given to observing how students learned best, deciding what they needed to learn and then prioritising. In many sessions, the emphasis was on the completion of tasks, sometimes by the teacher, rather than on the learning which could be undertaken through the tasks.

College D

Students previously receiving support in discrete programmes are now learning in a range of vocational classes. Resources for student support have been reviewed and now contribute to a learning environment which benefits all students. Teachers have changed the focus from previous practice where support was intended to match the perceived deficits in some students, to a new focus on creating learning environments, which takes account of the different requirements of learners. As a consequence, the learning support co-ordinator provides support for teachers rather than for individual students. The teachers still use detailed lesson plans, and specify individual learning objectives, which are recorded in learning agreements. However, they have created greater flexibility in the use of resources and different styles of teaching. The focus now is on promoting good support in subject classes rather than providing separate support for students, away from their peers. Students are encouraged to learn independently and to reduce their reliance on support staff. In the best classes it is not possible to single out the students with learning difficulties from the rest of the group.

College E

The purpose of many lessons is not clear and is not explained to the students. The activities and materials used within lessons are often more appropriate for children than young adults. Some staff require students to spend lessons completing worksheets or copying information from the board. Often, students are not able to read what they are copying. All students do the same tasks within a lesson even though they have very different levels of ability. The emphasis seems to be on the completion of tasks; little analysis is undertaken of what students can learn through doing them. Students' work folders contain many worksheets which have not been marked. Each member of staff plans his or her own work with the students. There are few opportunities to share ideas and to plan programmes together. Students spend the majority of their time on literacy and numeracy tasks, and often repeat work which they have done previously. Learning support workers are used to help students with their English and mathematics. Their advice often contradicts that of the teacher. Some of the support workers help the students by completing the tasks for them.

College F

The senior management team is particularly committed to providing programmes of high quality for students with learning difficulties and/or disabilities. Governors have been involved in producing the parts of the mission statement, strategic plan, and policies which relate to these students. There is evidence of widespread collaboration and consultation both within the college and with the local community providers to secure support. The vice-principal is knowledgeable about this area of work and has been directly involved in planning and implementing the provision. Staff speak highly of her vision and leadership qualities. The college's policy on inclusiveness stresses the importance of valuing each individual student. Staff across the college have had the opportunity to contribute to the development of this policy and there is a genuine concern to ensure that everyone adheres to its philosophy. Detailed procedures have been developed to monitor its implementation. The management structure of the college is clear, job descriptions are detailed and staff are well aware of their roles and responsibilities. Regular team meetings are held. These are scheduled in advance and are minuted. Part-time staff speak positively about the effort that is made to keep them informed of developments. Although management responsibility for the specially-designed programmes lies within one department, all departments are required to provide vocational courses at foundation level. This helps to ensure that all staff within the college accept responsibility for students with learning difficulties and/or disabilities. The operating statements of the departments clearly indicate how the objectives within the strategic plan will be implemented. A learning support development group, a subcommittee of the academic board, has been established. The current focus of the group is to ensure that there is a consistent approach to foundation level programmes across the college. Representatives from each department have been elected to the group. The learning support manager has established detailed systems and procedures to identify students' support needs on entry to college. Training has been provided for all staff to ensure that they understand their role in implementing the procedures and to support their understanding of how students learn best. Curriculum documentation is comprehensive and detailed.

College G

There is little interest from the senior management team in the provision for students with disability and/or learning difficulties. A small committed group of teachers has devised plans which the senior management team has chosen not to comment on, believing the work not to be of a high priority. All programmes for students with learning difficulties and/or disabilities are based within one department with no planned progression routes. The college's strategic plan indicates an intention to expand the college's recruitment of students with learning difficulties and/or disabilities but there has been no needs analysis and there is no evidence of planning for this within any of the departments' operating statements and no targets have been set. The college does not have a learning support policy and curriculum documentation is sparse. The section leader responsible for provision for students with learning difficulties and/or disabilities is committed to the work but has no qualifications relating specifically to the teaching of students with learning difficulties and/or disabilities. He does not have direct access to a member of the senior management team and feels somewhat isolated and unsupported. As a main grade lecturer he feels that he lacks status in the college and does not have the authority to ask other departments to make provision for students with learning difficulties and/or disabilities. He has little knowledge of how the financial allocation to his department is decided. The majority of staff involved in teaching students with learning difficulties and/or disabilities are on part-time contracts. They very rarely meet together as a team. They have been given little guidance as to what they should teach and are not required to submit schemes of work. A large number of learning support workers have been employed but criteria for their deployment have not been established. Students are highly dependent on them for support.

The factors that contribute to effective teaching

6.6 We found a mixed picture when we looked at the quality of teaching and learning. Students wanted to be welcomed and accepted, to have their contributions to college life respected and their achievements valued.[1] They agreed that the best teaching was where the teacher understood and responded to their individual requirements by:

- understanding how they learnt best
- demonstrating skill in meeting individual support requirements
- using a variety of imaginative and appropriate teaching methods
- monitoring progress and providing regular positive feedback to assist improvement
- spending time with individual students to get to know them and to develop rapport.

6.7 Although some students were rightly pleased with the teaching they received, others had good cause for dissatisfaction:

> *I learn well in some lessons, but the teachers do not tell each other how I learn best, so in some lessons I do not learn at all.*
>
> *The support assistant doesn't understand why I can't add up, so she just does the sums for me.*[2]

6.8 Other evidence supported the view that colleges themselves might prevent students from learning. For example, one college takes the view that:

> *The majority of difficulties experienced by disabled people in the social and educational context do not arise from an individual's particular impairment, but rather from society's reluctance to create physical and human structures which seek to accommodate its disabled members.*[3]

6.9 A support service commented that:

> *The environment, including the teaching approach, is the most disabling factor and little effort is made to shape teaching to individual learning needs. The practice of throwing support workers at courses where tutors are reluctant to change their teaching methods is questionable.*[4]

6.10 The most compelling evidence of the need for colleges to improve the quality of teaching and learning for students with learning difficulties and/or disabilities may be found in the inspection reports of the Council's inspectorate. The inspection grades awarded by the Council's inspectors for provision for students with learning difficulties and/or disabilities are, on average, the lowest for any programme area. The new focus provided by a continuation of the Council's funding, inspection and other arrangements and the commitment and effort of many colleges have not yet combined to produce nationally consistent high-quality provision. The committee has agreed that some fundamental and far-reaching co-ordinated action or initiative is needed to improve the quality of provision for students with learning difficulties and/or disabilities.

6.11 We wanted to understand why the grades should be poor. Some aspects are discussed in chapter 2. We found the following main weaknesses:

2 Improving the quality of teaching and learning

6.12 The quality of teaching and learning depends on a match between students' learning styles, learning goals and the teaching they received. Evidence from students provides examples of mismatch:

> *We are taught as a whole class, instead of as a group of individual students, everyone hurrying to catch up or waiting for the rest.*

> *I am really confused because all the teachers teach us different ways of doing the same things.*

> *When I have a problem, the teacher says, 'get on, I have taught you how to do that three times already'.*

> *The teacher doesn't understand my difficulties in learning. For example, I don't understand plans, diagrams and graphs.*

> *We are always given worksheets — some of the words I cannot read or understand. My folder is full of unfinished worksheets and my work is never marked, so I don't know how to make my work better. Nobody cares if you don't finish. The teacher always says my work is 'good' however hard I try.*[5]

6.13 Students know which style of teaching suits them best. They know what they want to learn and what they need to help them to learn. Students told us they wanted teachers to talk to them more positively during lessons and tell them how they were progressing. They also wanted their teachers to make clear to them the purpose of the activities they were carrying out. It was suggested to the committee that students with disability make a particularly valuable contribution to the college by helping staff and other students to understand more about the nature of disability. After careful debate, the committee concluded that all students contribute to their college to some degree or other, and no one individual or group should be valued more than another. Students want teaching activities which are relevant to their lives and are linked to their life experiences. They want vocational preparation courses related to available employment opportunities. We were struck by the number of students with learning difficulties and/or disabilities who said they wanted a policy which would allow them to enjoy a high profile and status in the college. Students told us:

> *My tutors really seem to understand what helps me to learn.*

> *Teaching materials and ways of learning are geared to my age, for example, we use newspapers, real money and adult text books.*

Our tutor often videos our work and then plays it back so that we can work out which bits need improving. We all comment on each others work. I find this really helpful.

My teacher makes sure I understand what I have learned from doing a particular job or task. The next task always seems to fit with what I did before.[6]

6.14 The inspectorate evidence told us that in many instances there is a considerable degree of mismatch between what students need to assist them to learn and what teachers offer them. Teachers often provide students with simulated, rather than real experiences. For example:

In one class, students learning how to swim were asked to cut out pictures of swimming trunks from a mail order catalogue and label them. In another, students tackling money concepts were asked to draw and colour over coins. In another lesson about the post office, students copied and coloured the post office sign instead of learning from operating in their own post office.[7]

6.15 One of the greatest barriers to improving the quality of provision is the poor quality of training for teachers, particularly for matching the requirements of students who have the most complex learning difficulties. Few teachers are specifically trained to teach students in further education who have learning difficulties and/or disabilities. Many teachers are unable to determine how the student learns best or to design the most effective learning environments to match students' requirements. The committee considered that this was of such importance, that it dealt with separately in chapter 10.

6.16 On the basis of the evidence we received, we decided that successful teachers meet their students' requirements because they:

- understand the different ways in which students learn and use a wide a range of appropriate teaching methods to match these
- explain abstract concepts in such a way as to develop students' understanding
- ensure that students understand processes of change and development by meticulously breaking down processes into small steps
- communicate with students in straightforward and unambiguous language
- turn the need for regular reinforcement of skills into enjoyable learning experiences
- have high expectations of their students as successful learners
- see learning difficulties as a challenge, to be tackled by creating stimulating and diverse learning environments in which students can learn, rather than by describing students as the problem
- enable students to succeed when previously they may have failed
- teach students to speak for themselves so that they can take on greater responsibility for their own learning (self-advocacy)
- provide learning activities which enhance the status of students as adults
- use the independent living programmes in specialist colleges to teach students about particular jobs; for example, how to be a waiter as well as how to learn what waiters do through using real work environments, the wearing of correct uniforms and an understanding of industrial standards
- understand the potential for furthering the personal and social development of students who learn in a residential environment.

3 The factors that contribute to the managment of good teaching and learning

6.17 The quality of students' experience is adversely affected if the college does not manage the match between what students need to learn and the physical surroundings in which learning takes place. For example:

> *[The] deputy head of school...complained at the lack of provision for students with profound and multiple learning difficulties, who are treated as second-rate citizens. Also, courses for students with severe learning difficulties do not have equal status with 'mainstream' courses and are always segregated. There is no evidence of differentiated planning or teaching — students have to fit into the college system. Their profile is very low and they are undervalued as people.*[8]

> *We have to do art in a classroom because the art room is always being used by other students. We never get to use the catering department, even though I want to work in an hotel.*[9]

6.18 Managers provide a framework within which good teaching and learning can take place. Management arrangements have a major impact on students' experience and on their opportunities to achieve. We received considerable evidence of this at college, faculty and course level. For example, accepting a student without a college strategy for providing support and a structure for curriculum and organisational planning can result in a student failing to make any progress. One teacher working with students with emotional and behavioural difficulties at a sector college said that:

> *A serious rethink on the strategy of colleges is needed if they are to realise the potential of these students, many of whom are clearly disenchanted with education.*[10]

Another noted:

> *A hearing-impaired student needs a notetaker who can sign but is provided with an unqualified notetaker who cannot sign — the support is disorganised and of poor quality and is destroying her self-confidence.*[11]

4 The role of senior managers in supporting and delivering high-quality learning programmes within an effective learning environment; and the role of the college co-ordinator

6.19 We found that 50% of the respondents to the committee's call for evidence referred to the importance of good college management. Inspection grades awarded to colleges by the Council's inspectors show that there is a correlation between good management and good teaching and learning. If colleges are to implement the committee's recommendations, then managers will need to have:

- an understanding of the benefits that inclusive learning could deliver for all students
- vision and leadership qualities
- the ability to support, help and guide staff to change their approach
- the will to reallocate resources to support training for teachers' development in general further education courses so that students with learning difficulties and/or disabilities can learn alongside their peers.

6.20 In addition, just under 200 respondents asked for the Council to disseminate models of good practice and to include some of the following:

> *...help with strategic planning for students with learning difficulties and/or disabilities, quality standards in management, standards for physical access and help to improve public reporting on students with learning difficulties and disabilities.*[12]

Management of the college's corporate strategy for inclusive learning

6.21 The college will need to ensure that teaching and learning benefits all learners, colleges will want to carefully manage the organisation and use of facilities and other resources. Some colleges told us that they have adopted a corporate approach to staffing, staff resources and staff development. They have set out to recruit well-qualified staff; implement a policy of continuing professional development for all staff; promote team-working within the college and with other external agencies; ensure that senior staff teach on pre-foundation and foundation courses, and aim to recruit experienced learning support assistants. Others have carefully briefed governors on inclusive learning and have asked them to monitor the college's progress towards inclusiveness.[13]

6.22 We were told that to adopt the principles of this report, colleges may need to review the organisation and use of resources; for example:

- developing a college accommodation strategy with incremental plans to improve physical access
- compare the status and quality of types of accommodation as used by different student groups
- review how easy it is to find the way around the college
- review the availability and accessibility of enabling technology.

6.23 Or through resourcing by:

- setting new targets and determining a broader range of unit costs
- clarifying the procedures, allocation and purposes of funding to develop learning environments which benefit a greater number of students
- identifying a separate budget for additional support and then monitoring its use
- creating policies and procedures on finance which support the development of learning opportunities from which all can benefit.

Managing a framework that co-ordinates all the college's systems

6.24 We found that progress in improving the quality of teaching and learning for students with learning difficulties and/or disabilities is slow when the different ingredients of successful teaching operate in isolation. For example, a system for assessing learning requirements may be working well but unless the outcomes of assessment influence the design of a student's individual learning programme, then the assessment has been of little value. An effective learning environment should take account of the outcomes of the assessment, decisions about how teaching styles might match students' learning styles, what needs to be taught when and by whom and within what timescale. Good management should ensure that these elements are co-ordinated. The beneficial impact on the student of this taking place was clear to us.

> *I get really confused going from class to class. I don't understand how all the lessons fit together.*
>
> *I don't understand why we do some classes, but we have to go. The things I said I wanted to learn have been forgotten — we all do the same things whether we need them or not, we just do the course.*[14]

6 SUMMARY OF MAIN FINDINGS

6.25 When we compared what we found with the principles set out in paragraph 6.2, we found the following main weakness:

- inadequate teacher training
- the lack of a corporate strategy for managing teaching and learning. This leads to an absence of leadership and support of staff teaching on courses specifically designed for these students
- the lack of a corporate decision to make provision for these students in all faculties, which means that co-ordinators attempt to develop progression routes and other courses for students by making *ad hoc* arrangements. They are not able to work systematically within a commonly agreed plan
- the lack of any overall plan for provision, which makes it difficult for staff to devise a curriculum framework for specifically-designed programmes
- the need to review the organisation of resources.

6.26 Absence of a management framework can lead to:

- the lack of a corporate working party or committee with representatives from each faculty to develop an action plan to implement the objectives stated in the strategic plan
- the lack of a curriculum framework for the programmes designed specifically for students with learning difficulties and/or disabilities
- poor management of the curriculum and the provision across faculties and college sites
- the segregation of provision for students with learning difficulties from provision in the rest of the college
- insufficient time for the co-ordination of specifically-designed programmes
- the lack of a cross-college co-ordinator for learning support
- insufficient leadership and support for staff
- incomplete data regarding students' achievements and destinations
- infrequent team meetings
- poor communication with part-time staff
- learning support assistants not deployed effectively.

6.27 Of particular concern is the partial understanding within some senior management teams of the Council's arrangements for funding additional support. This means that sometimes mechanisms for allocating and accounting for additional units are poorly developed.

6.28 We were told that the management team did not always scrutinise course documentation which sets out the aims, objectives and content of specifically-designed courses with the same rigour as other courses. In other colleges, no criteria had been devised for entry to courses. Elsewhere, some members of staff were given timetabled sessions which they fill with activities of their own choice, and since staff met rarely, they had no knowledge of the work students were involved in at other times in the week.[15]

Managing the college's quality assurance mechanisms and processes

6.29 Quality assurance mechanisms and processes are discussed in more detail in chapter 10.

ADDRESSING WEAKNESSES AND BUILDING ON STRENGTHS

6.30 We believe that the quality of teaching and learning will be improved if the principles of this report are adopted. Managers' commitment and understanding is crucial to the success of the ideas we are proposing in this report. We realise this will place a heavy burden on staff in colleges and implementing our recommendations will take even more of their time.

6.31 The committee recognises the scale of the changes required of sector colleges over the last three or four years. The Council has reported that over 18% efficiency savings have been secured. The committee received evidence showing that these economies have been achieved without too much apparent detriment to the support of students. These developments undertaken during a time of unprecedented change owe a great deal to the professionalism and commitment of college staff. We recognise that teachers feel burdened by the range and speed of change required of them in the past three years: for example, understanding the funding methodology, securing accreditation, responding to students with an increasing range of requirements and meeting efficiency targets.

1 The factors that contribute to effective teaching

6.32 In particular, we received evidence from teachers which suggested that staff strongly desire to reassert their professional status as teachers and to have their skills and knowledge of curriculum matters recognised. They wish to see a fresh focus on teaching and learning. Some have lost their confidence to develop imaginative and challenging programmes. We hope that the adoption of the ideas proposed in this report will help to revive a debate about teaching and learning.

Improving the quality of teaching and learning

Implications for teachers

6.33 We wish to see the creation of more inclusive learning environments with teachers expecting students to think more for themselves and lecturers having higher expectations of students.

6.34 We think that our approach would help to eliminate many of the shortcomings brought to our attention. For example, we would expect to see the increased use of 'real work' environments and specialist vocational workshops to teach students practical skills; teachers being more able to use a variety of activities within a session; students being less dependent for their learning on support staff and more supportive of one another; students more able to contribute to discussions and through the acquisition of self-advocacy skills, to assess their own performance.

6.35 To achieve this we realise the need for a comprehensive training initiative and chapter 12 addresses this in more detail.

6.36 The committee advocates inclusive learning because of the perceived benefits to students. We believe that a corporate adoption of our principles could allow the twin priorities of efficiency and student achievement to be properly balanced. We would like to see inclusive learning become a characteristic of further education.

The factors that contribute to the management of good teaching and learning

Implications for managers

6.37 We identified three key management roles which contribute to good-quality teaching and learning. These are the management of:

6

- the college's strategy for meeting the needs of all its students for inclusive learning
- a framework that co-ordinates all the college's systems
- the college's quality assurance policy and processes.

6.38 We want to see senior managers and governors who are supportive of the principles of inclusive learning. Their success will depend on the leadership and personal support provided by the principal, the corporation board and the heads of faculties. Governors will need to play a particular role in providing strategic guidance and monitoring and in promoting the colleges' new approach outside the college. Senior managers will need to be visionary because the changes proposed require a corporate response. They will need to be courageous because staff at all levels will have to be convinced that the new approach will bring long-term benefits to all learners.

6.39 Senior managers need to remove the isolation of students and staff. We wish to see the personal involvement of senior managers in a corporate restructuring. We wish to see the commitment of the college's corporation board in monitoring its strategic impact on the success of the college.

6.40 Our recommendations will require:

- an understanding of the principles and implications for the college
- a corporate strategy to ensure a consistent implementation of inclusive learning
- review of the equal opportunities policy to reflect the college's policy of inclusion
- college documentation on inclusive learning to be comprehensive and detailed
- the development of a college philosophy of inclusion clearly stated in documents such as the mission statement, charter and staff handbook
- staff awareness of this philosophy and commitment to implementation
- critical analysis of implementation and outcomes of the approach in the college's self-assessment report
- the appointment of learning support managers to have overall responsibility for inclusive learning across the college with direct access to all members of the senior management team and members of the college's curriculum team
- a restructuring of learning support across the college to a learning environment in which all students can benefit
- management of staff within learning support sections to work across the college to provide support to students with learning difficulties and/or disabilities on general further education courses
- redesign of responsibilities and training for staff providing different types of learning support (for example, language support, support for students with dyslexia, basic skills support, in-class support, one-to-one additional learning support)
- the inclusive learning organisers to be based within the departments and faculties and the learning support manager to hold regular meetings (weekly or fortnightly) with them
- inclusive learning organisers and tutors to attend course team meetings within other faculties
- allocation of time specifically for liaison purposes
- allocation of time for part-time tutors to enable them to be well supported and informed
- the aims of inclusive learning and the development of inclusive learning environments to be clearly stated in college documentation
- detailed management information systems and procedures to identify and cost students' support needs on entry to college

- recording of information relating to the support given to students to be entered on the college's management information system
- a strategy for the allocation of finance to learning support.

2 The role of senior managers in supporting and delivering high-quality learning programmes within an effective learning environment; and the role of the college co-ordinators

6.41 Colleges in the testing exercise told us that they will need to devise a comprehensive and detailed action plan with new management arrangements which extend the responsibility of teachers for students with learning difficulties and/or disabilities across the college. Colleges need to establish advisory boards and forums for those outside the college to share in the planning of the implementation. The strategy will need to take account of the varying stages colleges have reached. There may need to be a separation of programme management from the co-ordination of learning support. The provision may require a higher profile in the college. The development of inclusive learning may need to form a central part of discussions at academic and corporation boards. It will require new management arrangements at faculty level with a long-term strategy for the development of carefully thought out and well-documented support.

6.42 The role of the co-ordinator, at middle management level, is crucial for the college to achieve an approach to teaching and learning and management which allows all students to benefit. Much of the good work we saw in colleges is due to their hard work, imagination and professional skill. We were impressed, but concerned that the good practice is patchy. Our proposals will require an operational plan for delivery which will need careful liaison at middle management and programme level to ensure success. We were reassured on our college visits that co-ordinators wished to see their roles change to a college-wide function. We realise the transition to be made by co-ordinators will not be easy. Some will be reluctant to give up their current function, having fought long and hard to achieve their current position. Others commented on their frustration at having to work in cross-college roles without the support of senior managers or the time to do the job as they wished. The practice of special pleading to persuade heads of department to take students with learning difficulties into their departments is unacceptable. The practice of students being excluded from some accommodation in the college is also unacceptable. The fact that colleges handicap students from realising their full potential through unequal opportunities needs to be addressed. We are encouraged by the evidence that in some colleges this work is already under way.

RECOMMENDATIONS

6.43 The committee's key recommendations about teaching, learning and management:

The Council's role

6.44 The Council should support the evident wish of the sector to move towards inclusive teaching, learning and management and should encourage colleges to adopt the approach to teaching and management advocated in this report. Specifically, the Council should:

- review the factors which influence the quality of teaching and its impact on student achievement through the college self-assessment procedures using the criteria given in this chapter
- review the policy, resource allocation and management structures likely to provide learning which is inclusive and require these to be part of the colleges' self-assessment report.

College management

6.45 The Council should support college managers in developing a strategic approach to inclusive learning. Specifically, the Council should:

- encourage colleges to produce a long-term strategy and action plan to implement the principles identified in this report
- encourage colleges to establish forums for debate on management issues, to include all those agencies involved with students to enhance collaboration and partnership
- audit staff training requirements required to provide inclusive learning which provides opportunity for all to learn
- encourage colleges to review the role of the college co-ordinator and the establishment of inclusive learning managers
- offer briefings to college governors on inclusive learning
- involve corporation boards in monitoring the progress made by the college to provide learning which is inclusive.

References

1. SCPR *Student Voices: The Views of Further Education Students with Learning Difficulties and/or Disabilities: Findings From a Series of Student Workshops Commissioned by the Learning Difficulties and/or Disabilities Committee,* London, Skill: National Bureau for Students with Disabilities, 1996

2. *Ibid.*

3. Responses to the call for evidence, (unpublished)

4. *Ibid.*

5. SCPR *Student Voices: The Views of Further Education Students with Learning Difficulties and/or Disabilities: Findings From a Series of Student Workshops Commissioned by the Learning Difficulties and/or Disabilities Committee,* London, Skill: National Bureau for Students with Disabilities, 1996

6. *Ibid.*

7. Evidence from the FEFC inspectorate

8. *Ibid.*

9. SCPR *Student Voices: The Views of Further Education Students with Learning Difficulties and/or Disabilities: Findings From a Series of Student Workshops Commissioned by the Learning Difficulties and/or Disabilities Committee,* London, Skill: National Bureau for Students with Disabilities, 1996

10. Responses to the call for evidence, (unpublished)

11. *Ibid.*

12. *Ibid.*

13. Finding of the exercise to test the committee's approach to learning with colleges (see also annex D)

14. SCPR *Student Voices: The Views of Further Education Students with Learning Difficulties and/or Disabilities: Findings From a Series of Student Workshops Commissioned by the Learning Difficulties and/or Disabilities Committee,* London, Skill: National Bureau for Students with Disabilities, 1996

15. Evidence from the FEFC inspectorate

Chapter 7: Effective Support for Learning

The committee's focus on inclusive learning identifies support for learning as an essential component of the individual learning environment for many students. In this chapter, the committee examines college arrangements for support for learning, and describes how these might be made more effective.

THE ISSUES

1. organising and delivering effective support for learning
2. funding effective support for learning.

EFFECTIVE SUPPORT AND INCLUSIVE LEARNING

7.1 In chapter 2, we described some of the components of a learning environment. Amongst these were different kinds of support for learning. Support for learning is support which enables students to have access to the curriculum and to learn. This will often be organised by the college within a support system. The system will include a number of different services, for example, counselling and guidance, directed at enabling the student to learn successfully and to achieve their chosen learning goals. A support system within a college is:

> *a college-wide approach to meeting the individual requirements of a wide variety of learners, including those with disabilities and/or learning difficulties*[1]

7.2 Colleges provide support for learning delivered by generic and specialist services. Generic services are usually internal to the college and are available to every student. Specialist services are provided on an individual basis and are over and above generic services. They are 'additional'. Generic services typically include counselling and guidance, the college's library services and support for basic skills. Specialist services typically include converting written

7

material to Braille for a student who is blind, interpreting oral exchanges for a student who is deaf, or access to psychiatric nursing support for a student with mental health difficulties. Sometimes these services are provided from outside the college, for example, by the local education authority educational psychology service, a voluntary organisation or the health service.

7.3 The committee sees the support provided by colleges as extending in a continuum from, at one end, the support which is on offer to all students (generic support) to that which is *additional* or *specialist* and is only offered to meet the requirements of some students. Some of the following components may be included within that continuum,[2] and they illustrate the kinds of service a support system might provide.

Suggested generic service within a college's support system, for any student:

- an assessment of additional needs
- staff development for teachers and support assistants
- a confidential personal counselling service
- careers advice
- personal (one-to-one) tutorials
- study and basic skills help
- provision of first-aid advice
- accessible information on services
- a complaints procedure
- an individual support plan and learning agreement
- regular reviews of progress and support arrangements
- an induction programme
- a mechanism for referrals
- procedures for arranging support
- advice on, for example, finance, childcare.

Suggested additional and specialist support services which may be required by some students:

- specialist assessment
- specialist staff development and briefing
- an advocate, or advocacy support, for students with disabilities
- environmental audits and consultancy on physical access
- educational psychology help and assessment
- other specialist teaching (for example, sex education for disabled people)
- advice and help with the management of students' behaviour
- provision of specialist equipment (for example, adapted keyboards)
- notetaking for deaf and hard of hearing students
- interpreting for deaf students
- specialist teaching for deaf students
- communicating for deaf students
- nursing support (general)
- nursing support (learning disability)
- nursing support and psychiatric support
- medical support
- personal care support
- specialist counselling
- visual impairment support — Brailling, mobility training, etc.
- specialist teaching for blind people
- consultancy in respect of disabilities
- amanuensis
- maintaining specialist equipment (for example, repairing adapted equipment)
- technical advice and support on specialist equipment
- occupational therapy
- speech and communication therapy
- physiotherapy
- specialist transport support
- training to travel independently
- LEA adviser and advisory teacher
- social work support.

7.4 Students require different levels of support to meet their learning goals. Sometimes students cannot gain access to generic support services without appropriate specialist support. For example, a deaf student may require a signer before being able to talk to the college counsellor. A college must have the right identification and referral systems before a student can make use of specialist external services:

> *Provision to meet the full range of support needs usually requires both internal and external services. The mix of these varies considerably between colleges. In practice, internal resources are required in order to access external services.*[3]

7.5 A distinction is often made between *learner* support (defined as giving people the opportunity to acquire the status of learner, such as provision of childcare) and *learning* support (defined as enabling students to learn and have access to the curriculum, such as help with study skills). Both should be part of the college-wide approach. In 'support for learning' we include both these concepts of learner support and learning support.

THE COMMITTEE'S PRINCIPLES

7.6 Effective support for learning underpins inclusive learning because it can make the difference between a learning environment that matches an individual's requirements and one that fails to do so. Inclusive learning requires that support for learning is delivered as an integral part of the learning programme rather than as a separate and unrelated activity. It is essential to ensure, as the-then secretary of state for education wrote in a letter of guidance to the Council in June 1993, that 'learning difficulties are no bar to access to further education'.[4] The committee believes that support for learning is essential because it:

- enables all students in a college to have equal access to the curriculum they have chosen
- helps students to progress and achieve
- assists effective transition to college, between courses and beyond college.

7.7 It follows that:

- the responsibility for support within the college should be clearly allocated and recognised by all staff within the college and be evident to those outside it
- the organisation and provision of support must be systematic.

7.8 Evidence which might indicate the adoption of these principles includes:

EVIDENCE

- accessible information on support
- established links with schools, the careers service, voluntary organisations, the LEA and the community
- regular tutorials and reviews of students' support arrangements
- effective assessment processes which identify students' needs and the support required
- support for learning linked to a student's main programme, provided by well-trained staff, at a time or times convenient and appropriate for the student
- a range of advice and guidance and specialist support from external agencies, which assure good-quality services
- adequate systems for identifying what enabling equipment[5] is needed for an individual student, and for supplying and maintaining it
- strategic approach to improving physical access to college and within college.

7.9 The inspectorate gave us the following examples of good and bad practice in learning support:

EXAMPLES

College A

Well-established links with local schools, the careers service, the local authority and voluntary agencies in the community enable staff at the college to obtain detailed information about students prior to their starting college. Many of the students who go straight to college from school have attended link programmes at the college as part of a detailed assessment of their requirements. All students are interviewed and given clear information about the programmes available in college and the support available. Specialist guidance is available for students who need it. Staff at the college have planned a detailed induction programme for the students which is designed to familiarise them with the college, the staff and the requirements of their programmes. Weekly tutorials are held which are used to encourage students to express their opinions about their courses, their support and college life in general. On entry to college, all full-time students are screened to identify those who may need help with aspects of their programmes, particularly in literacy and numeracy. Where appropriate, the screening is followed by diagnostic testing, after which individual programmes of support are developed for the students. These are formally recorded and shared with the students' tutors. The extra support is carefully linked to the students' main programmes. Students are very positive about the support they receive and feel that it is helping them to succeed. The college has negotiated a contract with the local careers service which enables students to have good-quality advice and guidance at each stage of their college programme. A contract has also been negotiated with the local authority to secure specialist support from the educational psychology service and the peripatetic hearing and visual support service.

College B

There is little information within students' files about the students' levels of achievement on entry to college. There are also no agreed procedures for interviewing the students. Many of the students are unable to read the information which is given to them during the induction programme. Some departments have introduced screening procedures for students on entry to college, but there is no consistent approach to this across the college. Learning support is provided through a 'drop-in' workshop. Students are told about the workshop by their tutors but their attendance is voluntary and is not monitored. Course tutors are not aware of the support that is given to students within the workshop. The college has enrolled several students who have been diagnosed as having dyslexia. There is no-one on the staff who has a qualification relating specifically to this area of work. All full-time students are allocated a personal tutor, but there is no specific time allowance for tutorials and no tutorial programme. Many students on the specially-designed courses have emotional and/or behavioural difficulties but they do not have access to the college's counselling service or to any external support services.

1 Organising and delivering effective support for learning

7.10 There has been an evolution of support for learning in colleges. The *Further and Higher Education Act 1992* has provided a valuable impetus to this evolution. Previously, young people often had limited options, especially if their learning difficulties were complicated or rare. They could:

- go to an independent college
- negotiate an arrangement between the local further education college, LEA and school where appropriate support was being externally provided
- go to a 'designated college' in the LEA, which was expected to take the majority of students with learning difficulties and/or disabilities.

7.11 Support arrangements for some students with comparatively rare disabilities and learning difficulties are relatively expensive. Prior to the establishment of the new further education sector in 1992, some LEAs had designated a limited number of colleges in their area as providers for these students and resourced them accordingly. As a consequence, the range of choice of college or provision for these students was restricted. Some students had to spend considerable time in travelling to one of the designated colleges which could meet their particular requirements. At the time of their incorporation, some colleges were endowed with appropriate resources to meet the needs of students with disabilities and/or learning difficulties, while others were not.

External support for learning

7.12 Colleges told us that the organisation of external support for learning had become more complex as a result of incorporation. Some said it was not always possible for them to purchase services from the LEAs, partly because LEAs focused far more on their statutory responsibilities to provide support to schools. Others said that the LEAs' infrastructure for peripatetic sensory support services, educational psychology support and advisory support had declined in scale and effectiveness. Some colleges have started to shop around for good external support. Others have formed consortia, where services operate to support students in several colleges. Good intentions seem to have broken down in some areas because one or more colleges would not invest in the consortium.[6]

7.13 Prior to incorporation, some LEAs had dedicated, well-resourced services to colleges. Most external support was provided from largely schools-oriented services. The level of service which colleges received was often determined by the goodwill and commitment of individual staff. At the time of incorporation, some colleges were only at the early stages of developing learning support services.[7] Colleges and schools are now purchasers in the market for support; other colleges, LEAs and private and voluntary organisations are all potential providers of support. Some elements of support for learning are the responsibility of different statutory organisations. For example, LEAs have responsibility for transport, and social services departments for residential care. External support for learning has to be negotiated, contracted for and co-ordinated. This places additional administrative and co-ordination burdens on colleges which have varying degrees of expertise in managing external support for learning. Sometimes the arrangements colleges make with a provider of support are informal and of varying quality and are not subject to a service level agreement. Many colleges told us, in response to the call for evidence, that:

- upon incorporation they lost significant levels of support for learning from their LEA
- they were unable to afford the new charges being made by LEA services

- there is a shortage of communicators and communication support workers, signers and teachers of the deaf in further education
- there is an absence of training for classroom assistants and support staff and incentives for colleges to increase the effectiveness and raise the status of support staff through accredited training
- charges for LEA services are variable, sometimes unrealistic, and the level of service is not necessarily linked to real cost
- external support for learning can be delayed because of uncertainty about who should purchase and provide it.

7.14 Some voluntary organisations suggested that expertise had been lost to the sector following incorporation because colleges now bid piecemeal for specialist support rather than banding together, as they did formerly, to fund a specialist service.[8]

7.15 Some students and parents reported that students' requirements were not always properly identified. They said that some colleges lacked specialist knowledge, the necessary ability to understand learning difficulties or to detect particular requirements early enough in a student's programme:

> *General further education colleges without discrete learning units, and some sixth form colleges, were sometimes felt to be less successful in meeting the support needs of their students with disabilities. In these instances, students felt that their needs had neither been assessed nor addressed. Some students had responded by drawing their needs to the attention of the college authorities whilst others were reluctant to do so. As a consequence, some students felt they were not receiving sufficient learner support.*[9]

Students taking part in the workshop series also suggested that the support for learning was of poor quality. There were clear indications that staff in some colleges did not have the qualifications or experience to assess students' requirements for support effectively.

7.16 Poor assessment of students' support requirements means that staff were sometimes unprepared for students when they came to college or were slow to provide what was required. Students who took part in the workshops told us:

> *When I went in the class, she had no idea she had a wheelchair in the room so obviously she did not know what to do...what it was all about.*
>
> *I had to wait 10 weeks for them to do something for me...I was behind in my work because of it.*[10]

Effective internal support for learning

7.17 One parent told us that a college had pursued a policy of 'a fresh start' for all students and had deliberately ignored the significant work of earlier specialists from the LEA and the student's school. The result was that much time and effort was wasted as staff found out about the student's requirements by a process of trial and error. The way colleges manage support for learning can be vital. One voluntary organisation reported:

> *Support structures are not clearly defined and the quality of support is not monitored...no clearly-defined college policies for special exam concessions; current situations [are] inconsistent and ad hoc.*[11]

7.18 We found that:

- colleges vary in their understanding of what support for learning should be available

- staff in some colleges were poorly informed about the potential of enabling technology and the ways in which technology can help students to learn; inappropriate equipment had sometimes been purchased which was rarely used
- colleges did not always receive sufficient information from schools and services about the support already being given to students; others did not use the information they had
- some colleges were unaware of what information they should expect from schools
- some teachers were unaware of the importance of identifying particular support for learning requirements
- staff carrying out assessments to identify the support students needed were not always qualified or trained to do so
- class teachers were not always informed about students' requirements or the support they were receiving in other parts of the college
- some colleges considered that external specialist support services were offering poor quality and value for money but they had to use them in the absence of other options. For example, some educational psychology services used by colleges to assess students for exam dispensations, particularly those with dyslexia, were considered to be too expensive and that the providers were insufficiently informed about further education
- external specialist support services were charging very different rates and were of very different quality.

2 Funding effective support for learning

7.19 The Council has, with colleges, developed a new funding methodology during the course of the committee's work. This methodology is described in more detail in chapter 11. It includes additional support bands for those students for whom colleges need to provide learning support, whether internal or external. These bands start currently at a threshold of about £170 above the usual level of funding for each student. The threshold reflects the Council's assumption that colleges will provide some generic learning support for all students below the threshold, and specialist or additional support for some, above the threshold. However, we found no common understanding about what should reasonably be funded below the threshold, as generic support.

7.20 Colleges gave us generally very positive feedback about these new arrangements for funding support for learning. However, as we show later in chapter 11, colleges face particular difficulties in providing appropriate equipment for some students. The additional support bands do not include the costs of individual, enabling equipment, partly because of the limited extent of the capital funds allocated to the Council and partly because treasury rules have, to date, prevented any easy inclusion of equipment within a recurrent funding methodology. It can mean that students are slow to receive enabling equipment. Students taking part in the workshops told us that this made their learning much more difficult:

> *All our equipment was bought by charities — it is hard to believe but it is true. That is why it is all old and decrepit.*
>
> *It is difficult to get technology to help. There is no money for equipment, just funding for learning support workers.*[12]

7.21 This seems to have discouraged colleges from pooling enabling technology and from providing the equipment needed by some individuals. Some colleges told us that they felt they could no longer take part in collaborative or pooling arrangements for equipment, even though these arrangements can be particularly important for smaller colleges that want to provide support without investing large sums for small numbers of students.

7.22 A second innovation of the funding methodology is the learning agreement and additional support assessment form. We consider the advantages of this in chapter 6. In the context of funding support for learning, these arrangements should mean that students agree with the college the support that is to be provided for them. In the USA,[13] we found that students carry the assessment of their support needs with them from school to college and within college, as the basis for demanding the 'reasonable adjustments' to which they are entitled under the *Americans with Disabilities Act of 1991*. Whilst this places considerable responsibility on the students, they do have some statutory backing for their support, and they are given some control over its nature and extent.

SUMMARY OF MAIN FINDINGS

7.23 When we compared what we found with the principles set out in paragraph 7.6 and the evidence of their adoption in paragraph 7.8, the main weaknesses we found were:

- the limited range of support in some colleges, often because these were not designated, or resourced by their former LEA to provide for students with learning difficulties and/or disabilities
- the slow, sometimes ineffective, and hesitant responses to students with some disabilities which are comparatively rare and whose needs are considered relatively expensive to meet
- the lack of good-quality external support services for colleges, staffed by those who have experience in, and understanding of, further education
- the loss of LEA advisory and support services to colleges after they became incorporated institutions
- uneven charging for external services, such as educational psychology
- the confusion over who has responsibilities for the supply, maintenance and funding of enabling technology, and the lack of such technology in many colleges
- the lack of any consensus on what generic services should be provided to all students
- uncertainty, both within and outside colleges, about where responsibility lies in the college for the provision of support
- unsystematic organisation and provision of support.

ADDRESSING WEAKNESSES AND BUILDING ON STRENGTHS

Organising and delivering effective support for learning

7.24 Effective support for learning ensures that the learning environment for students is matched to their personal requirements. Support for learning should be organised and delivered to ensure that this match is sustained. Before any support for learning is given to a student, he or she should be involved in discussion about the nature of that support with parents where appropriate, or with carers. Students should be consulted about confidential information and given the opportunity to choose or influence the learning environment in which they are to work and the kind of support for learning they require. Students should be able to expect that college staff will have the appropriate expertise to help them, that their teachers will be well briefed about their requirements, and that the knowledge and skills of staff from any external services are appropriate to further education. Support for learning should be reviewed regularly. Organising and providing effective support for learning has the following components, which we discuss in turn in paragraphs 7.25 to 7.38:

- information for students
- clear and senior responsibility for support for learning within each college
- information for colleges about students and external support for learning
- staff training
- collaborative networks
- support to prepare students for, and during, examinations and assessments
- equipment and enabling technology
- physical access.

Information for students

7.25 The *Disability Discrimination Act 1995* places a duty on the Council to require colleges, as a condition of funding, to publish disability statements.[14] These statements are to describe the arrangements made for students with disabilities to learn and to give details of the support for learning which the college can provide. A student will be able to challenge a college if it does not fulfil the obligations to which it is committed on the statement. We consider this legislation has the potential to be particularly helpful to students. We are optimistic that the statements will be useful to prospective students, their parents and students' advocates. Information in the statements must be sufficiently detailed to give students a realistic idea of what support is or could be available. If colleges were to comment in their statements on both *internal* and *external* support, this would usefully mirror the duty on social services departments to inform disabled people of facilities available to them, even when those facilities are not directly provided by the social services department.[15]

Clear and senior responsibility for support for learning within each college

7.26 The delays we found in students' receiving the package of support for learning they needed could be successfully addressed if comprehensive information on funding were available to colleges and those working with students. Staff in social services departments and LEAs, parents and advocates need a straightforward guide to the Council's methodology to understand it better so they can make informed decisions and help students to do the same. We say more about this in chapter 11.

7.27 Colleges need to allocate the responsibility for managing the organisation and delivery of support for learning to a senior member of staff. Colleges should ensure that support for learning is the responsibility of one person or a properly co-ordinated team, and that it is well managed. Co-ordinating and tracking support for students with additional support requirements is complex and further research is required to highlight good practice in organising and managing caseloads. However, whilst some staff may have a particular responsibility in relation to the provision of support, all staff should have a commitment to help and assist students. Such a recommendation is in keeping with our thinking about inclusiveness and is essential if support is to be available and provided when it is needed. If support for students with disabilities and/or learning difficulties is organised and managed separately from the support provided for students on other courses, then the college should ensure that there are clear links between the two support systems, in order that students may progress from one kind of provision to the other, and that staff may share their expertise and good practice.

Information for colleges about students and external support for learning

7.28 The quality and extent of information about appropriate external support for learning vary between colleges. All colleges need to be well informed about sources of external support services, and receive information of better quality from schools, social services departments and other agencies about the support requirements of students.

7.29 Smaller colleges, including those for art and design, and agriculture, particularly need help from research and development organisations to find out how best to support students with particular needs such as specific learning difficulties (for example, dyslexia or dyscalcula). Whilst we were able to draw on the work of a number of experienced agencies in developing our thinking, colleges told us they needed more help to understand the effectiveness of different models of generic support and their suitability for different types of college.[16] We think that higher education and other training and staff development agencies could help here.

7.30 Colleges need to have assurance that the support for learning which they are purchasing from an external service meets the right standards. This assurance could be obtained if specialist services providing external support for learning were encouraged or required to obtain an appropriate quality mark which was nationally validated.

7.31 In order to provide the best support for learning, colleges also need to have the right information about their students. We say more about this in chapter 5. Such information about students and about the availability of specialist support for learning is essential if colleges are to provide the learning environment which best matches a student's requirements.

Staff training

7.32 Staff development plays a key role in helping all staff to identify and meet the requirements of individual students for support. The colleges which responded to the mapping project told the researchers that lack of staff expertise was a key reason for their inability to meet a student's particular requirements.[17] We endorse the views of many respondents to the call for evidence who recommend that staff carrying out assessments and providing support for learning require proper training.[18] This training should be given a high priority in each college, particularly in those colleges where there is less tradition of identifying the requirements and providing additional support for students with learning difficulties and/or disabilities.

7.33 All teaching staff need to become sensitive to the importance of identifying particular learning support requirements. Staff need to be briefed on the implications for their own preparation of lessons and material. All teachers can benefit from staff training to ensure that all learning in colleges becomes inclusive. Non-teaching staff too need access to accredited training, to raise their effectiveness and status. We say more about this in chapter 12.

7.34 One of the most common learning difficulties experienced by students in colleges is a specific learning difficulty such as dyscalcula. Some 9% of students with disabilities or learning difficulties overall have varying degrees of specific learning difficulty; in sixth form colleges, art and design and specially designated colleges nearly half of them do.[19] Colleges have increasingly used screening tests to identify students' additional support requirements for literacy and numeracy skills. As we noted in chapter 5, such screening should not be the only form of assessment used, and it should not replace individual or diagnostic assessment. We share the concerns expressed by some respondents to the call for evidence that colleges should use teachers who are properly trained to assess and support students with specific learning difficulties, such as dyslexia, and who can give advice on their needs to staff.[20] Each college should have at least one key member of staff who is trained to work with these students. If colleges are to do more for those who belong to under-represented groups in further education, then colleges will also need to ensure that staff development programmes help staff to meet their requirements.

Collaborative networks

7.35 Agencies need to ensure that effective networks for collaboration continue to exist and involve colleges. We found no good reason why the more local networks should have ceased with the advent of incorporation. College managers could help to re-establish them by encouraging staff to meet others providing support for learning in highly-specialist areas of disability or learning difficulty to exchange ideas, share expertise and keep their specialist knowledge up to date. For example, as we suggest in chapter 4, teachers who are working with students with mental health difficulties should receive relevant professional supervision. Colleges need to provide continuous support to staff who are giving at a highly-specialised level assistance to students, such as support for students who are deaf or hard of hearing, blind or visually impaired, dyslexic, or who have a mental health difficulty. Some networks at regional and national level still exist.

Support to prepare students for, and during, examinations and assessments

7.36 The committee heard from students that some accreditation arrangements require students to specify the help they have received. Students feel that this requirement is a disincentive to ask for additional help in exams. We discuss this in more detail in chapter 5. Although accreditation requirements are outside the Council's control, the Council could seek to influence awarding bodies and colleges to ensure that additional support received by students during examinations or assessment neither advantages nor disadvantages them, in terms of their examination result, nor discourages students from seeking appropriate support for their learning.

Equipment and enabling technology

7.37 We discuss in chapter 11 some changes to the Council's funding methodology which would significantly enhance colleges' ability to meet the support requirements of their students. In addition to those changes, which would apply to all colleges, we consider that regional arrangements are needed, especially for those students whose support costs are particularly high and occur infrequently. We do not consider it reasonable to expect every college to be able to provide every kind of support for learning. One of the tasks of the regional subcommittees we advocate in chapter 8 is the possibility of monitoring the provision of particularly specialist support as part of their arrangements for ensuring adequate and sufficient facilities in the region. In chapter 11, we also argue that start-up funding should be available, managed by these regional subcommittees, to fill any gaps in the provision of specialist support or enabling technology. Staff expertise to make proper use of enabling technology is also required. Implementation of the *Report of the Learning and Technology Committee*[21] recommendation for learning technology centres needs to be accompanied by funding to include a specified amount for the development and support of staff working with students with learning difficulties and/or disabilities using enabling technology.

Physical access

7.38 We also recommend in chapter 11 that the Council should pay more attention to the capital state of the sector if colleges are to be able to provide appropriately for students with disabilities and/or learning difficulties. A survey of the accessibility of sector colleges would also give the Council a better picture of whether and how the sector might respond to those groups currently under-represented. Such a survey, we propose, could be followed by a guide on good practice for colleges intending to make changes to their buildings in their accommodation strategy. Both of these recommendations will assist colleges to fulfil their general intention to make their accommodation more accessible to all students.

2 Funding effective support for learning

7.39 Most of our thinking on funding effective support for learning is set out in detail in chapter 11. That chapter addresses the important aspects of:

- understanding the methodology
- adjustments to the Council's additional support bands
- equipment and enabling technology.

7.40 Here, we address funding support for effective learning through:

- generic support for learning
- regional planning and collaboration
- quality of support for learning systems
- information on external services and their funding.

Generic support for learning

7.41 The additional support bands of the funding methodology assume that colleges make a certain level of support available to all students. Many respondents argued that they needed more guidance on what the threshold level of support might cover. Many argue that the lowest band for full-time students was set too high for the significant numbers requiring low levels of support. Full-time students include those with specific learning difficulties, such as dyslexia, those needing help with their literacy and numeracy, and those with moderate learning difficulties on vocational programmes.[22] There is currently no common understanding of what constitutes generic support. Such an understanding would, we believe, help colleges to identify a 'baseline' that should be available for all students and against which colleges can measure themselves. This would promote both consistency of practice and cost-effectiveness across the sector.

Regional planning and collaboration

7.42 The Council could play a more active regional role to ensure that there is adequate provision of specialist support within each region. Regional and local networks are important in making sure that students continue to receive support when they join and leave college. Students might attend their local college more readily if they could be assured that there were arrangements whereby smaller colleges, and those with less developed support systems, could borrow essential equipment and provide access to the expertise, both within and outside the college, which they needed. The regional subcommittees we propose in chapter 8 could review these arrangements; help colleges to understand what is available and required in a region; and recommend to the Council where start-up funding or other action might be required.

7.43 As a result of such work, the Council would know comprehensively what generic and additional specialist support services are available at most colleges. It could then establish some benchmarks for additional or specialist services and require colleges to identify in their strategic plans and disability statements how they aim to provide this support.

7.44 More effective systems for hiring enabling technology and arranging specialist advice and support could also be promoted by joint working with bodies outside the sector such as the Higher Education Funding Council for England (HEFCE), LEAs, health authorities and social services departments, and specialist voluntary organisations. The development of collaborative networks to provide support for learning would assist smaller colleges which may only need to hire equipment or purchase specialist support for a few students, for a short time. It could also build on the expertise of those colleges with the greatest experience in providing specialist support. Such sector colleges might be best placed to tender for such regional roles.

7.45 A recent Council circular[23] took pains not to discourage collaboration between sector and specialist colleges outside the sector. We believe that these colleges could be further encouraged to share their expertise in the provision of support for learning, and that a flexible approach to funding would enable more students to make the best use of the range of support for learning available.

Quality of support for learning systems

7.46 The components of support for learning identified here need to be provided through a support system which is coherent and consistent. An effective support system has the following characteristics:

- operational across the whole college
- centralised admission procedures
- procedures for early identification and assessment of support requirements
- support for staff and students across the whole curriculum
- specialist staff and vocational teachers working together
- a variety of cost-effective strategies for delivering support.

7.47 Internal support services are usually covered by college quality assurance systems, involving activities such as student perception questionnaires and course reviews. We explore this further in chapter 10. Colleges need to ensure that students' perceptions are obtained in ways which enable the students to communicate their views clearly and effectively, through an appropriate medium.

7.48 To address colleges' concern about the quality of some support for learning which they purchase from an external service, we believe specialist external support services should be encouraged to establish good quality assurance procedures, perhaps through obtaining a nationally validated quality mark. This would enable colleges to be confident they are using services of proven quality and to know they are getting value for money.

Information on external services and their funding

7.49 Managing specialist support for some students is complicated. It requires an understanding of the benefits and limitations of support and how support contributes to students' progress, performance and success. It also requires an understanding of the legal duties of the respective agencies and how they fund their services. College staff may need clarification about specialist health services. They may also require encouragement to purchase such services and to claim additional units accordingly. Little is known in some colleges about the potential role of language and communication therapy services, physiotherapy, occupational therapy and educational psychology, and the support they could provide, even though these services can be critical to a student's educational success. Some professional bodies told us of their concern at the lack of joint working between colleges and external services. Forty-four respondents to the call for evidence told us of the significant role of speech and language therapy in further education. Almost all (colleges, careers services, parents, NHS trusts, voluntary organisations) complained of its absence, the difficulty of obtaining commitment from health units and its essential role for particular students.[24] Others reported on the valuable work of educational psychologists. In some areas there are service level agreements between educational psychology services and colleges which cover the provision of direct support for students and recommendations to examining bodies on behalf of students. However, more needs to be done to ensure that colleges and external services each have a clear understanding about the level of service and fees involved.

7.50 Colleges need better information on funding arrangements for specialist support and on models of service agreements with specialist support services. Some colleges are heavily dependent on these external services and spend considerable resources upon them; one sixth form college reported that in 1994, it spent some £37,000 on external services for its visually-impaired and hearing-impaired students and for educational psychology. Middle managers in colleges and managers from other agencies stressed how better information on funding for students with additional support requirements helped them to avoid having to make contracting arrangements at the last minute, and how it could prevent late assessment and delay in the provision of support.[25] On the basis of the evidence we received, we consider that guidance on service level agreements with specialist support services should include:

- scale of charges
- methods of assuring quality
- roles and suggested salaries of support staff
- right of access to existing information about students prior to their entry
- the use of the current regional access centres
- payment for educational psychology assessments for exam dispensations.

RECOMMENDATIONS

7.51 The key recommendations in relation to effective support for learning are:

FUNDING

7.52 The Council should ensure that its funding arrangements continue to enable colleges to meet the costs of individual support for learning, currently achieved through the additional support bands. Further recommendations are made in chapter 11 on funding. Specifically, the Council should:

- work with colleges to derive a clear statement which indicates what generic support students can expect in every college
- require colleges to review and report on the effectiveness of their support for learning as part of their self-assessment within the inspection framework
- ensure that learning technology centres are funded for the development and support of staff working with students with learning difficulties and/or disabilities using enabling technology
- investigate the costs of external specialist support on a national basis with a view to identifying quality standards and reasonable levels of charges.

REGIONAL ARRANGEMENTS

7.53 The Council and colleges should work with other agencies at regional level to ensure that internal and external support for learning is available throughout the region. Specifically, the Council should ensure the remit for regional subcommittees includes review of the support available for students in their region in order that:

- there is adequate provision of specialist support for students throughout the region

- regional gaps in the provision of enabling technology may be identified
- start-up funds may be allocated to fill any gaps in the availability of support for learning
- collaborative arrangements between colleges, including specialist colleges, are promoted.

INFORMATION

7.54 The Council, through its regional committees, should encourage the agencies which provide and use support for learning, to provide information for each other on the standard, level and cost of the services each provides and on how funding is allocated.

QUALITY OF EXTERNAL SUPPORT FOR LEARNING

7.55 The Council should encourage specialist support services to develop quality assurance systems, perhaps using a recognised, nationally validated quality hallmark.

7

References

1. Further Education Unit *Supporting Learning: Promoting Equity and Participation Part 1. A Model for Colleges,* London, FEU, 1992

2. Further Education Unit *External Support Services: Meeting Additional Support Needs in Further Education,* London, FEU, 1994

3. *Ibid.*

4. Secretary of state's second letter to the Council, FEFC Circular 92/08 *Establishment of the FEFC,* London, FEFC, July 1992

5. By 'enabling equipment' we mean equipment especially for students to enable them to participate in further education, such as a word processor with spellchecker for a student with dyslexia. 'Enabling equipment' is intended for individual use as opposed to a computer suite which is available for all students.

6. Responses to the call for evidence, (unpublished)

7. Further Education Unit *External Support Services: Meeting Additional Support Needs in Further Education,* London, FEU, 1994

8. Responses to the call for evidence, (unpublished)

9. SCPR *Student Voices: The Views of Further Education Students with Learning Difficulties and/or Disabilities: Findings from a Series of Student Workshops Commissioned by the Learning Difficulties and/or Disablities Committee*, London, Skill: National Bureau for Students with Disabilities, 1996

10. *Ibid.*

11. Responses to the call for evidence, (unpublished)

12. SCPR *Student Voices: The Views of Further Education Students with Learning Difficulties and/or Disabilities: Findings from a Series of Student Workshops Commissioned by the Learning Difficulties and/or Disablities Committee*, London, Skill: National Bureau for Students with Disabilities, 1996

13. Committee visit to USA, April 1996 (see also annex C)

14. *Disability Discrimination Act 1995,* London, HMSO, 1995.

15. See DES Circular 2/88 (Joint Circular with DHSS-LAC(88)2 and Welsh Office 3/88) section VIII [417] and IX [418] which amends the *Chronically Sick and Disabled Persons Act 1970* through section 9 of the HMSO *Disabled Persons (Services, Consultation and Representation) Act 1986,* London, HMSO, 1986

16. Responses to the call for evidence, (unpublished)

17. Responses to the mapping project, (unpublished)

18. Responses to the call for evidence, (unpublished)

19. 41.8% in sixth form colleges; 43.5% in art and design colleges; 43.1% in specially designated colleges. See Meager, N *et al. Mapping Provision: The Provision of and Participation in Further Education by Students with Learning Difficulties and/or Disabilities: A Report to the Learning Difficulties and/or Disabilities Committee*, London, HMSO, 1996, tables 3:1 and A:21.

20. Responses to the call for evidence, (unpublished)

21. *Report of the Learning and Technology Committee,* Coventry, FEFC, January 1996

22. Responses to the call for evidence, (unpublished)

23. FEFC Circular 96/02, *Analysis of Institutions' Strategic Planning Information for the Period 1995-96 to 1997-98,* Coventry, FEFC, January 1996

24. Responses to the call for evidence, (unpublished)

25. *Ibid.*

Chapter 8: Collaboration

In this chapter, the committee addresses the role of collaboration between agencies and colleges in promoting inclusive learning.

THE ISSUES

1. collaborating effectively to bring about inclusive learning
2. providing the essential components for a framework for collaboration at national and local level.

COLLABORATION AND INCLUSIVE LEARNING

8.1 Through collaboration, different agencies and colleges can, at national and local level, work together within a framework of legislation, policy and resource allocation, to make the best use of resources and to assist individuals to achieve their potential.

8.2 Collaboration is important to secure inclusive learning because:

- a number of agencies are likely to be involved in supporting young people with learning difficulties and/or disabilities, as they make the transition to adult life
- the support of more than one agency may be required for some adults with learning difficulties and/or disabilities, for them to take a full part in society.

8.3 Agencies must work together to provide a coherent service for the individual and to use resources effectively. By agencies, we mean statutory and voluntary organisations and services and authorities. Lack of co-ordination leads to confusion for students, parents and carers and a waste of talent and opportunity. Public money is used ineffectively whilst the efforts of individuals and services are duplicated.

8.4 Whilst further education will do much to develop the knowledge, skills and understanding that students with learning difficulties and/or disabilities require, it is not in itself sufficient to realise their aspirations for an ordinary life. There needs, for example, to be wider training and employment opportunities or facilities for independent living or residential care. In addition, the further education sector cannot on its own ensure that all those who wish to benefit from further education are able to do so; some students will require social services support or health services, such as physiotherapy in order to participate.

8.5 It follows that:

- further education colleges need to collaborate with other agencies in order that as many learners as possible can participate
- the Council needs to collaborate with other agencies in order to make the most effective use of resources and to ensure that it provides adequate and sufficient provision.

The secretary of state's letter of guidance to the Council[1] indicates that 'the Council should encourage inter-agency collaboration in order to ensure the best possible response to students' needs.'

THE COMMITTEE'S PRINCIPLES

8.6 In relation to collaboration, we adopted the following principles concerning inclusive learning, which depends upon:

- the Council and colleges entering into mutually helpful agreements with other agencies that plan, fund, provide and monitor related services
- the Council actively encouraging colleges and other providers to work together collaboratively where students with learning difficulties and/or disabilities are concerned
- effective collaboration is based on the principles that:
  - –individuals have the right to say what they want to do with their lives
  - –individuals' aspirations should be respected and acted upon by the organisations that work with them.

8.7 Evidence which might indicate that our principles have been adopted includes:

EVIDENCE

- a mission statement which declares the college's commitment to meet the needs of all those in the community
- a thorough community needs analysis, involving consultation with other providers, health and social services, voluntary organisations, advocacy groups, the careers service, and the local education authority
- co-ordination by senior managers of collaborative activities
- well-developed links between the colleges and the community, including links with employers, TECs, schools, health and social services, and voluntary organisations
- membership of local transition planning groups, health and social services planning groups
- accessible information for students and parents, about local further education, training and support services, produced jointly with other organisations
- effective arrangements to take account of students' transition and care plans
- effective arrangements for joint assessment and reviews with other services
- jointly-managed school and college link courses
- effective schemes for providing support for students who are entering employment and further training.

8.8 Inspectorate evidence gave us the following examples of good and bad practice in collaboration:

EXAMPLES

College A

The college's mission statement indicates clearly the college's commitment to meeting the needs of the community. Liaison with other organisations is part of the college co-ordinator's job description. She reports regularly on its effectiveness to her line manager. The college is represented on the local transition planning group with the local education authority, schools, careers service and support services. This assists the college to identify students and to plan programmes which meet their requirements. Collaboration with social services and the local health authority has enabled the college to plan provision for people with mental health difficulties. Local advocacy groups and groups representing people with articular disabilities are consulted before new provision is planned. A joint project has been undertaken with one of these groups to identify the employment opportunities in the area. A short course to support students with learning difficulties who are starting employment has been introduced with assistance from MENCAP. A jointly-managed link programme for pupils from local special schools provides opportunities for assessment and guidance before students choose their full-time course at college. Parents and pupils are invited to attend an evening meeting with the teams before the link programme begins. The programme's objectives are explained and parents are able to meet staff and ask questions about the college. A senior member of staff is responsible for ensuring that a student's transition and care plans are used for assessments and reviews.

College B

A good working relationship has been established between staff at the college of agriculture and horticulture and staff in a number of special schools. A two-day residential summer programme has been planned jointly by the college and these schools. This provides opportunities for prospective students to try out different activities and to find out more about the college. These close links have resulted in the development of a two-year full-time course in land-based studies for these students. Consultation with the careers service and local employers indicated a demand for the course and the availability of possible employment once the students left college.

College C

The college indicates in its strategic plan an intention to develop provision for students with learning difficulties and/or disabilities but there has not been a comprehensive analysis of needs within the community to identify the type of provision that is needed. A local long-stay hospital for people with learning difficulties moved its residents into the community six years ago. However, they travel considerable distances to another college for their further education. The college does not take part in regular meetings convened by the local education authority for special schools, careers service and educational psychology service where pupils' futures are discussed. The college withdrew its link programme when local special schools requested changes in what was provided. Full-time courses designed for students with learning difficulties have not recruited well in the last two years. Staff spend considerable time making individual arrangements with social and health services, often to the detriment of their other duties. These arrangements break down when a member of staff leaves. Parents' groups complain that they feel unwelcome in the college and that it is difficult to find out about provision. An NVQ level 1 course in hairdressing has been established recently although local employers report the closure of an increasing number of hairdressing salons.

1 Collaborating effectively to bring about inclusive learning

8.9 The evidence we received showed us that colleges and students find the present situation confusing and unsatisfactory. Some 25% of all respondents to the committee's call for evidence dealt with collaboration between further education and other services.

8.10 However, there were some encouraging examples of the provision of clear and helpful information for students. We received evidence of initiatives which indicated what could be achieved when local providers worked in tandem with schools, the LEA and the careers service. For example, several local education authorities provide a handbook for post-16 year olds with learning difficulties and/or disabilities. A careers service has this year mounted a convention at which all the local colleges and some specialist colleges took stands to offer guidance; and at which voluntary and statutory agencies were also represented. This kind of development can do much to redress the pressure young people and their parents felt about making decisions about the future. We heard from some students who were not aware of various options available to them and who were not fully involved in decisions about their future. They experienced pressure to attend certain provision or felt that the choices presented to them were restricted because of their learning difficulty or disability rather than being based on their aspirations. For example, students said:

> *There wasn't really a choice...there was only one course.*
>
> *School pushed us into specialist colleges or specialist units. I wanted to be told what is available.*
>
> *Visually-impaired people need to be encouraged to know what they want to do. There seems to be so much of this steering people into things.*[2]

8.11 On the whole, we heard about the absence of collaboration rather than its effectiveness. We were told that:

- before the *Further and Higher Education Act 1992*, the best local education authorities had provided a framework and support for colleges and others to work together. In some LEAs, for example, Stockport and Manchester, this co-ordination and support still exists. Colleges, schools, other providers and services are able to meet to share their strategic planning for these students and to agree on their individual responsibilities
- other evidence told us that many LEAs reorganised or cut their staff with responsibilities for further education after the *Further and Higher Education Act 1992*. This meant that it was hard for even the most committed LEAs to continue to support such groups[3]
- competition between colleges and schools, between neighbouring colleges and between colleges and other providers of post-school education and training is a major barrier to joint planning[4]
- responsibility for initiating and sustaining many important relationships with other agencies rested on the college co-ordinator for students with disabilities and/or learning difficulties. Sometimes their job description included a responsibility for maintaining collaborative links with other organisations and in some instances time was allocated for the work, but this did not always happen
- the processes involved in collaboration are not understood by all managers and are not evaluated rigorously
- some middle managers in particular doubted the benefits of collaboration and that its effectiveness could be evaluated rigorously. They also did not know how much time they should spend on collaboration. Some middle

managers have changed their roles since their colleges were incorporated, and it was now difficult for them to allocate time to supporting and monitoring collaborative activities[5]

- colleges and other agencies do not always work sufficiently closely together
- links between colleges and schools are not always effective; some colleges find it difficult to get information from schools about young people who are starting college courses. Some schools told us that it is difficult sometimes to influence the content of link courses provided by the college
- parents and students cannot always find out about the learning opportunities and support services that are available.

Transition from school to college

8.12 Parents have high expectations of colleges and these are not always met. At school, pupils with statements will have been the focus of co-ordinated efforts between the school and different services. When these young people enter further education, they should not necessarily assume that they will continue to receive the same degree of support to which they were accustomed at school. Many colleges, however, have service level contracts with careers services and educational psychology services and these benefit students with learning difficulties and/or disabilities. In addition, the transition plan is intended to ensure some continuity of support for these young people.[6] We wish the principles and recommendations in this chapter to apply to all young people with learning difficulties and/or disabilities.

Role of careers service

8.13 The role of the careers service in providing independent advice is crucial. The committee was concerned that as a result of the re-organisation of the service and the development of generic rather than specialist services, access to specialist careers officers had become more difficult for some students.[7] Sometimes, careers officers were able to act as a continuous point of referral for young people as they moved from school, through college and into employment and further training. We anticipate that referral will be strengthened as transition planning becomes better developed. We consider it essential that all students have easy access to a careers officer who is well informed about the variety of options available to a young person with learning difficulties and/or disabilities, and who knows the young person well. We say more about the important role of the careers service in chapter 5. The need for a single point of continuity is addressed in our recommendations later in this chapter at paragraph 8.48.

Collaboration with health and social services

8.14 We were told that the quality and extent of collaboration had deteriorated since the incorporation of colleges and other legislative and organisational changes in health and social services. Inadequate relationships have an adverse effect, particularly on adult learners, for whom social services purchase education provision. College staff told us that they had to spend excessive amounts of time to obtain what are often small amounts of money from health and social services in order to provide educational opportunities for students.[8] On the other hand, social services told us that colleges are not always clear about the benefits or costs of their provision and do not take into account sufficiently the care plans of adult learners when they devise learning programmes.[9]

2 Providing the essential components for a framework for collaboration at national and local level

A national framework

8.15 Much of the evidence concerned the absence of a national framework for collaboration. The lack of clarity over different agencies' legislative responsibilities was considered to be a major barrier to collaboration at regional and local levels. We were told that there is no single, unifying framework within which agencies could work together.[10] Respondents suggested that there is a pressing need for a joint circular from the Department of Health, social services and the Department for Education and Employment which would outline their respective responsibilities for young people and adults with learning difficulties and/or disabilities:

> *The remit of different bodies and the relevant legislation may overlap or leave gaps. These gaps/overlaps should be identified, especially where bodies have power but no clear duty to provide. The links between FEFC and LEAs are as important for colleges as between FEFC and social services.*[11]

A local framework

8.16 Without the assistance of a national framework, colleges must establish their own networks for collaboration. Sometimes, the LEA has retained a role in drawing agencies together; one LEA convenes regular meetings of colleges, schools, careers service and other agencies and assists them to co-ordinate provision. Although colleges and agencies were keen to co-operate with one another, they were unclear as to how they should do so.

8.17 We were told that there is a need for the Council to support and assist the development of existing good practice in collaborative planning of provision for students with learning difficulties and/or disabilities and to take action with others to promote collaboration where it is needed. One country-wide transition group commented that:

> *While dialogue between agencies remains optimistic, success will ultimately depend upon a clearer lead from central government. In this respect, the role of the FEFC regional officers appears crucial. They must assume more than an 'arms length' operational brief if inter-agency collaboration is to remain a reality.*[12]

8.18 We found that the absence of good local networks and opportunities for collaborative planning meant that:

- some colleges had difficulty in analysing local community requirements effectively
- provision might be duplicated by different providers
- some groups of learners might not have provision made for them
- it was difficult to track students as they moved from school to college and on to employment or further training and to ensure that they received the right services at the right time
- support services were not used effectively.[13]

The student

8.19 Lack of clarity over the responsibilities of different services and of different parts of the education service often led to confusion for students and their parents or carers. Sometimes students were passed from one service to another and no single agency assumed responsibility for them.[14]

8.20 Collaboration is essential when more than one service is involved in assessing a student's requirements for provision or for support. The transition plan serves as a focus to draw agencies together. There was considerable evidence to suggest that colleges should make more use of the potential the plan offers to continue the planning process.

8.21 Unless agencies work together over assessment, its purpose and nature are unclear and students and their families or carers lose a sense of control and power over decision-making. There is an urgent need for agencies to bring their individual assessments together. There is, however, evidence to indicate that it is increasingly difficult for professionals to devise and maintain effective co-operative assessment.[15] Other evidence indicates the assessment procedures of health and social services do not always identify the educational requirements of individuals.

8.22 The transfer of information about individuals varies. Some colleges do not want much information on pupils and prefer to operate a 'clean slate' policy. Some schools provide inadequate information. Health and social services do not always supply relevant information about the care plans of adult learners. Some colleges either do not ask for, or do not make good use of, the information on care plans when putting together individual learning programmes. Under the code of practice, information on younger learners must be relayed to the college, but this requirement does not extend to information about adult learners. As a result, learning that colleges provide for adults may not be relevant to other aspects of these students' lives nor assist them to reach broader goals.

8.23 Some students with learning difficulties and/or disabilities require support from a number of services throughout their time in college. Colleges vary in the effectiveness with which they record and track the involvement of different agencies with a student.[16]

8.24 There is no equivalent of a transition plan in further education and it is not clear what entitlement students have during their time in college. The Council requires that each student should have a 'learning agreement' but this is mainly concerned with the on-entry stage of the learning programme. The requirement for colleges to produce disability statements should result in greater clarity over what a student can expect to receive.

Self-advocacy

8.25 Learners need the opportunity to develop skills which enable them to state what they require from further education and which help them to make decisions about their future. These skills are essential if learners are to find their way through the maze of provision, services, sources of funding, assessment regimes and qualifications that constitute further education.

8.26 The committee was concerned to find that awareness of self-advocacy was low amongst students attending the workshop series. Where students have attended self-advocacy groups, they are enthusiastic about the opportunities they provide to raise important issues about their future.[17] However, teachers did not always recognise the potential of self-advocacy to assist students to make decisions about their current learning and future plans.[18] It was difficult to see how some students could acquire the skills they required in order to articulate their views, influence decision-making and take charge of their own lives if colleges did not provide opportunities for these skills to be developed and used. Once they had begun to develop self-advocacy skills and to enjoy the personal autonomy that they gave, students wanted opportunities to have their say:

> *Our college is good for self-advocacy. Every week we have a meeting where we get things sorted out.*
>
> *We do not have tutors chasing us. I wouldn't like that: it would be like school. We need to be treated like people capable of making our own decisions.*[19]

Transition from college

8.27 Colleges find it difficult to fund and provide support for the vital transition from college to employment or further training. There is considerable international and national evidence to demonstrate the overall cost-effectiveness of even short periods of support during this transition period.[20] Unless this support is provided, much of the investment made in the individual by the family, school and college may be wasted or put at risk. It is clear that a high percentage of young people with severe disabilities or learning difficulties are capable of employment and independent living, providing they have the appropriate education and support which continues to be available to them when needed.[21]

8.28 Colleges are well placed to work with TECs, employers and voluntary organisations to provide the support which is vital to the students when they start work. Some are beginning to think along these lines, for example, setting up job-coaching schemes or providing short 'day release' courses to support students and their employers in the early stages of employment or training. Sometimes these opportunities are planned in conjunction with a local voluntary organisation or TEC.[22]

SUMMARY OF MAIN FINDINGS

8.29 In the light of our principles and indicative evidence, we found that the main weaknesses in relation to collaboration are:

- the absence of a national framework for collaboration
- difficulty in maintaining regional and local collaboration
- too much depends upon individual commitment and energy and not enough on formal arrangements for collaboration
- the lack of formal arrangements for collaboration leads to insufficient identification by colleges of local needs and of individual requirements
- there are insufficient opportunities for students to develop their ability to make informed and independent choices.

ADDRESSING WEAKNESSES AND BUILDING ON STRENGTHS

1 Collaborating effectively to bring about inclusive learning

8.30 The committee wishes young people with learning difficulties and/or disabilities to progress easily and smoothly to adult life through a 'seamless robe' of provision and support services. We wish to see adult learners able to move in and out of opportunities for learning as and when they require them. We want to see everyone with a learning difficulty and/or disability claim their entitlement to lifelong learning.

8.31 In order to address the weaknesses and build on the strengths we have identified, we want to see a framework for collaboration operating at four levels:

- national
- regional and local
- college
- individual.

8.32 Effective collaboration is likely to have the same features at each level:

- an agreed framework of common principles, aims, outcomes and quality indicators, described in a common language
- evaluation in terms of direct or indirect benefits to students
- a shift of power and decision-making from professionals to individuals with learning difficulties and/or disabilities and their parents and carers by increasing opportunities for self-advocacy and choice
- good deployment of resources which allocate clear responsibilities to different services, and by providing mechanisms for co-ordination, monitoring and review.

2 Providing the essential components for a framework for collaboration at national and local level

National framework

8.33 *The Children Act 1989*[23] and the code of practice on the identification and assessment of special educational needs[24] are welcome indications of a growing understanding of the importance of collaboration between different government departments where children are concerned. The Act and code, together with the *Disabled Persons (Services, Consultation and Representation) Act 1986* constitute a national framework which provides guidance on the responsibilities of local services and requires agencies to work together. Where the code is concerned, the transition plan provides a focus for collaboration.

8.34 There is no comparative framework for young people beyond school age or for adults. In order for a framework to be established, we wish to see a joint departmental circular which sets out the powers and duties of education, health and social services where students with learning difficulties and/or disabilities in further education are concerned. The circular must:

- identify where departments have the power as well as the duty to work with or take account of the work of other departments
- encourage and support collaboration at a national level
- promote planning between local services by providing guidance on their responsibilities.

8.35 The circular might serve a similar function to that issued by the Scottish Office which describes the responsibilities of different services towards students with learning difficulties and/or disabilities in further education.[25]

Information for students, parents and advocates

8.36 It is important that students and those most closely concerned with them understand the duties and powers of various departments if they are to exercise choice and control in their lives. We see a need for easily-accessible information for students, parents and their advocates on the duties and powers of respective departments and relevant agencies.

8.37 This information is different from that provided in the circular and should be readily available through careers services, colleges and schools. It should be easy to read and in an attractive format. Its purpose would be to assist students, parents and their advocates to know what they are entitled to receive in the way of educational and relevant support services, and from which department or agency these may be obtained.

Regional and local further education planning groups

8.38 There is a need for two types of planning groups at regional and local levels:

- *subcommittees of the Council's regional committees;* which would draw together senior representatives from colleges, schools, TECs, LEAs, careers services, health and social services, voluntary organisations, advocacy groups, parents and students' groups with a remit to advise the Council's regional committees on the adequacy and sufficiency of provision for students with learning difficulties and/or disabilities at regional level and to act as a focus for collaborative strategic planning
- *local further education transition groups;* with a remit to plan the transition from school to further education and from further education to employment or training of individual students; the groups to involve practitioners from schools, colleges, careers service, TECs and others. Students should be represented.

8.39 Our intention here is to encourage the development of existing good practice and to encourage colleges and others to take account of a student's transition plan.

8.40 We attempt to take account of different regional and local circumstances in our vision of a national, regional and local framework for collaboration. Whilst the Council must be sensitive to the good work that has already taken place in some areas, evidence indicates that a more proactive role by the Council would be warmly welcomed by the sector and others.

The college

8.41 In England, as elsewhere, continuity of planning and support for people with learning difficulties and/or disabilities and their families through transition between phases of their lives is rare.[26] We have described briefly how schools provide a single point of delivery for many of the services provided for children and their families.

8.42 However, once a student leaves school, there is no single person with continued responsibility for their successful transition whilst they are in college and on to employment or training. Although some colleges take account of students' transition plans, there is, as yet, no clear idea in colleges of the best way of dealing with these or using them as a basis for co-ordinating the supporting sessions. In particular, we wish to see colleges take greater responsibility for supporting the students' transition from college. In this context, we are impressed by some of the possibilities presented by the *Kurator* or advocate role, one which is familiar in colleges and schools in Denmark and Sweden. There, a member of staff has received special training in order to take on the role of education advocate throughout a student's school and college career and initial employment. Regular planned contact is maintained through a series of reviews and visits. The *Kurator's* job is to:

- plan for the young person's education and training with them and on their behalf
- ensure that they receive the right education and support services at the right time
- assist them to articulate their own ambitions and aspirations and to work towards them
- convey information and liaise between different services on behalf of the young person
- offer relevant support to the young person's family.[27]

8.43 Whilst the careers service in England fulfils some of these functions, it does not have the broad remit to draw together and co-ordinate the many different and complex processes in which students are involved. The mass of evidence we received from students, parents and colleges, together with the findings of national and international research referred to earlier in this chapter, make a strong case for such a central co-ordinating role. We think this role is best fulfilled by the establishment of a named person in each college who would have similar functions to the *Kurator* and who would be responsible for:

- co-ordinating and managing the student's further education plan (see paragraph 8.46) with and on behalf of the student
- ensuring the student receives their further education entitlement
- assisting the student's transition to and from college
- liaising with other services, including careers service, health and social services
- ensuring the student receives opportunities to develop and use self-advocacy skills or receives advocacy support
- liaison with parents and carers
- ensuring that information about the student is conveyed appropriately

from school and other services to the college; from the college to employment, training or other placement, and from college to subject teachers and from course to course as the student progresses.

8.44 Where the tutorial systems are well developed in a college, then the named person role will be an extension of the tutor's present role. In some colleges, the role will be a new one. We suggest that a small-scale pilot project is established in order to assist colleges to test out and refine the role.

The individual

8.45 We have remained conscious of the importance of the individual student amongst these new structures and arrangements. We asked ourselves:

- how did colleges ensure that the students' total experience had a sense of unity and purpose?
- how could the student find out what they were entitled to?
- what would assist them to ask for and receive this entitlement?

8.46 We were loathe to invent something new. Instead, we looked to see what was already in place that might be developed or enhanced in order to serve our purposes. At present each student in Council-funded provision must have a learning agreement as a requirement for funding. In future we wish to see this used as a starting point for a *further education plan* (FE plan), perhaps supported by an further education code of practice, similar to the code of practice used in the school sector. Where students have transition or care plans, the FE plan will carry forward the further education component. The FE plan will move with the student through college and beyond, complemented by the enhanced national record of achievement. The plan must ensure that the student receives their entitlement whilst at college. It would comprise:

- access to information – as part of the college's disability statement
- independent counselling and guidance – from the careers service
- opportunities to develop and use self-advocacy skills and advocacy support
- assessment of learning styles, learning goals and learning environment, including learning support
- record of progress and outcomes of regular reviews
- national record of achievement
- access to high-quality accreditation
- access to a named person.

A diagram showing the different components of the plan is on page 131.

8.47 The named person in each college would be responsible for ensuring that the FE plan is devised and implemented.

RECOMMENDATIONS

8.48 The key recommendation in relation to collaboration is that the Council should work with other agencies and government departments to create and define a framework for collaboration. Specifically, the Council should:

- urge the drawing up of a joint departmental circular setting out the powers and duties of education, health and social services where students with learning difficulties and/or disabilities are concerned; the circular would draw attention to the duties of these services, and the powers they have to work with, and to take account of, the work of other departments
- work with others to provide easily accessible information for students, parents and their advocates on the duties and powers of respective departments and relevant agencies
- establish subcommittees to its regional committees which include senior representatives from colleges, schools, TECs, LEAs, careers services, health

and social services, voluntary organisations, advocacy groups and others, with a remit to advise the Council's regional committees on the adequacy and sufficiency of provision at regional level and to act as a focus for collaborative, strategic planning

- work with others to encourage the support and development of local further education transition groups with a remit to plan the transition of individual students
- work with colleges and others to establish the concept of the 'named person' in each college and to test and refine the concept through a small-scale pilot project
- work with colleges and others to develop a further education plan, using the existing learning agreement as a starting point, together with a code of practice for its use
- encourage the undertaking of research on the cost benefits of collaboration to the Council, colleges and the individual.

The Further Education Plan

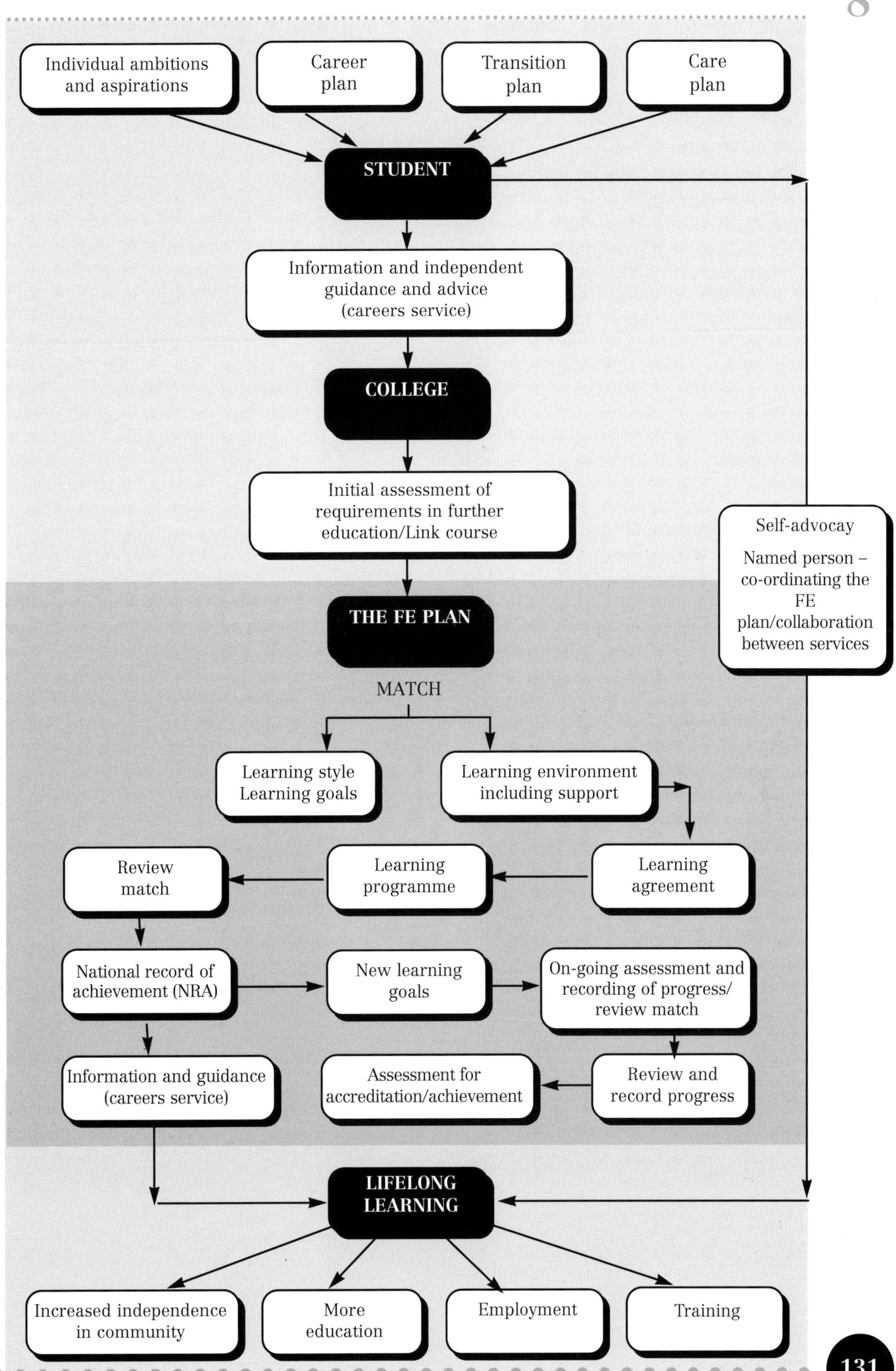

8

References

1. FEFC Circular 92/08, *Establishment of the FEFC,* London, FEFC, July 1992

2. SCPR *Student Voices: The Views of Further Education Students with Learning Difficulties and/or Disabilities: Findings From a Series of Student Workshops Commissioned by the Learning Difficulties and/or Disabilities Committee,* London, Skill: National Bureau for Students with Disabilities, 1996

3. Responses to the call for evidence (unpublished)

4. *Ibid.*

5. *Ibid.*

6. Peter Lavender, *Special Needs Occasional Paper: Care and Education in the Community,* Harlow, Longman, 1988

7. Response to the call for evidence, (unpublished)

8. *Ibid.*

9. *Ibid.*

10. *Ibid.*

11. *Ibid*

12. *Ibid.*

13. *Ibid.*

14. Responses to the call for evidence, (unpublished) and seminar for parents' organisations, 12 July 1995

15. Responses to the call for evidence, (unpublished)

16. Evidence from the FEFC inspectorate

17. Skill & SCPR *Student Voices: The Views of Further Education Students with Learning Difficulties and/or Disabilities: Findings From a Series of Student Workshops Commissioned by the Learning Difficulties and/or Disabilities Committee,* London, Skill: National Bureau for Students with Disabilities, 1996

18. Evidence from the FEFC inspectorate

19. Skill & SCPR *Student Voices: The Views of Further Education Students with Learning Difficulties and/or Disabilities: Findings From a Series of Student Workshops Commissioned by the Learning Difficulties and/or Disabilities Committee,* London, Skill: National Bureau for Students with Disabilities, 1996

20. *Disabled Youth: From School to Work,* Paris, OECD-CERI, 1991; *Enabled to Work: Support into Employment for Young People with Disabilities,* FEU; *Transition to Employment; Proceedings of the 1990 International Symposium on the Employment of Persons with Disabilities,* University of Maryland, 1991

21. *Transition to Employment; Proceedings of the 1990 International Symposium on the Employment of Persons with Disabilities,* University of Maryland, 1991

22. Visits to colleges

23. *The Children Act 1989,* London, HMSO

24. Department for Education and Employment *Code of Practice on the Identification and Assessment of Special Educational Needs,* London, HMSO, 1994

25. Scottish Office Circular (FE)13/95: *Further Education Colleges: Students with Disabilities and/or Learning Difficulties,* Scottish Office, July 1995

26. *Young People with Handicaps: The Road to Adulthood,* Paris, OECD-CERI, 1986

27. *Disabled Youth: From School to Work,* Paris, OECD-CERI, January 1991; FEFC *Post-16 Vocational Education and Training in Sweden: International Report from the Inspectorate,* Coventry, FEFC, May 1994; FEFC *Post-16 Vocational Education and Training in Denmark: International Report from the Inspectorate,* Coventry, FEFC, May 1994

Chapter 9: Assessing Students' Achievements

In this chapter, the committee examines how students' achievements are assessed in the light of the objective of promoting inclusive learning.

THE ISSUES

1. what constitutes achievement
2. the availability of good-quality accreditation
3. interpreting schedule 2(j) to the *Further and Higher Education Act 1992*
4. transition from college.

ASSESSING ACHIEVEMENT AND INCLUSIVE LEARNING

9.1 The achievements of the majority of students with learning difficulties and/or disabilities will, in common with most students in further education, be concerned with developing knowledge, skills and understanding in order to achieve qualifications. For some students with learning difficulties or profound and multiple disabilities, achievement will be concerned with developing the knowledge, skills and understanding which will enable them to lead a more independent, ordinary adult life in the community.[1] We ascribe equal dignity and importance to these different types of achievement. It is important to restate this because in the past many students with learning difficulties and/or disabilities have followed separate and different courses from other students; they have received separate, if any, assessment or recognition of their achievements, sometimes based on different standards and procedures. The principles that follow, with their emphasis on inclusive learning, represent an important step forward.

9 THE COMMITTEE'S PRINCIPLES

9.2 We set out the principles which should inform all assessment in further education in chapter 5. The assessment of students' achievements should be inclusive, in that the achievements of all students are given equal value and status; and in that it is:

- *based on self-advocacy;* students are involved in deciding what they wish to achieve and in evaluating their progress towards these achievements
- *fair*; assessment regimes are fair, impartial and objective
- *transparent*; the purpose of criteria for and outcomes of assessment should be understood by students, parents and employers
- *accessible*; assessment is conducted in a way that enables the individual to participate fully.

9.3 Evidence which might indicate that a college has adopted our principles for assessing students' achivements includes:

EVIDENCE

- achievement of relevant and realistic learning goals
- validation of achievement by nationally-recognised external bodies
- accreditation which supports rather than determines the learning programme
- accreditation which is recognised and valued by employers
- evidence that assessment has helped the student to develop more self confidence, self-esteem, autonomy and responsibility
- careful recording of assessment of the student's achievements covers all aspects of the curriculum
- teachers are able to identify, assess and record small steps of progress and achievement
- students' awareness of their achievements
- systematic use of national records of achievement
- the high status given to a variety of students' achievements, for example, displays of students' work and prize-givings.

9.4 Inspectorate evidence gave us the following examples of good and bad practice in assessing students' achievements:

EXAMPLES

College A

All the students who are following specifically-designed courses will have their achievements validated by external bodies. Great care has been taken to ensure that the accreditation supports rather than determines their programmes. The college has deliberately opted for accreditation which will be easily recognised by employers. Many students undertake vocational training within the college's simulated work environments such as the training restaurant which is open to the public. They dress smartly in the uniforms provided and perform a variety of tasks efficiently. The students have developed confidence and self-esteem; they are able to use their initiative and to accept responsibility; they work independently and will take the initiative in asking for help. Some students take part in work experience placements in local hotels; their achievements here count toward their final assessment. All the students are aware of their achievements and are justifiably proud of them. National records of achievement are used to record students' achievements in other aspects of the course, for example, during a short residential experience. Last year, nearly all the students on these courses progressed to other provision within the college or to further training.

College B

Students' work is accredited by a variety of awarding bodies. Many students achieve a considerable number of accredited modules but it is difficult to understand what these signify in terms of their ability. The rationale for entering students for the accreditation is unclear. Very few students achieve a full qualification. Several students have been attending the college for a number of years but there is little evidence that they have made progress. The students themselves complain that they are simply repeating a lot of what they have already done at school. There are no clearly-defined progression routes from discrete provision to vocational or academic programmes. The lack of opportunity for the students to undertake vocational training which would enable them to build on their strengths is resulting in many of them underachieving and becoming disillusioned with college.

College C

Students with learning difficulties and/or disabilities follow a variety of academic programmes. Three students with visual impairment are taking A level English with the support of a Brailling tutor. Two students who are deaf are working toward science A levels with the support of an interpreter. Other students with physical disabilities receive carefully-tailored individual support. All students benefit from a short study skills course which is run as part of the college's induction programme. There are well worked out procedures with examination boards for securing Brailling and other support during examinations. These arrangements are made in time for students to feel confident about the support they will receive. The college reviews regularly the effectiveness of its learning support by comparing the achievements of students receiving support with others in the same class. Last year, their examination results compared favourably.

College D

The college has few students with learning difficulties and/or disabilities following academic programmes. Learning support arrangements are poor, with support staff unsure of their roles. Subject teachers receive little information about students' requirements and find it difficult to adapt their teaching styles and learning materials to suit them. One class teacher did not know that a deaf student used lip-reading to follow the lesson. The teacher frequently turned away from the students as he explained important concepts. Students with learning difficulties and/or disabilities find it hard to keep up the same pace of work as other students. Staff provide little clear guidance on how best to revise for examinations. Students are not sure what support will be available during examinations and express considerable anxiety about them. Last year, two deaf students and two students with physical disabilities left their courses before the examinations.

College E

The college provides a part-time programme for older students with learning difficulties who live in nearby residential bungalows which are managed by social services. Each student takes part in an individual assessment where they are encouraged to say what they wish to achieve by coming to college. Their social services key worker takes part in the assessment and helps to identify longer-term goals for the individual. A learning programme with clearly identified learning goals is then devised for each student. Three students have learnt to travel to college on their own by following a carefully-staged programme devised and implemented by the group's support worker. Other students are now able to use the college canteen and library without assistance. Two students who became anxious when asked to talk in front of others have learnt to take part in group discussions. Some students are learning how to prepare simple meals, and other skills for independent living. These classes take place in a purpose-built flat attached to the college. A recent sightseeing trip to London provided opportunities for students to budget for the day, travel on a variety of transport and make a tape-recording of their impressions. A high-quality, well-labelled photographic display in the classroom records the event. Students discuss their progress with the course tutor on a regular basis and are encouraged to set new targets. The group spends some time each week reviewing the achievements of its members. These sessions provide opportunities for students to practise their self-advocacy skills. Course tutors are evaluating various forms of accreditation to decide which best meets their students' requirements. They wish to enhance the rigour of their work but do not want to change the topics they cover, which have been carefully worked out with social services. At present, students use individual portfolios to record their achievements. Last year, four students moved from the bungalows to more independent living in shared flats.

1 What constitutes achievement

9.5 Students who took part in the workshop series offered us important evidence about their expectations of achievement and the extent to which those were realised. They told us that:

- most of them attend college because, like the majority of other students, they want experience, skills and a recognised qualification which will open further doors to them
- a qualification had an additional value; as one commented, 'You can't deny our disabilities, but certificates prove our abilities.'[2]

9.6 One student who took part in the workshops told us:

> *I have actually got certificates I went to college to get and what I am doing now is to continue upgrading the work I am doing and at the end of the day the idea is to get a position in a transport office and get a position as a transport manager.*[3]

Respondents to the committee's call for evidence shared these views. One day-care service told us that a local survey to find out what people with mental health difficulties wanted from education and training showed that 80% of them wanted some form of progression, leading towards work.[4]

9.7 In addition, we received considerable evidence about the benefits of learning which aims to increase or maintain skills for adult life. This kind of learning contributes to the economic well-being of the country because it increases the capacity of the individual to lead an ordinary independent life, thereby reducing their need for support services. Parents, in particular, stressed the value of this learning to the individual and the community. Students described how it increased their confidence, developed their ability to travel alone, enabled them to handle money, manage their physical care requirements and relate more easily to others.[5] Students want these skills assessed properly. One student who took part in the workshops told us:

> *They should write reports about what you are as a person. They always focus on the things you can't do. We have a right to be here. It's society that makes you think disabled people are useless.*[6]

9.8 For a small number of students, including those with profound or multiple learning difficulties, a significant achievement may be represented by a turn of the head to indicate 'no' consistently, or by making the connection between a given signal and an event, such as a move to another room. These achievements are an indicator of the individual's developing independence. They show how the student relates to others, instructs carers or expresses preferences. These achievements are small in their scale but huge in their importance. We found that colleges often have difficulty in recording them consistently and thoroughly.

2 The availability of good-quality accreditation

9.9 There was considerable evidence of concern of a lack of consistency in the standards by which students' achievements are assessed. Local or regional centres can determine and moderate standards for different awards with varying degrees of rigour. Standards can differ between centres and between providers. There are no national standards for many of the awards and types of accreditation used with students with learning difficulties and/or disabilities.

9.10 The quality and appropriateness of some accreditation used by students with learning difficulties was a common theme. Some teachers lacked the skills to adapt accreditation requirements to suit their students. The inspectorate told us that, in effect, the assessment and record-keeping systems for accreditation are used as an inadequate substitute for a curriculum.

Sometimes the modules leading to accreditation are combined in ways that do not match students' learning requirements. It can be difficult for students to work out the relevance of the different modules to one another and to the learning programme as a whole, or how they relate to their lives outside college. Students' achievements are presented as a list of modules they have completed. This makes it hard for an employer, parents or a tutor interviewing a student for another course to identify what they can and cannot do. Furthermore, it does not help the student to understand what they have achieved in order that they may explain their achievement clearly to others.[7] We were told that some qualifications are inaccessible to students with learning difficulties and/or disabilities because:

- the qualification is not broken down into sufficiently small units
- the first level of the qualification is at too high a level
- some of the assessment processes, such as written tests, cannot be carried out by them
- language used in the specification for some standards assumes that candidates can see or hear
- standards in core skills are sometimes set at a higher level than standards for practical skills
- there is inconsistency between awarding bodies in relation to the nature and extent of the support that may be given to candidates during examinations.

9.11 The inspectorate also told us that different forms of accreditation sometimes have different assessment regimes. Many students have parts of their learning programmes accredited by different awarding bodies, each with different assessment regimes.[8]

9.12 About 20% of students in colleges currently follow programmes which are accredited by bodies other than the National Council for Vocational Qualifications (NCVQ) or are not accredited at all. A significant number of these students have learning difficulties and/or disabilities. There are 11 national bodies which offer a variety of certification for use with students with learning difficulties and/or disabilities. In addition, there is a plethora of local arrangements for accrediting their courses.

9.13 There are no systematic arrangements for accrediting the skills, knowledge and understanding which students with learning difficulties and/or disabilities may have before they come to college. Their prior learning is not recognised or accredited in the context of foundation or NVQ level 1 awards. There are no planned progression routes and no continuity between the various types of accreditation. OFSTED told us that the absence of appropriate accreditation for pupils at the end of key stage 4 continues to make it difficult for special schools to construct an appropriate curriculum. There are inadequate opportunities for students to accumulate credits for units of learning which start whilst they are still at school. Even though many students achieve a considerable number of accredited modules, it can be difficult to understand what these signify in terms of the student's ability or achievement.[9]

9.14 More than 380 respondents to the call for evidence provided evidence on assessment, over 200 about accreditation. Over 100 respondents, including employers, stressed the need for nationally-recognised vocational qualifications at pre-foundation and level 1 stages. Others referred to the need to acknowledge and fund units of accreditation for small steps of progress. One college told us that 'partial units of accreditation may represent superb achievements for some students'.[10]

9.15 Some 5% of all GCSE candidates come from further education. The proportion of GCE A level candidates from further education is much higher. Amongst these will be students who have learning difficulties and/or disabilities. Two students who took part in the workshops described conflicting experiences of examination arrangements:

> *I took a maths exam and I had the use of a CCTV and when I looked at the exam paper I just looked at it because when you come to blow the diagrams up for the pie charts I couldn't do it and she knew I couldn't do it and I just failed the exam.*

> *When I used to do exams at my last college they were very good. They used to do exam papers in very large print, and Braille, and the staff used to negotiate extra time, in fact.*[11]

9.16 We were told that there are five main difficulties with assessment for academic qualifications:

- GCSE examining bodies need to find appropriate ways, within the terms of their assessment criteria, of assessing candidates with disabilities; for example, in GCSE music for candidates with hearing impairment and GCSE geography for students with visual impairment
- the costs of meeting individual requirements, for example, providing papers in Braille or on audio-tape; or providing examination rooms which are accessible to students with disabilities
- the cost to the student and educational establishment of providing evidence of individual requirements, for example, the cost of a report from a recognised psychologist for candidates with specific learning difficulties
- the volume of requests for individual arrangements. At present each request is dealt with by the examining body rather than by the head of the examination centre[12]
- the need for examining and awarding bodies to understand the Council's funding arrangements for students who may require additional support during examinations.[13]

3 Interpreting schedule 2(j) to the Further and Higher Education Act 1992

9.17 Schedule 2 to the *Further and Higher Education Act 1992* defines the kinds of courses which the Council has a duty to fund. It also defines the courses for which funding was transferred to the Council from LEAs upon incorporation. It applies to students over the age of 16 studying part time and to students over the age of 19 studying full time. The legal aspects to the schedule are described in more detail in chapter 3. Schedule 2(j) refers to:

> *(j) a course to teach independent living and communication skills to persons having learning difficulties which prepares them for entry to another course falling within paragraphs (d) to (h) above.*

9.18 The further education sector and other services perceive the Council to be a stable source of funding. The Council is managing finite resources and changing priorities. We recognise that it must discharge but not go beyond its legal duties. It follows that the Council must draw parameters around what it will fund. The legislative framework indicates what it must fund but there will be areas of discretion or ambiguity which are open to interpretation. The way in which the Council interprets its discretion has consequences for some students with learning difficulties. Their learning may be funded by the Council or be subject to the exigencies of LEA funding or social service budgets. The Council has published criteria to help define the scope of schedule 2(j). These criteria are given in chapter 3.

9.19 We found that schedule 2(j) issues were of considerable concern to colleges, parents and other agencies. Over 100 respondents to the committee's call for evidence addressed these matters, and over 60 were concerned specifically with the criteria used for identifying courses within schedule 2(j).

9

At the time of the call for evidence (1993), the criteria and their interpretation were seen by these respondents as:

- unclear
- too narrow in that they fail to relate to provision which, although not externally accredited, enables students to make progress and experience achievements
- to place undue importance on external accreditation.[14]

9.20 We found a different picture during our visit to Scotland. There, students who are making progress in parallel to their previous learning, through the practice and transfer of existing skills into other settings, are to have their achievements recognised within the Skill Start qualifications framework. In England, we found that progress in parallel would probably fall outside the scope of schedule 2(j) as it was then defined. There is no equivalent of the distinction between schedule 2 and non-schedule 2 funding in Scotland.[15]

9.21 Evidence from national organisations and others indicated the consequences of the *Further and Higher Education Act 1992* had led to the loss of some non-schedule 2 work. Local education authorities felt they did not have enough funds left to continue to provide such provision. The local infrastructure had been depleted when LEA responsibilities changed. Sometimes social service departments had insufficient funds. In a national survey of 280 respondents:

- 30% reported that emphasis on accreditation for funding purposes has excluded people with learning difficulties
- older adults with learning difficulties and/or disabilities were starting to miss out on education
- there had been cuts in provision for people with severe and profound learning difficulties.[16]

9.22 Respondents to our call for evidence highlighted wide variation in the way colleges interpreted schedule 2(j).[17] They said that students had difficulties with progression between schedule 2 and non-schedule 2 provision because each was funded from different sources. Many respondents had considerable unease about the unintended effects on students' learning of schedule 2(j) requirements. Some said there was lack of consistency in the Council's interpretation of schedule 2(j). Others referred to concerns that particular groups of learners had been excluded, whether deliberately or otherwise, from the scope of the schedule when it was constructed by parliament. The Council's inspectorate told us that the curriculum was being determined by the perceived demand by the Council for qualifications, rather than the needs of the student. Students were seen to spend too much time on the completion of tasks to meet the requirements of validating bodies. The inspectorate provided evidence of the lack of quality assurance of some validation and accreditation arrangements currently used by colleges.[18]

9.23 This view was reinforced by OFSTED, which told us that the move to meet the perceived requirements for schedule 2(j) funding has led to changes in what is taught, dictated by what is fundable rather than what is appropriate for the learners.[19]

9.24 The 20 colleges participating in the committee's testing exercise agreed unanimously that the prevailing interpretation of schedule 2(j) prevented them from meeting individual requirements as effectively as they would wish. They advised us that it would be a barrier to colleges adopting the committee's recommendations about inclusive learning.[20]

9.25 We were told that students with profound or complex learning difficulties and/or disabilities were likely to be most affected by these issues, because their achievements are not readily recognised and valued within the prevailing interpretation of schedule 2(j).[21]

4 Transition from college

9.26 Some students benefit from a short period of support whilst they make the transition from college to employment or training. Considerable international and national evidence indicates that a relatively small extra investment in the student at this point assists them to make good use of their further education. Support may take the form of a job-coaching scheme, short bridging course or visits from tutors. Employers are more confident about offering work to people with learning difficulties and/or disabilities if they know they will receive expert support from staff who know the student well.[22] During our visit to the USA, we found the value of job-coaching schemes widely accepted. People with severe learning difficulties or physical disabilities were able to hold down a job with the assistance of trained job coaches and to earn a wage, thus enabling them to live more independently.[23]

9.27 Time should not be a barrier to achievement by students with learning difficulties and/or disabilities. Some students may learn more slowly and require more guided learning hours over a longer period of time. They may require more time in college than other students in order to make a successful transition to adult life. We found some concerns amongst colleges that the Council's funding methodology did not recognise this.

9.28 The careers service provides an important link to initial employment. However, despite its important role, we found that the careers service duty towards students with learning difficulties and/or disabilities until they are settled in their career intentions is interpreted inconsistently.

SUMMARY OF MAIN FINDINGS

9.29 When we analysed this evidence in the light of the principles set out earlier, we found the following main weaknesses in the way students' achievements are assessed:

- barriers in the way some qualifications are designed
- no nationally-recognised and quality assured third pathway for independence skills for adult life, to parallel the academic and the vocational pathways
- difficulties for some students in obtaining appropriate examination arrangements.

In respect of schedule 2:

- the potential for uncertainty and inconsistency in its interpretation between colleges and the Council
- the available accreditation routes are not appropriate and some students are following programmes because they lead to accreditation rather than the right programme in which their learning is then accredited
- it appears to exclude students with profound and multiple disabilities from its scope
- some teachers are not able to break down learning programmes into small steps to facilitate learning for all their students.

ADDRESSING WEAKNESSES AND BUILDING ON STRENGTHS

What constitutes achievement

9.30 We want to see all students' achievements recognised within a national framework that gives value to their learning.

We would wish to see:

- the development of skills for adult life recognised as being of importance to society and the nation's economy
- a more inclusive qualifications framework that recognises the achievements of all young people
- greater rigour, coherence and relevance in the learning of students at pre-foundation level
- colleges improving their recording of progress made by students with learning difficulties and/or disabilities.

9.31 Good provision is where students who are on specifically-designed courses have their achievements validated by external bodies. Learning is broken down into small units for which high-quality accreditation has been arranged. The different units accumulated by a student make up a coherent programme of learning.[24]

2 The availability of good-quality accreditation

A third pathway for learning for adult life

9.32 In keeping with our principle of inclusive learning, we wish to see recognition accorded to learning which will assist students with learning difficulties and/or disabilities to achieve greater independence in their adult life. The importance of this learning must be recognised. We proposed to Sir Ron Dearing that he include a recommendation for a pre-foundation Skills for Adult Life award in his review of the 16 to 19 curriculum. This award might be made up of the following units:

- employability, preparation for working life
- understanding roles in the family, including parenting skills and relationships
- understanding the local community, including travel, leisure pursuits, and voluntary work
- understanding the society we live in, including the laws and individual benefits and allowances.

9.33 Skills for Adult Life should be available as an award within the national qualifications framework at pre-foundation level. It should also be included among the core skills at the foundation level of GNVQ. In this way, these skills could be acquired by young people with moderate learning difficulties or with emotional and other difficulties. Opportunities for progression to foundation level Skills for Adult Life should be built into the design of the pre-qualification award. The award should not be seen as a separate qualification only for students with learning difficulties: other young people would also benefit from developing these skills and having them recognised.

9.34 The new award was proposed in Sir Ron's report.[25] It must be designed to be relevant to the needs of students who are making the transition to adult life or who want to develop skills to live more independently. It must be assessed in such a way that small steps of learning can be recognised. Colleges and others emphasised that the development of the new Skills for Adult Life awards should take account of the lessons learnt in the design of GNVQs and NVQs. Consultation with teachers and others working with students with learning difficulties and/or disabilities will be essential for the new award to properly meet the requirements of these students.[26] Evidence from Scotland indicated the effectiveness of involving teachers in the early stages of designing new qualifications.[27] The National Council for Vocational Qualification's Access and Fair Assessment Forum provides welcome opportunities for teachers' views to be heard.

9.35 We are pleased to see our proposals reflected in their entirety in Sir Ron's final report and look forward to the development of the award.

Existing qualification design and assessment arrangements

9.36 We want to see greater consistency of assessment arrangements. This could be achieved by:

- ensuring that awarding and examination bodies are better informed about the Council's funding arrangements for students with learning difficulties and/or disabilities
- encouraging examining and awarding bodies to allow examination centres greater freedom to make individual arrangements for students
- encouraging these bodies to find a common language to describe students with learning difficulties and/or disabilities and their assessment requirements.

9.37 The existing GNVQ and NVQ qualifications should become more accessible to students with learning difficulties and/or disabilities. To this end, the Council should encourage the National Council for Vocational Qualifications (NCVQ), the School Curriculum and Assessment Authority (SCAA) and others to review the assessment requirement for written tests at GNVQ foundation and level 1. Furthermore, we ask that the Council should encourage the development of rigorous, alternative and more flexible approaches to assessment.

Continuity between school and college

9.38 To promote continuity between school and college, we want to see:

- more units of NVQs and GNVQs available for young people in schools
- colleges taking more account of a student's transition plan
- promotion of an enhanced national record of achievement.

3 Interpreting schedule 2(j) to the Further and Higher Education Act 1992

9.39 We want to ensure that the Council's — and colleges' — interpretation of schedule 2(j) is in keeping with the spirit of the legislation. We recognise that the Act is designed, in part, to ensure that national training and education priorities are met. This places importance on learning programmes that contribute to economic productivity, directly or indirectly. Programmes which contribute to independent adult living should be included because they facilitate economic productivity.

9.40 It is the committee's view that the Council's present interpretation of schedule 2(j) and that of some colleges does not take properly into account the value to society of this kind of learning. As we argued in chapter 3, our focus on inclusive learning requires new standards for judging the adequacy of provision. Using those new standards, we think the present interpretation of schedule 2(j) falls short of the interpretation we would wish to see of the *Further and Higher Education Act 1992*. We have concluded on the basis of the overwhelming evidence we have received that the emphasis on accreditation has led to some students being subject to inappropriate accreditation. We believe that the learning needs of some students are being overlooked in an attempt to secure funding by practitioners who fear that provision may be lost if it is not funded by the Council, and who perceive accreditation to be essential for that funding.

9.41 However, it is vital to retain and improve the rigour and standards of learning falling within schedule 2(j). Accreditation is not in itself a guarantor of quality and standards. Nor does accreditation guarantee that a student will progress onto another schedule 2 course. Accreditation is suitable for most learners, but not for all. It is one method of demonstrating that progression is likely.

9.42 A wider interpretation of schedule 2(j) is required. The standards we advocate involve a broader view of economic activity, and of students' progress. We believe that this is in keeping with the intentions of the legislation because:

- it is likely to lessen the individual's requirement for other services later in life, thereby contributing to the nation's economy in an indirect but important way
- it recognises new ways of measuring progress and achievement which parallel those already included.

9.43 Because of its emphasis on preparation for another course in the schedule, a student must be able to demonstrate an intention and a capacity to move on to such a course if their current learning programme is to be funded within schedule 2(j). There are two kinds of progression: progress in learning within a programme of study and progression from one programme of study to another at a higher level.

9.44 The committee wishes to see progress within the learning programme used as one of a group of indicators of whether the individual is likely and able to move on to a higher level of study. We propose that three definitions of progress should be used within a learning programme to indicate that the requirement for preparation for another course is met:

i. *incremental progress;* this relates to the acquisition of knowledge, skills and understanding which build on the student's existing achievements. Evidence of progress is found by comparing the student's level of attainment when they started their learning programme with that which is expected of them at the end. The student's acquisition of knowledge, skills and understanding would be assessed and recorded throughout their learning programme. Their standard of achievement would be assessed at its end

ii. *lateral progress;* this relates to the student's ability to transfer and practise the knowledge, skills and understanding they already have, in a range of new settings. Evidence of progress is found in the student's understanding of different settings and their ability to transfer and generalise. For example, a student who had achieved the skills of working with one other person might progress to working in a group of two or three others. Or, a person who had completed a particular task with assistance, might progress to working successfully without help. The learning environment would have to provide a variety of appropriate settings in which students could demonstrate their knowledge, skill and understanding. Evidence of progress is found by identifying how settings differed from each other and how successfully knowledge, skills and understanding had been transferred and generalised. What constituted a reasonable 'range and variety of settings' would require careful consideration

iii. *maintaining knowledge, skills and understanding;* this relates to the maintenance of skills, knowledge and understanding that are threatened by degenerative illness or the effects of medical trauma. Evidence of progress is found by identifying the student's existing knowledge, skills and understanding; identifying which of these is most threatened; the development of strategies and goals for their maintenance; the assessment and recording of the degree of maintenance that takes place. There might be a 'cut-off' point at which it becomes necessary to ensure that students retain physical skills such as the ability to feed themselves. The student's programme might cease to be educational and become one of nursing or therapeutic care. At this point, the Council would not continue to fund the programme.

9.45 In order that a student's progress can be identified within a programme, it would be necessary to:

- assess the student's existing knowledge, skills and understanding (the 'baseline')
- assess the student's individual approach to learning (that is, find out how the student learns best)
- identify the student's learning goals (what student wants and needs to learn both long and short term; the desired learning outcomes)
- assess the learning environment that matches each of the elements of the learning environment, together with the percentage of resources and time allocated to each, including learning support
- record arrangements for regular assessment and reviews
- ensure arrangements for systematically recording the outcomes of assessment in an appropriate form that indicates whether progress, using the definitions we suggest, is taking place
- ensure arrangements for assessing and recording the student's standard of achievement at the end of their programme either through accreditation which is within the GNVQ/NVQ framework or which has received the 'quality kite mark' that we have suggested, or through the use of the national record of achievement
- describe how the learning programme fits with, and is affected by, any care, transition, rehabilitation or nursing plan or with services provided by other agencies
- ensure that the student is involved in the assessment, review and recording of their learning; provide advocacy support if this required.

9.46 Judgements about whether a student is able to progress are best made by the teachers and other professional staff who are most closely associated with him or her, and who are able to track the progress that has already been made.

9.47 There would need to be rigorous and systematic assessment and recording procedures in place designed to track even small steps of educational progress. In this way, it would be clear whether the main focus of the programme was educational, therapeutic, social, leisure or recreational, or care. The Council would fund those elements that were designated as educational or that were considered to be learner or learning support.

9.48 The committee tested this thinking about progress within a programme with the experts responsible for the legal analysis commissioned for us.[28] On the basis of their advice and the work we have undertaken on progression, we would like to the Council to accept the following as constituting evidence that a student's programme of learning fits within schedule 2(j):

Either:

i. progression to another course within schedule 2 is a stated aim of the student's learning programme: the student intends and has the ability to achieve progress onto another course and is able to demonstrate that ability by providing evidence of incremental or lateral progress or the maintenance of skills; or

ii. progression to another course within schedule 2 is a stated aim of the student's learning programme and the student is working toward accreditation which meets the quality criteria described in paragraph 9.49.

9.49 The most problematic of these for the Council is to record the maintenance of skills as progress and therefore as evidence that the student is able to move on to another programme at a higher level of study. It is not our intention that the Council fund provision which should be funded by health and social services. Evidence from the legal analysis indicated that, at present, it would be difficult for the Council legally to fund learning which is concerned primarily with the maintenance of skills because the capacity to progress — and hence to achieve progress — could not be easily demonstrated. However, we believe that this kind of learning sustains the capacity of a student with terminal or degenerative conditions for independence, relationships with others and a role in the community for as long as possible. The ability of students to retain their skills whilst their medical condition is deteriorating represents real progress. We do not wish to see this valuable learning excluded from funding by the Council. We ask therefore that the Council gives further attention to this important issue, perhaps on the basis of additional analysis and the production of guidelines for providers. These might be drawn up in discussion with providers of other services such as therapy, to establish the balance of individual programmes.

9.50 There is also a fundamental need to improve the quality of accreditation. We wish all students to have access to accreditation that allows them to record and measure their learning in ways which can be generally recognised. Carefully-designed and properly used accreditation brings important benefits to students. It can, for example, help to structure learning programmes and focus attention on the assessment and recording of learning. Its use can also bring together staff to share successful approaches to teaching and learning, and assessment arrangements.

9.51 In order to strengthen and improve good-quality accreditation, we want to see the development of quality criteria by NCVQ, SCAA and others. These criteria should be used as a 'kite mark' for accreditation which is outside the national vocational qualifications framework. We have made this proposal to Sir Ron Dearing and are pleased that his report reflects our views.

9.52 In order to stimulate awarding bodies to adopt such criteria and to encourage providers to use 'kite marked' accreditation, we recommend that only those accredited according to these criteria should be accepted for funding by the Council within schedule 2(j).

9.53 It is important that the right course should be available to those students who have the capacity to progress. Evidence indicated that students with profound and multiple difficulties, in particular, were able to continue in their learning but courses within the schedule did not offer suitable progression opportunities. We wish to see the list of courses within the schedule amended by order of the secretary of state to include certain specified courses which meet the quality criteria.

4 Transition from college

9.54 We wish to see colleges take greater responsibility for managing a student's transition from further education. This is an important part of the job of the 'named person' referred to in chapter 8. The careers service must be available to provide independent guidance and advice until the student is settled into the next stage of their career. Colleges should work with voluntary organisations, TECs and others to devise strategies to support students in the early stages of employment or training. This support enables students to make the best use of their achievements at college.

9.55 The Council's funding arrangements should be flexible enough to fund additional time at college for some students with learning difficulties and/or disabilities if the time is required to complete their studies.

RECOMMENDATIONS

Pre-foundation award

9.56 The Council should support the development of a pre-foundation award called Skills for Adult Life which is relevant to all students, made up of the following units:

- employability (preparation for working life)
- understanding roles in the family, including parenting skills and relationships
- understanding the local community, including travel, leisure pursuits and voluntary work
- understanding the society in which we live, including the laws and the individual benefits and allowances.

9.57 Skills for Adult Life should be:

- available as an award within the national qualifications framework at pre-foundation level
- incorporated with core skills into the GNVQ foundation level of courses
- designed to include opportunities for progression from pre-foundation to foundation level
- subject to quality criteria based on the assessment and recording arrangements set out in paragraph 9.45.

Enhanced national record of achievement

9.58 The Council should encourage the development and use of an enhanced national record of achievement (NRA). Specifically, the Council should:

- consider how it might be used to contribute to evidence of progress in schedule 2(j) courses
- request evidence of its use during inspection
- support the development of quality criteria which draw on current or commissioned work on the value-added factor in programmes for students with learning difficulties and/or disabilities.

Accessible and consistent assessment

9.59 The Council should encourage accessible and consistent assessment. Specifically, it should:

- encourage NCVQ, SCAA and others to review the assessment requirement for written tests at GNVQ foundation and level 1 and consider the development of alternative, rigorous and more flexible approaches to assessment
- consider whether its funding methodology could do more to encourage colleges to offer units of accreditation by ensuring that colleges which offer them are not disadvantaged financially
- ensure that awarding and examination bodies are better informed about the Council's funding arrangements for students with learning difficulties and/or disabilities
- encourage these bodies to find a common language to describe students with learning difficulties and/or disabilities and their assessment requirements
- encourage examining and awarding bodies to allow centres greater freedom to make individual arrangements for students.

Schedule 2(j)

9.60 The Council should review its interpretation of requirements for schedule 2(j) by taking a wider view of the meaning of progression. Specifically, the Council should:

- allow colleges a choice of two sets of criteria to demonstrate that a programme falls within the schedule; either:

i. progression to another course within schedule 2 is a stated aim of the student's learning programme: the student intends to progress to another course and is able to provide evidence of incremental or lateral progression or the maintenance of skills; or

ii. progression to another course within schedule 2 is a stated aim of the student's learning programme and the student is working towards accreditation which meets the quality criteria described below;

- seek to have the list of courses under schedule 2 amended to include specified courses which meet agreed quality criteria and which provide suitable progression opportunities for students with profound and multiple learning difficulties. This recommendation is aimed at clarifying the intention of the Act rather than seeking new legislation. It is not the committee's aim that the Council should fund courses which are presently funded by local authorities and which are primarily leisure or recreational in purpose. Specifically, the courses should be concerned with the further development of life skills rather than with leisure or with recreational activities
- review the funding for programmes which help students to maintain the skills they have by conducting further analysis and discussion with providers and professionals who are experts in this area of work
- review the effects of implementing these recommendations after a certain period of time.

References

1. David Towell *Enabling Community Integration: The Role of Public Authorities in Promoting an Ordinary Life for People with Learning Disabilities in the 1990s*, London, Kings Fund Centre, 1991

2. SCPR *Student Voices: The Views of Further Education Students with Learning Difficulties and/or Disabilities: Findings From a Series of Student Workshops Commissioned by the Learning Difficulties and/or Disabilities Committee,* London, Skill: National Bureau for Students with Disabilities, 1996

3. *Ibid.*

4. Responses to the call for evidence (unpublished) and seminar for parents' groups, 12 July 1995

5. *Ibid.*

6. SCPR *Student Voices: The Views of Further Education Students with Learning Difficulties and/or Disabilities: Findings From a Series of Student Workshops Commissioned by the Learning Difficulties and/or Disabilities Committee,* London, Skill: National Bureau for Students with Disabilities, 1996

7. Evidence from the FEFC inspectorate, (unpublished)

8. *Ibid.*

9. Evidence from OFSTED, (unpublished)

10. Responses to the call for evidence, (unpublished)

11. SCPR *Student Voices: The Views of Further Education Students with Learning Difficulties and/or Disabilities: Findings From a Series of Student Workshops Commissioned by the Learning Difficulties and/or Disabilities Committee,* London, Skill: National Bureau for Students with Disabilities, 1996

12. Evidence presented to the assessment working group on 16 June 1995 by the examining groups inter-group advisory committee

13. *Ibid.*

14. Responses to the call for evidence, (unpublished)

15. Evidence from the visit to Scotland, presented to the committee on 19 December 1995 (see also annex C)

16. Evidence from NIACE presented to committee on 16 November 1995, based on NIACE/Rowntree survey

17. Responses to the call for evidence, (unpublished)

18. Evidence from the FEFC inspectorate, (unpublished)

19. Evidence from OFSTED, (unpublished)

20. Finding of the exercise to test the committee's approach to learning with colleges

21. Responses to the call for evidence (unpublished)

22. Matthew Griffiths *Enabled to Work: Support into Employment for Young People with Disabilities*, London, FEU, 1991; *Disabled Youth: From School to Work,* Paris, OECD/CERI, 1991; *Education of the Handicapped Adolescent: Transition from School to Working Life*, Paris, OECD-CERI, 1983; *Supported Employment for People with Learning Difficulties: The Real Jobs Initiative 1990-92: An Evaluation*, Manchester, National Development Team, 1992

23. Committee visit to the USA April 1996 (see also annex C)

24. Evidence from the FEFC inspectorate, (unpublished)

25. Sir Ron Dearing, *Review of Qualifications for 16 to 19 Year Olds,* Middlesex, SCAA, 1996 paras 12.44 to 12.51

26. Evidence presented to assessment working group on 16 June 1995

27. Evidence from the visit to Scotland, (see also annex C)

28. Beachcroft Stanleys (1996) *Duties and Powers: The Law Governing the Provision of Further Education to Students with Learning Difficulties and/or Disabilities: A Report to the Learning Difficulties and/or Disabilities Committee*, London, HMSO, 1996

PART THREE

Implementation

Chapter 10: Quality Assurance

In this chapter, the committee examines how the quality of further education can be assured for students with learning difficulties and/or disabilities and considers the arrangements that are required on the part of colleges and the Council.

THE ISSUES

1. developing the Council's arrangements for quality assurance to support the committee's principles
2. enhancing the quality assurance arrangements in the colleges to ensure inclusive learning
3. the factors that contribute to effective quality assurance
4. the requirements for quality assurance for provision funded at specialist residential colleges
5. the need for high standards to be set.

QUALITY ASSURANCE AND INCLUSIVE LEARNING

10.1 The committee understands quality assurance to refer to the checks and audits used to ensure that quality arrangements are followed. We have used the word 'standards' to refer to the levels and targets of good practice to which a service or agency agrees to conform. We have used performance indicators to mean the quantitative or qualitative measures used to demonstrate that a target set, for example, for students' achievements, has been reached. We are interested in quality assurance because changes will need to be made to current quality assurance arrangements to accommodate the main principles contained in this report. Standards may need to be revised.

10 THE COMMITTEE'S PRINCIPLES

10.2 We have set out our principles for inclusive learning and for inclusive participation in earlier chapters. These principles informed our thinking about the fitness for purpose of quality assurance arrangements. The committee's principles in this chapter are that:

- quality assurance arrangements must be fit for the purpose of monitoring learning, participation and achievement
- good-quality assurance arrangements will apply to provision made for all students
- effective quality assurance arrangements use clearly-defined standards and are consistently implemented
- the Council's quality assessment arrangements should apply equally whether operated in independent or sector colleges.

10.3 Evidence which might indicate that colleges have adopted our principles for assessing achivement includes:

EVIDENCE

- comprehensive course review and evaluation procedures carried out as part of a college-wide formal quality assurance system
- questionnaires and discussion groups for students to enable all students to comment on the quality of their programmes, using Braille and audio-tape, and enabling technology (that is, technical equipment which enables students with physical and/or sensory difficulties to learn)
- monitoring of performance indicators such as student enrolments, attendance, achievements, destinations and the colleges' responsiveness to a wide variety of individual requirements, (for example, facilities); set targets for under-represented groups developed in needs analysis, such as favourable comparison of profiles of achievement for students with learning difficulties with their peers
- production of reports analysing statistics on performance indicators for inclusive learning and participation shared with the academic board and governors
- published information on the achievements and destinations of students
- staff awareness of how to develop learning environments which support all students' learning
- opportunities for advanced training of staff in understanding students' cognitive development (including studies in perception, reasoning and intuition) and in developing inclusive learning
- analysis of data on the benefits of learning support on students' achievements
- evidence of progress towards implementing the college action plan to create learning which is inclusive and which benefits all learners.

10.4 The inspectorate gave us the following examples of good and bad practice in quality assurance:

EXAMPLES

College A

The college has developed a formal quality assurance system, managed by the vice-principal. All programmes across the college are subject to the same review and evaluation procedures. A questionnaire is used to enable students to comment on the quality of their programmes. The questionnaire has been produced in different forms such as in Braille and on audio-tape to enable all students to participate in the process. Senior managers have made it clear that they expect the same level of rigour to apply to the management of all courses across the college. It is the responsibility of programme leaders to monitor performance indicators such as students' enrolments, attendance, achievements and destinations. A formal report analysing these statistics and their implications for future planning has to be submitted to senior managers and the academic board. Information about the achievements and destinations of students with learning difficulties and/or disabilities is carefully recorded and published alongside that relating to other students. All staff in the college have been required to attend training sessions to raise their awareness of inclusive learning and of learning support systems and procedures. Staff who work with students who have learning difficulties are required to undertake advanced training to help them to understand cognitive development and the effect that a learning difficulty can have on this. Regular classroom observations contribute to this. Time has been allocated to inclusive learning managers to enable them to work together with vocational and academic staff who teach students with learning difficulties and/or disabilities within their classes. This evidence contributes to their appraisal. A recent project aimed at developing inclusive learning environments focused on the provision of learning support through team-teaching. It included the classroom observations of teachers. The evaluation of the project indicated that there were benefits to be gained by offering support in this way, particularly for those students who were previously reluctant to attend additional sessions in the learning support workshop.

College B

Quality assurance systems and procedures are at an early stage of development in the college. A policy document has not yet been implemented. Some departments have established their own system, but there are no formal review procedures for the programmes which have been designed specifically for students with learning difficulties and/or disabilities. Some course teams meet regularly but without the involvement of part-time teachers. Enrolment targets are not set and there is no requirement to record information about students' achievements or destinations. There is little opportunity for students, their parents, carers, advocates or representatives from other agencies such as social services to comment on the quality of the college's provision. Training opportunities for staff who work with students who have learning difficulties and/or disabilities are limited to voluntary awareness raising sessions. Teachers rarely observe each other teach and there are few opportunities for staff to work together in classrooms.

1 Developing the Council's arrangements for quality assurance to support the committee's principles

10.5 The *Further and Higher Education Act 1992* requires that the Council shall:

> *...secure that provision is made for assessing the quality of education provided in institutions within the further education sector*[1]

The Council has a legal responsibility to assess the quality of the provision which it funds. However, it is the colleges' responsibility to provide high-quality provision for all students.

10.6 In the secretary of state's second letter of guidance of March 1993, additional guidance was given to the Council in respect of quality assessment. For students with learning difficulties and/or disabilities the Council was asked to:

> *...cover the provision made for students with learning difficulties and/or disabilities in its reports on individual colleges and provide survey reports on provision for such students from time to time.*

10.7 We considered the Council's current arrangements for assuring the quality of provision in colleges, though we are aware that a proposed new framework is being considered by the sector. In the Council's framework for inspection, *Assessing Achievement,*[2] a distinctive approach to quality and its assessment in further education has been developed which recognises that provision:

- must fit its purpose by being capable of delivering the intended learning outcomes
- should be of a high standard and excellent
- should satisfy and involve customers by involving them in planning, review and evaluation
- lead to improved performance on the part of students
- should be of sufficient quality to assure the taxpayer that the money devoted to this sector of education is being well spent.[3]

10.8 The Council has set up an inspectorate to inspect the quality of provision which it funds. Through the work of its inspectorate, and by publishing inspectorate reports on individual colleges in the further education sector, the Council demonstrates that there is quality assurance and control over the way it spends public funds. To some extent, the publication of inspection reports helps students to find out about the quality of the provision in colleges they may attend. We believe that the Council's inspection framework and its efforts to discharge its legal duties constitute a major impetus for the sector to improve the quality of further education provision.

10.9 The work of the inspectorate plays a central role in determining what constitutes quality for the whole sector. Inspection evidence is powerful because it is comprehensive and gathered against inspection criteria for quality and standards. Within a national context, the Council is able to act as a catalyst for the improvement of the quality of provision against these criteria. This means that students can expect the same quality of provision regardless of where they live or what they study. The Council uses low inspection grades to encourage colleges to improve their provision by not allowing them to increase provision in a curriculum area graded 4 or 5 (that is, where the weaknesses outweigh the strengths).

10.10 The Council also sets out to assure the quality of the provision it funds through the conditions it attaches to its funding arrangements. These include the use of six performance indicators related to funding targets; student enrolment trends; programme effectiveness; learning goals and qualifications; contribution to national targets; value for money and the scrutiny of the college charter and requirement for colleges to produce and share strategic plans. These matters are dealt with elsewhere in this report.

10.11 The committee considers that the inspection framework used for assuring the quality of provision funded at sector colleges is sufficiently flexible to be used for inspecting provision funded by the Council at specialist colleges outside the sector. At these specialist colleges, the Council inspects only the quality of the provision it funds, not the college as a whole. It does so primarily to ascertain that the quality of provision offered to students in these establishments is the same as that in sector colleges. Inspection also identifies whether or not the Council's contract is being complied with.

10.12 Unlike the inspection reports on sector colleges, reports on provision funded by the Council at independent specialist colleges are not published. Both specialist colleges and sector colleges are subject to a number of different quality assurance requirements, for example, from the social services inspectorate, from commissioned independent inspections or from moderators and awarding bodies. Training and Enterprise Councils (TECs) require evidence that standards are achieved and where there are students of school age or adults in non-schedule 2 provision, OFSTED may also require evidence of certain standards. The committee believes that more consistent improvements in the quality of provision for these students could be achieved through more collaborative inspection. Though we were told by the inspectorate that there has been some collaboration, this has been insufficient, as yet, to secure systematic joint working with other inspectorates.

2 Enhancing the quality assurance arrangements in the colleges to ensure inclusive learning

10.13 The responsibility to develop quality assurance arrangements rests with the colleges. Analysing and acting on the outcomes of quality assessment is a major way of improving the quality of students' experience and raising their achievements. The inspectorate told us that a number of the grades for quality assurance were low as well as the grades for the provision for students with learning difficulties and/or disabilities. We were told also that few colleges have quality assurance arrangements that are well developed for this provision. Some colleges have failed to agree a definition of 'high quality' for work with students with learning difficulties and/or disabilities. Many colleges, committed to betterment, are unclear about what they need to do to improve quality or to demonstrate that they have achieved the requisite standards. We were concerned particularly at evidence that some teachers and managers have low expectations of students with learning difficulties.

10.14 We wanted to know what factors contribute to effective quality assurance arrangements. We were mindful of the evidence from the inspectorate which showed that inspection grades for provision for students with learning difficulties were generally lower than those for other programme areas, and that therefore the quality of this provision needed to be improved.

10.15 Several colleges told us that while they had policies for quality assurance the procedures for their implementation were not well developed.[4] The inspectorate also told us that quality assurance arrangements are not comprehensive nor applied consistently to all provision for students. Some of the weaknesses drawn to our attention included:

- insufficient monitoring of the quality of provision specifically designed for students with learning difficulties
- the absence of course reviews
- lack of a consistent system for responding to issues raised through course reviews.[5]

10.16 We have found that it can be hard for teachers of students with learning difficulties and/or disabilities to understand why inspection grades are poor when they are conscientious, have good relationships with their students, are caring and put a great deal of effort into their work. The reasons are complex. Poor teaching in other areas often results from inexperienced or inadequate teachers. This is not necessarily the case in provision for students with learning difficulties and/or disabilities. There are complex reasons why inspection grades for this area of work are poor. Some teachers are uncertain what to teach and they are unsure of the standards of work they should expect from their students. Furthermore, they may be over-protective towards their students and wish to prevent them from failing. Cumulatively, these factors can have an adverse effect on the quality of the teaching and the students' learning and can lead to the awarding of low inspection grades.

10.17 Often standards for this work are not set by the college in the same way as they are for students on other courses. This is unlike some other areas where the industry, lead or awarding body sets national standards. In many instances, the quality assurance arrangements do not have sufficient impact on teaching and learning for students with learning difficulties and/or difficulties. Furthermore, quality assessment arrangements are inadequate to identify the range of factors which affect poor quality. For example, evidence from observation of work in the classroom is seldom used. Relying on evidence of what students and teachers say about the quality and effectiveness of teaching is not sufficient.

3 The factors that contribute to effective quality assurance

10.18 We concluded that there are a number of factors which contribute to effective quality assurance. Colleges will need to implement a number of changes to their quality assurance systems if our principles are adopted. These are:

- the development of a policy on quality assurance to include the main principles of this report
- to review quality assurance arrangements to ensure that they cover learning for all students
- a review of standards set and the consistency of their application
- clarification about the evidence which is required to substantiate that standards have been met.

10.19 From the evidence we received and from our college visits, we concluded that colleges recognise that they need support and assistance with quality assurance of provision for students with learning difficulties and/or learning disabilities. We have set out what we would like to see developed as a result of the committee's work. We have used inspection evidence to indicate the good and bad practice which already exists in colleges and we have offered some guidelines on how colleges might assess the quality of their current provision. We anticipate that colleges will want to develop their own self-assessment and quality assurance arrangements so that they embrace the principles proposed in this report.

10.20 Throughout our work we have taken the interests of the students very seriously. We asked students in the workshops for their views on quality assurance. Opportunities for students to say what they want from colleges are a fundamental element of good quality assurance arrangements. Our findings indicate that generally students are given insufficient opportunity to comment on the quality of their programmes. They need to understand the procedures for quality assurance and acquire the skills to put their views forward. Some of the factors preventing their contribution are: student questionnaires which use language too complex for them to understand; insufficient teaching to assist students to understand relative concepts such as 'how good' and 'what changes would you like to see'; fear that being critical will result in the withdrawal of support and help; inadequate variety of ways of making their views known; and an over-reliance on ticking boxes on questionnaires.

10.21 In the examples we found of best practice, colleges valued and gave credence to students' views which were expressed in students' forums. Students were enabled to develop skills of self-representation and self-expression (self-advocacy) by following an appropriate syllabus of the English Speaking Board or through their tutorial programme or their membership of a local self-advocacy group.

10.22 We were encouraged by evidence from social services inspectors of the way the views of people with learning difficulties and disabilities are valued. When planning the inspection of a day-centre, the social services inspectors had sought the views of members of a self-advocacy group at the centre, on what they should inspect and what standards they should expect to find.[6]

4 The requirements for quality assurance for provision funded at specialist residential colleges

10.23 The main issues facing the specialist residential colleges are the same as those facing sector colleges. For example, we were disappointed to see how few have information about complaints in formats which are accessible to students. Few, too, appear to enable ready access to independent outsiders for students with concerns.

10.24 The residential nature of the provision requires a more extensive range of quality assurance arrangements. Sometimes extensive and expensive quality assurance systems are not appropriate for teaching and learning. At other times, systems are used effectively for specific practical administrative activities. For example, BS5750 and ISO9000 were used in a residential college to cover the disposal of waste from medical procedures and the dispensing of drugs to students. Given the diversity of the activities in inclusive learning environments, it is likely that a careful combination of arrangements, tailored to monitor inclusive learning and participation, will be required.

10.25 The legacy of many of the residential colleges is a focus on care rather education. Some of the specialist residential colleges, especially the smaller ones, we found to be struggling to come to terms with the rigours of the Council's inspection regime, which focuses on educational objectives and achievements against a contract specifying each student's programme and expected outcomes. For example, staff sometimes step in too early to help a student; they can be afraid to allow students to risk failure; they can set tasks which are insufficiently demanding; and they sometimes record activities and not learning.

5 The need for high standards to be set

10.26 Colleges anticipate that if they adopt the principles of the report then students' achievements will improve.[7] Achievements will usually be assessed against a set of defined standards. We found considerable evidence that in many colleges, the standards set for students with learning difficulties and/or disabilities are too low and that teachers' low expectations of these students lead to teaching and learning of poorer quality.[8] Sometimes teachers considered it inappropriate or unkind to challenge or make rigorous demands of students who have disabilities or learning difficulties. Effective quality assurance arrangements will need to set standards which reflect higher expectations of students' achievements.

10 SUMMARY OF MAIN FINDINGS

10.27 When we examined the evidence on quality assurance in the light of our principles and indicative evidence, we found the following main weaknesses:

- the absence of comprehensive quality assurance arrangements suitable for monitoring learning
- the lack of high standards for provision designed specifically for students with learning difficulties
- a focus on care rather than education in some of the residential specialist colleges.

ADDRESSING WEAKNESSES AND BUILDING ON STRENGTHS

Developing the Council's arrangements for quality assurance to support the committee's principles

10.28 We compared the current and the proposed revised inspection framework against our principles of inclusive learning. We concluded that the inspectorate's approach to assessing the quality of provision has within it many of the elements of the committee's thinking. It recognises that quality in further education is dependent on and demonstrated by:

- responsiveness to the requirements of individuals and groups in the community
- choice and diversity in the range and type of provision offered to students
- order and structure whereby governors and senior managers have responsibility to provide education which is strategically planned and which is efficient and effective and promotes students' achievements
- the maximum engagement of students in the processes of learning
- high achievements of students
- high standards set and achieved
- the pursuit and achievement of scholarship and competence.

10.29 We concluded that *Assessing Achievement*,[9] the inspectorate's main reference document, has proved to be sufficiently flexible to cover provision made by both sector and independent specialist colleges. Inspection focuses on an establishment's particular aims, objectives, targets and criteria for success. Not least, the framework appears to us to be sufficiently flexible to cover provision for a wide range of students with learning difficulties and/or disabilities.

10.30 The Council's consultative circular[10] proposes a review of the inspection framework to see how it can better reflect the growth and maturity of the sector. We consider it essential that the Council considers our recommendations for quality assurance as part of this review. The Council's new proposals reflect a number of our concerns; namely the need for:

- more rigorous evaluation of teaching and learning
- compatibility between inspection methods and the quality assurance systems of other agencies
- closer scrutiny of the college's mission to ascertain whether there is a commitment for the college to be responsive to the needs of all its students
- greater account to be taken of students' views
- joint planning between the college and external groups to ensure that the needs of students with learning difficulties and/or disabilities are fully met.

10.31 Our findings support the Council's proposed intention for colleges to undertake a greater degree of self-assessment. Parts of this report are intended to help colleges set standards and be more self-critical. Throughout, we have stressed that students' views should contribute to effective quality assessment. Some students will need to be taught new skills in speaking and representing themselves (self-advocacy) if their views are to be properly articulated and heard.

10.32 Through the process of self-assessment and improvement, some colleges will develop consistent and high standards and be ready at the end of the next quadrennial cycle to apply to the quality assessment committee for accreditation as self-assessing institutions. Some colleges may fail to obtain this accreditation because of their low grades for their work with students with learning difficulties and/or disabilities.

10.33 In our view, the proposed inspection framework needs significant but minor adjustments to reflect better the principles advocated throughout this report. These adjustments are:

- a separate inspection grade awarded which judges the extent to which the college provides learning which is inclusive. This grade should draw on evidence from across the college. To assist colleges to achieve this, the committee recommends that the Council establishes a development fund for colleges to apply for funds to support implementation of their action plan to achieve inclusive learning. We envisage that funds should be drawn from the residue of those allocated to fund placements at independent specialist colleges. Since more of these students are receiving their education in sector colleges, it would be fair to divert resources to sector colleges for this purpose
- a separate inspection grade for the quality of provision for students with learning difficulties and/or disabilities (where the provision constitutes 5% of the college's provision). We recognise that inspectors will draw evidence for this grade from their inspection of curriculum areas and subjects across the college. We envisage that in time a separate grade will be redundant. Until that time, we recommend a separate grade be required as a safeguard and for monitoring purposes.

10.34 The Council may want to review the guidance on its published performance indicators to include monitoring of inclusive learning and levels of participation. The Council has identified areas for further work, such as the calculation of the value-added factor in a student's learning experience and the responsiveness of colleges to the needs of employers and the demands of the labour market. The extent to which colleges have responded to the individuals and groups with learning difficulties and/or disabilities identified in the mapping exercise could be the subject of further funding for the Council. We wish to see a wider definition of responsiveness.

10.35 The committee is aware of the government's desire, set out in *Competitiveness: Forging Ahead*,[11] that there should be a reduction in the number of different inspection regimes and improvement in the links between those responsible for quality assessment. We wish to see this achieved through joint inspection particularly with social services, health authorities and with OFSTED. Our wish is consonant with our views expressed in chapter 8.

2 Enhancing the quality assurance arrangements in the colleges to ensure inclusive learning

10.36 We examined what type of quality assurance arrangements would be needed if our principles were to be adopted. We examined the fitness for purpose of colleges' quality assurance arrangements and their capacity to monitor inclusive learning and participation. The committee believes that if colleges use the quality assurance arrangements, they will be able to check whether inclusive learning has improved students' achievements.

10.37 Our view is that individuals learn in different ways and that they come to learn with different experiences. Thus, it is unrealistic to expect that there is a single way of ensuring that all students have learning experiences of high quality. Any quality assurance process must be sufficiently and finely tuned to ascertain whether provision for students with learning difficulties and/or disabilities is subject to the same criteria for quality as that for all other students in a college.

10.38 Improvements in the quality of provision can only be achieved by developing:

- learning environments which allow all students to participate fully and which are subject to continual improvement
- a co-ordinated college approach to systematic improvement
- training all staff on issues relating to quality assurance and on developing learning environments which benefit all students
- arrangements and procedures for quality assurance, which include the establishment of criteria and targets for developing learning environments within which all students can benefit
- a college-wide system which uses evidence from the assessment of quality to systematically improve learning which is inclusive.

3 The factors that contribute to effective quality assurance

10.39 We recognise that the Council and colleges will require a redefinition of the criteria for high-quality provision if they adopt and act upon the principles of this report. They will need to consider, and fully understand, the criteria for awarding inspection grades. For example, a grade one ('provision which has many strengths and very few weaknesses') would only be awarded for a programme area which was able to offer high-quality provision for a wide range of students, including those with learning difficulties and/or disabilities. Some colleges may have to redefine their own criteria for standards and quality in the light of the need to ensure that all programme areas are capable of offering high-quality teaching and learning to all students, whatever the abilities, aptitudes and circumstances of those students may be.

10.40 We wish to see the following taken into account by colleges when developing quality assurance arrangements:

- standards which are agreed and understood across the college
- a quality assessment policy with a detailed plan for implementation of inclusive learning
- an action plan to provide inclusive learning with funds from the Council to support its implementation
- performance indicators and targets at course, faculty and college level to monitor the effectiveness of learning
- staff development to help teachers to identify and support a whole-college approach to inclusive learning
- the dissemination of good practice across the college with opportunities for staff to identify and discuss teaching and learning methods which are inclusive and which result in high levels of achievement
- regular meetings with managers responsible for inclusive learning to disseminate information to the faculties about successful learning which is inclusive
- an induction policy for new staff to secure understanding of inclusive learning
- regular staff training to increase competence in developing learning which benefits all learners
- the provision of an externally accredited co-ordinated programme of

training to support the development of learning which is inclusive

- staff appraisal which is part of the college's plan to improve the quality of students' learning and achievements
- evaluation of the cost of developing learning environments which are designed so that all learners can benefit
- quality assurance covers provision for all students, including those with learning difficulties and/or disabilities who are potentially vulnerable to abuse and who are learning in sector or specialist residential colleges.

4 The requirements for quality assurance for provision funded at specialist colleges

10.41 Quality assurance arrangements should apply whether the student is in a sector college or placed in an independent establishment. Arrangements will need to be fit for the purpose of monitoring learning and achievement for learners with a wider and more complex range of learning difficulties and disabilities studying in a residential setting.

10.42 All establishments where the Council places a student have a contract accepting inspection. The standards of procedures for inspection and reporting by the Council are equally rigorous in both sector and specialist colleges. Reports on specialist colleges are not published but may be issued by the establishment inspected. There is some evidence that some establishments are reluctant to issue their reports when their grades are poor. This means that students, careers services, schools, LEAs and those responsible for the placement of students are not able to make fully-informed decisions about the available provision. We strongly advocate that the inspection reports for specialist colleges should be published. Students who wish to attend these colleges are entitled to be fully informed about the quality of their provision which is funded by the Council.

10.43 The committee is aware of the public concern to safeguard vulnerable students from abuse. Publishing inspection reports does not in itself protect students, although it does allow the evidence gathered on inspection to be available in the public domain. We are aware that the government has set up an enquiry under Sir William Utting to establish whether the measures implemented since the *Children Act 1989* have been properly enforced.[12] The committee thinks that the government should improve arrangements to protect potentially vulnerable students in residential settings. As the first stage towards this, the Utting review could consider an extension to their brief which would allow them to examine the protection afforded to students with learning difficulties and/or disabilities attending either sector or residential specialist colleges. We believe that colleges would welcome this proposal. However, a more extensive enquiry is required in the longer term.

10.44 We think that the Council should establish public criteria by which it decides at which specialist colleges it is prepared to fund students. The committee agreed that the Council should only contract with specialist residential colleges which are registered under the *Registered Homes Act 1994*.[13] The committee also agreed that the Council should only contract with specialist colleges which have an effective students' complaints procedure. These might be two of the criteria for future funding.

5 The need for high standards to be set

10.45 The Council monitors standards in sector colleges by gathering information on performance indicators. The Council may want to review the guidance on its published performance indicators to include monitoring on inclusive learning and participation.

10.46 The key recommendation is that the Council should encourage sector colleges to promote learning which is more inclusive. Specifically, the Council should:

- establish a development fund to support colleges to deliver their action plan on inclusive learning (see chapter 12 on the quality initiative)
- inspect colleges on the extent to which they provide learning which is inclusive and which benefits all students and publish a specific grade for this
- give a specific inspection grade for provision for students with learning difficulties and/or disabilities where this constitutes 5% or more of the college's total provision
- review its performance indicators to include inclusive learning and participation
- ensure that the committee's recommendations in this chapter are reflected in inspection arrangements for further education
- encourage colleges to ensure that students receive support to participate in both formal and informal quality assurance activities, using the approach developed in the workshop series.

10.47 The Council should help specialist colleges to promote learning which is more inclusive and should adopt more demanding quality assurance arrangements. Specifically, the Council should:

- publish the inspection reports about provision it funds in specialist colleges
- encourage colleges to set standards for achieving high-quality learning for students with learning difficulties and/or disabilities.

10.48 The Council should ensure that students with learning difficulties and/or disabilities in residential settings are properly protected. Specifically, the Council should:

- suggest to the government that it extends the Utting review of the *Children Act 1989* to include potentially vulnerable students with learning difficulties and/or disabilities in further education
- take steps to secure the protection of vulnerable students in further education provision, for example by requiring that staff be subject to police vetting
- contract only with specialist colleges registered under the procedures of the *Registered Homes Act 1994*; and which have an effective students' complaints procedure.

10.49 The Council should ensure through its inspection process that all colleges make good-quality provision for students with learning difficulties and/or disabilities. Specifically, the Council should:

- require an annual report on the colleges' self-assessment of their development of learning environments for all students
- secure systematic joint working with other inspectorates responsible for assuring the quality of provision for students with learning difficulties and/or disabilities in further education
- provide training for inspectors on inclusive learning and participation and on how best to deliver joint inspection with other agencies responsible for the quality of provision for students with learning difficulties and/or disabilities
- encourage colleges to develop quality assurance arrangements which are fit for the purpose of inclusive learning
- ensure that the committee's recommendations in this chapter are reflected in inspection arrangements for further education.

References

1. *Further and Higher Education Act 1992*, London, HMSO, chap. 13, Section 9(a)

2. FEFC Circular 93/28, *Assessing Achievement,* Coventry, FEFC, September 1993

3. *Ibid.*

4. Evidence from the FEFC inspectorate, (unpublished)

5. Evidence from the FEFC inspectorate presented to the committee on 28 September 1995

6. Evidence from the FEFC inspectorate, (unpublished)

7. Finding of the exercise to test the committee's approach to learning with colleges

8. Evidence from the FEFC inspectorate, (unpublished)

9. FEFC Circular 93/28, *Assessing Achievement,* Coventry, FEFC, September 1993

10. FEFC Circular 96/12, *Review of the Further Education Funding Council's Inspection Framework,* Coventry, FEFC, June 1996

11. *Competitiveness: Forging Ahead,* London, HMSO, May 1995

12. Department of Health press releases: 96/198 (13 June 1996) and 96/200 (17 June 1996)

13. *Registered Homes Act 1994,* London, HMSO and *Registered Homes (Amendment) 1991 Act,* London, HMSO

Chapter 11: Funding

In this chapter, the committee considers how the Council should obtain, allocate and account for funds to colleges for students with learning difficulties and/or disabilities, so that learning can be inclusive.

THE ISSUES

1. obtaining enough funds to ensure that further education can match the number and individual requirements of those who might participate
2. the best way of allocating the funds available to the Council
3. accounting for the funds allocated by the Council for students with learning difficulties and/or disabilities
4. the best way of funding students at specialist colleges.

FUNDING AND INCLUSIVE LEARNING

11.1 The way funds are obtained, allocated and accounted for by the Council directly affects the volume and kind of further education provision available. We therefore paid particular attention to funding issues during our work. The Council must allocate funds to colleges in a way which ensures that the facilities offered by colleges are sufficient and adequate, in accordance with the requirements of the *Further and Higher Education Act 1992*. The Council is also required to avoid disproportionate expenditure. Through its funding methodology, the Council has a powerful instrument for influencing colleges, and thus the extent to which learning is inclusive.

11.2 There is a direct relationship between the way funds are allocated to colleges and the way they organise and deliver their provision. We found two powerful examples of this during our work, the first in the contrast in further education before and after incorporation, and the second from the present-day United States of America:

- whilst English colleges received the bulk of their funding from local education authorities (LEAs), prior to the incorporation of colleges, most authorities only allocated extra funds for students with learning difficulties and/or disabilities for those students enrolled on discrete courses. Few had allocation mechanisms which could reflect easily the extra costs of supporting students across the range of the college's programmes. As a result, provision for these students tended to be on discrete courses. One college told the researchers in the mapping project:

The college has been able to offer appropriate support at a level which would have been impossible prior to incorporation. Banding may have its limitation[s], but it is immensely better than anything we had before with the LEAs. We have been able to access student mainstream provision as part of a student entitlement and it is accepted that this is the right way to proceed by the majority of college staff.[1]

- in the USA, we were told that the federal government is currently proposing to change its funding system for schools away from an allocation based on the number of disabled pupils to stop the labelling of pupils and encourage earlier intervention in the lives of children with disabilities.[2]

11.3 We also believe that the way funds are allocated has a significance beyond a simple transfer of funds from one public body to another. The scale of the funds involved — over £3 billion a year — is enough to ensure public interest in the policy choices made by the Council. We saw those choices as a crucial way of influencing the scope and nature of provision, which has immediate impact on students and those who work with them.

11.4 The Council must first be allocated an appropriate level of resources. The funds it allocates to colleges are first allocated to the Council in the annual public expenditure settlement (PES), voted by parliament. The Council is in competition with others for public expenditure to be allocated. The Council must provide robust evidence to justify its case.

THE COMMITTEE'S PRINCIPLES

11.5 The NFER report commissioned for the committee observed, 'to be considered effective, the funding system should work for young people with learning difficulties and/or disabilities, for education providers and for the wider community.[3] Our analysis and recommendations have been guided by four principles which we consider will promote this community of interest and which we believe should inform the Council when it reviews its methodology, as we understand it will do during 1997. The committee's principles are that, to have regard for these students' requirements and to avoid disproportionate expenditure, the way these public funds are obtained, allocated and accounted for should aim to:

- maximise the extent to which learning is inclusive
- maximise the rate of change by which the sector is able to offer inclusive learning, consistent with realistic but demanding expectations on colleges
- operate for those with learning difficulties and/or disabilities in the same way as for other students
- retain both the college's responsibility to plan its provision and allocate funds and an allocation methodology from the Council which is based on students' individual requirements.

11.6 To help us to apply these principles, we took evidence to ensure that we understood the Council's current policies as well as their impact on students and colleges. We also considered alternatives to these policies, derived from prevailing higher education and social care policy, as well as from some international evidence, to see if these alternatives would be more effective.

1 Obtaining enough funds to ensure that further education can match the number and individual requirements of those who might participate

11.7 The Council offers its advice to the secretary of state on an annual basis, detailing the funds it considers necessary to discharge its duties, within the framework of the public expenditure settlement. The secretary of state requires this submission to be confidential. So far, the Council has been allocated funds which are intended to enable colleges to deliver ambitious rates of growth in student numbers, largely through substantial and demanding efficiency savings.

11.8 The funds allocated by the Council are not the only funds available to support students with learning difficulties and/or disabilities. Many receive social security benefits by virtue of their disability or income. Some learners are on TEC-funded programmes. Some receive discretionary awards or transport provided by their home local education authority or social services department.

11.9 We have three main concerns about the funds which the Council has been able to obtain, in the light of the rest of this report. These are:

- the funds currently available for the entry phase of the learning programme are not likely to enable colleges to assess each student's learning requirements properly in the way which we believe is needed. We have discussed this in chapter 5. We do not think that reallocating units to this phase, which the Council could decide to do, will be enough
- the now overwhelming evidence of the capital famine in the sector, which affects equipment and buildings. This is preventing some colleges making their learning as inclusive as they would wish. Colleges responding to the mapping project told the researchers:

The college is multi-sited. There are three main areas with lifts. There are still two areas where physical access is a problem. Future building programmes will address the problems.

The FEFC's inability to fund capital works for wheelchair-bound students has been the major drawback in our 'open access' policy.

The majority of the college's building stock is poorly equipped for disabled access. Although the college is striving to address the issue, the costs involved with some buildings is prohibitive.[4]

These findings were echoed by the students who took part in the workshops. They commented:

All the library shelves are really close together. For me in the wheelchair, you can just get through them and I have knocked them down before: all the books, it was quite embarrassing really.

I think, as a matter of fact, colleges who accept students with disabilities should have libraries to suit them.

All our equipment was bought by charities — it is hard to believe but it is true. That is why it is all old and decrepit.

It is difficult to get technology to help. There is no money for equipment, just funding for learning support workers.[5]

The Hunter survey conducted by the Council identified significant urgent work needed to address immediate health and safety concerns. We know that capital matters have featured prominently in the Council's representations about the resources needed by the sector. The chief inspector noted in his annual report for 1994-95 that 'The sector still has a substantial amount of accommodation which is of poor quality.'[6]

A number of colleges told us that the only factor inhibiting the provision they could offer was the state of their accommodation or their equipment[7]

- colleges will need extra funds to be able to enrol the groups of people whom we have identified as under-represented in further education in chapter 4. The policy of growth will of itself encourage and enable colleges to enrol more students, supported by the funding methodology. However, we found concern that a changing student profile will be expensive. In the climate of efficiency savings and concerns about staff pay awards, it should not be assumed all colleges can manage within their existing resources.

2 The best way of allocating the funds available to the Council

11.10 The Council and the sector have developed a new methodology for allocating recurrent funding to sector colleges, external institutions and higher education institutions. It has a number of key components. These are:

i. stability year on year is offered through core funding, by which the college receives 90% of its previous year's allocation in return for 90% of that activity, leaving the college to apply to cover any additional activity for which it seeks funds;

ii. allocations are made to colleges in response to applications from them. The college's application is intended to be consistent with its strategic plan. Whilst colleges are encouraged to include a needs analysis within that plan, the Council does not currently seek to influence colleges' missions or their strategic direction;

iii. allocations are made to a college in return for a given volume of unit of activity, expressed in conditions of funding. This is effectively a contract between the Council and the college;

iv. funds are allocated for activity which is measured in units. The Council specifies the rate or sum of money it is prepared to allocate for each additional unit above the core. It also determines the relativities between the numbers of units for different sorts of activities in the tariff, on the advice of the tariff advisory committee;

v. the tariff is currently intended to be neutral between different activities, that is, the relative number of units assigned to different activities is intended to reflect what is known about their relative costs;

vi. the tariff includes units for additional support, where a student needs extra help to enable them to complete their further education. Additional support is currently defined as:

Any activity which provides direct support for learning to individual students, which is over and above that which is normally provided in a standard learning programme which leads to their primary learning goal. The additional support is required to help students gain access to, progress towards and successfully achieve their learning goals. The need for additional support may arise from a learning difficulty or disability or from literacy, numeracy or language support requirements.[8]

11.11 From 1996-97, funding for equipment is allocated within the rate set for each unit of activity. For adaptations to buildings or for new buildings, the emphasis is on colleges obtaining funds under the private finance initiative (PFI), and on colleges having in place an accommodation strategy.

11.12 We received much evidence that testified to:

- the positive impact of the additional support funds within the methodology on sector colleges' ability to make provision for students with learning difficulties and/or disabilities, leading to an increase in the range of this provision

- the way the Council has designed the methodology to attach funds to the additional support needed by individual students as a central component within the main framework
- the determination with which colleges have grappled with the new methodology and, in many cases, used it with persistence and imagination to develop and enhance their provision.

11.13 During the course of our work, we initially met with some scepticism about the Council's commitment to students with learning difficulties and/or disabilities, and the practicality of an apparently complex methodology. The scepticism was, however, replaced by enthusiastic approval for the methodology from those who had to put it into practice in colleges. Colleges responding to the mapping project told the researchers:

> *The college is inclusive in its approach. Additional support is firmly embedded within an equal opportunities perspective and is provided through a range of cross-college teams. We have not changed our approach since incorporation but the funding methodology has allowed for greater access for students across the full curriculum range.*

> *The college has set challenging targets for meeting the needs of learners with disabilities/learning difficulties, which represent a significant increase of provision since 1992-93. These targets have been made more realistic by the operation of the provision in the recurrent funding methodology for additional support units. This provision is central to the achievement of these targets.*[9]

11.14 The emphasis on guidance and assessment for each student which drives the entry phase of the methodology and the learning agreement is clearly having a positive impact on college practice and on the quality of teaching and learning for students. One college told the researchers in the mapping project, 'all students in the first year of their course are screened for possible learning difficulties as soon as possible in their first term'.[10] The chief inspector's annual report for 1994-95 describes the impact of the methodology:

> *The clear identification of entry, on-programme and achievement elements in the funding methodology and the innovative student learning agreement have had many beneficial effects. These include the greater emphasis placed in pre-programme and on-programme guidance and counselling by colleges; the increased attention paid to student retention to avoid funding penalties; and an increased awareness that the college's primary duty is to make sure that students achieve the qualifications for which they are aiming...The funding allocated to help colleges meet the needs of students with learning difficulties and/or disabilities has enabled colleges to increase provision for such students.*[11]

11.15 Our evaluation identified a number of strengths in the methodology, which make it well suited to deliver inclusive learning:

- the methodology is designed to allocate funds for successful learning. It reflects the way learning is organised and delivered by colleges. This focus chimes with ours
- the additional support bands cover a range of types of support. Colleges can use the funds flexibly. The bottom threshold of the band assumes that colleges will offer students support below this point. In principle, this is consistent with our thinking about inclusive learning since it enables and encourages colleges to meet a wide range of individual requirements
- the additional support bands are designed to reflect the costs to colleges of making a match between the student's learning requirements and the learning environment. This means that there should there be no disincentive to a college to enrol a student with a learning difficulty and/or disability

- each student (or advocate on their behalf) signs their learning agreement. This is a potentially powerful statement of the entitlement of the student; the obligations of the college and the responsibilities of the student as a learner
- colleges are expected to offer guidance and an assessment to each student. This expectation is exemplified in the entry phase of the learning programme and the guidance on audit arrangements
- students with learning difficulties and/or disabilities are included within the methodology on the same basis as any other student
- the methodology allocates funds to a college based on its strategic plan whilst reflecting the support needed by individual students.

11.16 We met some criticism of aspects of the methodology:

- some colleges were uncertain about what they were expected to provide for students before the bottom threshold for additional support is reached. Smaller colleges expressed particular concern about their ability to deliver support for large numbers of students with small support needs. One college told the researchers in the mapping project, 'the majority of students with learning difficulties, at this college, have levels of literacy and numeracy which do not attract additional units of support but nevertheless require additional support if they are to be successful'[12]
- some colleges were uncertain about how to claim and use funds for additional support, especially how to calculate costs and account for expenditure.

11.17 These criticisms, as well as our desire to ensure the best possible allocation mechanism, led us to consider whether there might be alternative ways of allocating funds which better reflect the principles set out in paragraph 11.5.

Allocating funds directly to students

11.18 The first alternative we explored was to allocate funds directly to students. This would establish a direct relationship between the Council and the student, who could then use the funds in whatever way they saw fit to secure their access to further education. This would be comparable with:

- the approach which has been introduced for youth credits for young people involved in training schemes
- the scheme the government intends to pilot for some people under the community care direct payment arrangements
- higher education, and other thinking about individual learning accounts or vouchers.

11.19 We considered whether this method of funding could benefit students with learning difficulties and/or disabilities in further education. Its advantages for students would be:

- that they could determine exactly what support they wanted and especially, if student financial support (for example, for transport) was included in the funds available, students would also have greater flexibility to obtain the right package to meet their requirements
- the principles behind such an approach would promote self-reliance, independence and choice
- such an approach might secure greater integration between support for students with their learning, and financial support available from other sources, such as the LEA.

11.20 However, we consider that the disadvantages of allocating funds directly to students would outweigh these apparent advantages. Our rejection of this model is based on principle and practice:

- it would remove responsibility from colleges and place too great a burden on students. The current methodology should give proper regard to the views of students. Whilst students should have a greater say in the support they receive, colleges must remain responsible for responding in a planned and systematic way to the needs of their local populations, in order to make effective use of resources and ensure that needs are met in a locality

- if such a model applied only to students with learning difficulties and/or disabilities, it would fail the test set out in our third principle (paragraph 11.5) and run counter to colleges achieving inclusive provision. If it applied to all students, we consider it would dangerously destabilise existing provision
- the existing methodology has the potential to deliver the 'consumer view' and responsiveness to demand, often put forward as the justification for allocating funds directly to students
- the higher education and social care models would be inappropriate for further education. The number of higher education students with support needs is smaller. Furthermore, the range of these needs are relatively narrow and most of the students will be clear about the support they need to achieve their learning goals
- a mechanism which allocates funds to individuals would be administratively cumbersome and expensive.

Allocating funds to managing agents

11.21 The second alternative we explored was to allocate funds to managing agents rather than to each college. This model appears to have worked well in some parts of the country already, where one college manages specialised support for students attending a number of local colleges. The advantage of this model would be that:

- the Council would specify the level and type of learning support needed in an area and invite bids from managing agents to deliver it
- the managing agent would be responsible for all the funds currently available for learning support and for students as learners, such as transport
- it might stimulate provision where a potential shortfall in provision emerges, or stimulate sector college provision where currently only specialist college provision is available
- if the quality of the support was an explicit criterion in allocating the funds, it might also be a way of ensuring that responsibility for delivery is in the hands of the highest-quality providers
- it might promote collaboration, as bids could be explicitly sought from collaborative partners, for example, between a sector and specialist college.

11.22 However, we do not believe that this approach would benefit students with learning difficulties and/or disabilities. They need the Council to be confident in discharging its duties of sufficiency and adequacy. They need colleges to be responsible for deciding on the provision they make, including additional support for local students based on a local needs analysis. Specifically:

- allocating funds to managing agents would give responsibility for determining the level of service to the Council, rather than to the college through its needs analysis. We did not think the Council could ever, in general, know better than the local college the broad scope of provision needed by a local community and therefore create a better pattern of provision
- the Council would have effectively passed over key aspects of its role to the managing agent
- the current methodology already enables colleges to buy in specialist support from expert services and to collaborate.

11.23 We therefore strongly rejected both these alternatives. They compare unfavourably with the existing methodology in terms of the benefits for students. We do not believe they would promote inclusive learning.

3 Accounting for the funds allocated by the Council for students with learning difficulties and/or disabilities

11.24 The Council's chief executive is accountable to parliament for the administration of funds available to it. Colleges are accountable to the Council for the funds allocated to them. They are required to meet certain conditions to ensure the funds are used for the purposes for which they are allocated. These conditions are set out in the financial memorandum and funding agreement between the Council and sector colleges and the contract with specialist colleges.

11.25 The Council has included in the funding agreement for sector colleges that each college must aim to enrol at least the same number and proportion of students with learning difficulties and/or disabilities as the previous year, in order to ensure that these students benefit from the general policy of growth in the sector. From 1996-97, the Council will be required to make it a condition of funding that each sector college has a disability statement. This is a requirement of the *Disability Discrimination Act 1995.*

11.26 The three main ways of ensuring accountability are:

- the external audit of the individualised student record (ISR), which records volumes of provision at each college. We have already explored how far the ISR meets our expectations for monitoring participation in chapter 4
- the inspection programme, which judges the quality of provision delivered by each college
- the internal and external audit regimes, which check that colleges are using appropriate systems for taking financial decisions.

11.27 We found some evidence that the external audit system had yet to establish itself. Evidence suggests that colleges do not always understand the rules of the methodology against which they will be audited or how to cost their additional support properly across the college. We are concerned that colleges can be awarded low inspection grades for their cross-college activities where those represent significant proportions of their income, but that, under the current arrangements, those activities are not then reinspected.

4 The best way of funding students at specialist colleges

11.28 We were told that funding for students at specialist colleges has been handled differently. The Council has paid fees for each individual whom it decides to place at a specialist college outside the sector. It has increasingly sought to control the amounts paid to specialist colleges in the light of the funds available to it; the need to have regard to value for money; and the efficiency savings demanded by the PES settlement. The contract with each specialist college:

- sets out the conditions which govern the financial relationship with each college
- gives the Council the right to inspect the quality of the provision which it funds and to receive audited accounts
- is accompanied by a specific contract for each student describing their programme and any particular support which is to be provided for them.

11.29 In principle, we consider this contract to be a useful vehicle for ensuring a match between each student's requirements, learning goals and learning environment. However, at present, inspection reports about the provision funded by the Council at these colleges are not published. We discuss this further in chapter 10.

11.30 We found general support for the Council's approach amongst sector and specialist colleges, although the latter were, during the course of our work, increasingly concerned about the level of fees which the Council told them it is prepared to pay. Some argued for the greater stability which they perceived to flow from the core and margin funding for sector colleges. Some colleges within and outside the sector wanted more encouragement within the funding arrangements to collaborate. Some sector colleges wanted the Council to exert more pressure on specialist colleges to make them reduce their costs or to focus more on students' achievements. Some sector colleges argued that levels of funding for students with learning difficulties and/or disabilities should be the same between sector and specialist colleges and they perceived that it was not.

SUMMARY OF MAIN FINDINGS

11.31 When we compared what we found against the principles described in paragraph 11.5, we found that:

- there are serious shortcomings in the funds available to the sector for capital, both for buildings and for equipment for students. This is affecting the ability of colleges to match the number and individual requirements of those who might participate
- the funding methodology has potential as a way of supporting inclusive learning in sector colleges. The strengths of the current methodology mirror fundamental weaknesses in the alternatives we considered for allocating funds to colleges
- there are some weaknesses in the methodology that can, we believe, be addressed quite easily. These relate to the scope of the additional support bands; and the arrangements for helping colleges to make new provision. We discuss these below
- it is acceptable to retain a different way of funding provision for students at specialist colleges, but more attention needs to be paid to ensuring the quality of what is funded.

ADDRESSING WEAKNESSES AND BUILDING ON STRENGTHS

Obtaining enough funds to ensure that further education can match the number and individual requirements of those who might participate

11.32 We consider that there are four pressing issues upon which action is needed:

- systematic investment in staff development. This is discussed in chapter 12
- capital funds, based on a thorough survey of the sector. This is discussed in more detail in paragraph 11.33
- action to redress the current under-representation of certain groups of students in further education in order for the Council to be able to continue to ensure it is making sufficient and adequate provision. This is discussed in more detail in paragraphs 11.34 to 11.37, and in chapters 3 and 4
- more thorough assessment of each student's learning requirements during the entry phase of the current methodology. This is discussed in more detail in chapter 5.

Capital funds

11.33 Colleges have very different starting-points in their buildings and equipment.

Many of them told us they needed help to know what to do to create a suitable learning environment as well as funding to do it. In our view, it is no longer acceptable to rely on colleges' goodwill to make the necessary adjustments to enable students to participate. The Council should carry out a thorough survey of the accessibility of colleges in order to have strong evidence when it next represents the resource needs of the sector. The Council should also issue guidance to colleges on how to make their provision more accessible in cost-effective ways. This guidance could be usefully derived from the survey.

Participation

11.34 Chapter 4 shows that certain groups of students are not yet properly represented in further education. We have two concerns. The first is that if the present policy of overall growth is curtailed or reversed, then the prospects for increasing the participation of these students will be slim. Our second concern is that some colleges may have to make some provision which is relatively more expensive if they are to match the requirements of those who might participate.

11.35 Chapter 4 also showed that some learners cannot take part because of reasons outside the control of the Council or colleges. The evidence we collected from colleges indicates that a significant number consider non-educational needs to be a key reason why students cannot participate.[13] The mismatch between the provision made by a college and the ability of a student to participate can be stark. The source of funds can distort choices about learning. This makes no sense. One way of tackling this particular issue would be to transfer to the Council all those funds currently allocated by other agencies for post-16 further education, such as discretionary awards and transport. The Council would then allocate these to colleges. These funds could be designated for learner support, alongside the existing hardship funds. Alternatively these funds could be added to the funds allocated through the additional support bands, thereby broadening the scope of additional support. Either option would enable colleges to guarantee students' access to college and the full range of support they require, determined by the colleges' strategic priorities and views of the needs of the local community. The implementation of either option would do much to increase participation. The transfer would apply to all students and not only those with learning difficulties and/or disabilities.

11.36 Coherence in post-16 funding arrangements would be addressed most thoroughly if a single post-16 funding agency were to be established. Such an agency might stimulate more radical thinking about the use of overall funding, in the way that we have suggested here.

11.37 We considered whether social security benefits should be included in this new package. Some aspects of some benefits are allocated for activities which arise because the recipient is a student. We were therefore keen to offer the Council advice on how, if at all, it should take account of benefits in its funding arrangements in order to promote coherence and to help it avoid double funding. We concluded that we should avoid any changes which would discourage students from participating. Nevertheless, we believe there is a case for some benefits and social services funding being offset in a more equitable and systematic way against the costs of further education where they are provided to meet certain costs incurred by the recipient. This applies most obviously to residential and social costs in specialist colleges.

Assessing students' requirements

11.38 Colleges will need to do more to assess each student's requirements properly in order to deliver learning which is inclusive. We considered whether this could be achieved by reallocating some of the units currently allocated to the 'on-programme' element of the funding methodology to the 'entry' element. We concluded that more than this is needed because we are dealing with an overall increase in college activity, not a reallocation of that activity.

2 The best way of allocating the funds available to the Council

11.39 This report focuses on providing a match between the individual, their learning goals and their learning environment. Allocating funds to support such a match requires a flexible approach. As the NFER report noted,

> *The range of disabling conditions and learning difficulties and their variable impact on the learning needs of young people tend to militate against the systematic categorisation of disability as a basis on which to consider possible funding levels...the nature of a student's disability or learning difficulty is not necessarily a good indicator of the additional costs of the provision needed.*[14]

We want to see the Council allocate funds in a way which maximises the extent of that match for individual students.

11.40 We evaluated the effectiveness of the current funding methodology in enabling colleges to provide inclusive learning. In the light of that evaluation, we considered first how the current methodology could be enhanced first to secure the changes we advocate in this report; and secondly what principles should inform the Council's long-term review and development of the methodology, particularly as it reviews this for 1997-98 and beyond.

Enhancing the current methodology

11.41 We concluded that:

- the general design and purpose of the methodology is extremely positive for students with learning difficulties and/or disabilities because they are included within its design and because the additional support units enable colleges to offer a learning environment that matches their requirements
- there would be resistance from colleges to a major change in the methodology
- the methodology recognises the extra costs that may be involved in providing an appropriate learning environment for some students and allows those costs to be met without needing to label the students or their provision. It emphasises the importance of an agreement between the college and each student about their learning goals
- the current methodology goes further towards ensuring that individual learning requirements are met than either of the alternatives we considered. These alternatives fund provision for students with learning difficulties and/or disabilities separately. They also sever the link between the allocation and the college's strategic responsibilities
- some form of recognising the costs of creating a learning environment that matches individual learning requirements, currently represented by the additional support bands, must be retained.

11.42 To improve the capacity of the methodology to reflect and deliver our inclusive approach, the following aspects needed further refinement:

- allowing colleges to include the cost of personal equipment and enabling technology and minor adaptations within the scope of additional support. This is vital for those students for whom access to the right technology or a minor adaptation to the college is the main or only barrier to their ability to learn. We understand the Council's current stance. However, we think that it is now timely to allocate funds for equipment and adaptations for individuals, both because of what we have learnt about the impact of technological change and accessibility on learning and participation, and because of the change in the conventional boundary between recurrent and capital funding

- requiring students and the college to sign a learning plan which is represented, in financial terms, in the additional support form. This would underline the importance to the student and the college of the assessment process. Moreover, it would emphasise that the student has an entitlement to the support described in the plan and costed on the form. This would considerably enhance the ability of the external auditors and the Council's inspectorate to check that the support described has been delivered
- extending the range of costs covered by the additional support above the value of the current top band by introducing further bands. Whilst we think that the current arrangement whereby the Council allocates funds individually against published criteria has been appropriate to date, extending the bands would be more consistent with the responsibilities of colleges and could do more to ensure that colleges are able to match the individual requirements of more students
- giving guidance to colleges on what should usually be provided before the threshold to the bottom band is reached. We heard some representations that the bottom threshold should be lowered. On balance, we thought it should be retained because this makes colleges responsible for responding to the requirements of the majority of their learners. However, if the threshold is retained at its present level, we think colleges need more guidance about what they are expected to provide as core support for students before the threshold is reached.

11.43 We also considered whether it is prohibitively difficult for colleges to offer provision of a new kind, for example, residential support. We were told that this is a particular concern of the smaller colleges, including the sixth form colleges. Some of these doubt their ability to tackle some of the issues raised in this report, especially in the face of competition from school sixth forms which they feel to be more generously resourced.

11.44 We considered these arguments carefully, to see how far they applied to any new or residential provision which a college wanted to offer and how far only to students with learning difficulties and/or disabilities. Although the arguments are general, they might have particular relevance to students with learning difficulties and/or disabilities where there is evidence:

- of an emerging insufficiency or inadequacy of provision in a local area which needs to be remedied as a result of the Council's legal duties and/or
- that over time, significant numbers of students from a local area are being placed at a specialist college for whom provision could be found locally if the same or fewer funds were available to the local college, with no diminution in quality.

11.45 Where either of these conditions are met, the Council should consider taking the initiative, through its regional offices and the subcommittees of the regional committee, to see that new local provision can be established. One way of doing this would be to invite the colleges concerned to write new strategic plans which better address these emerging needs. Another would be to invite local colleges to make proposals for new provision, giving details of their recurrent or capital costs over the foreseeable future and of local collaboration with relevant agencies. The subcommittee could then advise the Council to endow a college with funds or with an advance of funds which could be offset against future allocations. It would be important to ensure that, where residential provision was proposed, this would honour the principles of the 24-hour curriculum offered by residential colleges.

Identifying the principles that should inform the longer-term development of the methodology

11.46 As well as considering short-term enhancements to the methodology as it is currently designed, there are a number of principles which should inform its longer-term development. These principles should be based on those set out in paragraph 11.5. The aim should be to maximise inclusive learning at the levels of the sector, college and individual student. We feel particularly strongly that in any new methodology, the Council should retain a way of allocating funds to colleges based on the individual costs of providing a learning environment that matches learning requirements.

Accounting for the funds allocated by the Council for students with learning difficulties and/or disabilities

11.47 We support the Council's current approach to accountability, which combines a set of funding conditions and ways of measuring activity through an external audit of the ISR; the rigours of the inspection programme; and visits from the Council's own audit staff. We are aware, however, of the Council's review of the inspection and audit frameworks, in the light both of the growing maturity of colleges and the restrictions in the running costs available to it to fund such activities. We are also aware that some colleges want more help in costing and accounting for their additional support arrangements, and that there are some inconsistencies in costing and accounting practice between colleges.

11.48 We have made a number of recommendations about the inspection framework in chapter 10. The publication of inspection reports on the provision funded in specialist colleges outside the sector would do much to make them more accountable. In addition, we would like the Council to consider reinspecting cross-college learning support where the additional support funds represent a significant proportion of the college's total allocation and where inspection grades indicate that weaknesses outweigh strengths.

11.49 The ISR obviously has the potential to monitor any given activity of any college. It needs to be adapted to monitor provision for students with learning difficulties and/or disabilities more accurately than at present. To this end, we consider that there should be changes to the ISR, and these are described in chapter 4.

11.50 On external audit, colleges need more guidance on how to cost additional support and how to apportion those costs centrally or to the individual. We also think that there should be closer collaboration between the Council's inspectorate and the external auditors to ensure that these funds are being used properly.

The best way of funding students at specialist colleges

11.51 We support the Council's current approach to funding students to attend specialist colleges. We note the Council's recent efforts to ensure value for money for the funds allocated by paying comparable fees for comparable provision. The Council is likely to continue to need to use such placements to ensure a learning environment that matches the learning requirements of a small number of students. We regard this provision as forming a valuable part of the whole pattern of facilities available for students. We were concerned that there is not more collaboration between sector and specialist colleges even though they have much to learn from each other, for example, on initial assessment and on providing effective support for learning. Although we could not quantify any savings that might result from such collaboration, we consider that collaboration might enable the available funds to be put to better effect. Furthermore, we were concerned that specialist colleges are currently exempt from the pressures that follow from the achievement element of the funding allocated to sector colleges; and for the publication of inspection reports.

11.52 We do not advocate the wholesale incorporation of the specialist colleges and their evidence to us did not seek this development, although we note that individual specialist colleges may consider it the best way forward. We consider that greater rigour could be brought to the current arrangements if the Council published a list of approved specialist colleges, the fees it is prepared to pay, and the inspection reports.

RECOMMENDATIONS

11.53 In the light of the evidence presented to us and our guiding principles, the committee makes the following recommendations to the Council:

Understanding the methodology

11.54 The Council should promote the ability of the methodology to secure inclusive learning. Specifically, therefore, we recommend that the Council:

- publish an accessible guide to the funding methodology designed for students, parents and those who work with them.

The Council's current funding methodology

11.55 The committee recommends that the Council make a number of limited refinements to the current funding methodology that would help sector colleges to offer inclusive learning. Specifically, therefore, the committee recommends that the Council:

- include individual equipment, learning technology and minor adaptations within the scope of the additional support bands
- require colleges and students to sign the additional support form
- introduce new arrangements for regional subcommittees to recommend funding new provision where there is evidence of emerging need for this and/or it can be done more effectively than at specialist colleges
- introduce more bands above the value of the top band
- allocate new funds to the entry component to enable proper assessments of students' requirements.

Funding provision at specialist colleges

11.56 The committee recommends that the Council continue to fund individual placements at specialist colleges where necessary. Specifically, the Council should:

- ensure that these colleges give value for money, with particular reference to profit-making providers
- continue its policy of convergence between fee levels for comparable provision
- develop a list of approved specialist colleges which make high-quality provision and give better value for money, based on explicit criteria
- publish its inspection reports on provision it funds at these colleges
- promote funding arrangements that enable and encourage collaboration between specialist and sector colleges.

Capital funding

11.57 The committee recommends that if colleges are to be able to provide appropriately for those groups currently under-represented and to offer the technical support which individuals need to learn effectively, then more attention needs to be paid to equipment for individual students and to the capital state of the sector. Specifically, the Council should:

- commission a survey of the accessibility of the sector colleges to students with learning difficulties and/or disabilities
- publish a guide about good practice, on the basis of the survey of accessibility
- include likely costings about individual equipment, enabling technology and accessibility in its representations on behalf of the sector about needs, in the light of the survey.

Long-term principles to underpin the development of the funding methodology

11.58 The committee recommends that the Council apply the following principles to any review of the methodology in order that it promotes inclusive learning and participation. To have regard for these students' requirements and avoid disproportionate expenditure, the way these public funds are obtained, allocated and accounted for should aim to:

- maximise the extent to which learning is inclusive
- maximise the rate of change by which the sector is able to offer inclusive learning, consistent with realistic but demanding expectations on colleges
- operate for those with learning difficulties and/or disabilities in the same way as for other students
- retain both the college's responsibility to plan its provision and allocate funds and an allocation methodology from the Council which is based on students' individual requirements.

Other sources of funds

11.59 The committee recommends that, whilst the Council's primary focus must be to allocate the funds put at its disposal, it should also have regard to the wider pattern of funds from other sources. Students and the public purse would benefit if these were delivered on a more coherent basis. Specifically, therefore, the committee recommends that the Council:

- meet with the Department of Social Security (DSS) and the Department of Health (DoH) at the highest level to explore the scope for co-operation and simplification in the allocation of funds to ensure that funding opportunities for students are maximised and double funding minimised

11

- negotiate an agreement with the DSS and specialist colleges about the appropriate role of student benefits in meeting the costs of residential provision
- seek to have transferred to it funds currently allocated by LEAs in discretionary awards and transport to further education students, or, in the short term pending such a transfer, to help colleges and LEAs negotiate management agreements whereby the college manages the funds nominally allocated by the LEA
- explore the establishment of a single post-16 funding agency.

References

1. Responses to the mapping project, (unpublished)

2. Committee visit to Washington DC, April 1996 (see also annex C)

3. J. Bradley, L. Dee and F. Wilenius *Students with Disabilities and/or Learning Difficulties in Further Education; A Review of Research Carried out by the National Foundation for Educational Research*, Slough, NFER, 1994, p. 25

4. Responses to the mapping project, (unpublished)

5. SCPR *Student Voices: The Views of Further Education Students with Learning Difficulties and/or Disabilities: Findings from a Series of Student Workshops Commissioned by the Learning Difficulties and/or Disablities Committee*. London, Skill: National Bureau for Students with Disabilities, March 1996

6. *Quality and Standards in Further Education in England: Chief Inspector's Annual Report 1994-95,* Coventry, FEFC, 1995, para. 55

7. Meager, Nigel *et al. Mapping Provision: The Provision of and Participation in Further Education by Students with Learning Difficulties and/or Disabilities: A Report to the Learning Difficulties and/or Disabilities Committee*, London, HMSO, 1996

8. *How to Apply for Funding 1996-97*, Coventry, FEFC, 1995

9. Responses to the mapping project, (unpublished)

10. *Ibid.*

11. *Quality and Standards in Further Education in England: Chief Inspector's Annual Report 1994-95,* Coventry, FEFC, 1995, para. 16

12. Responses to the mapping project, (unpublished)

13. Meager, Nigel *et al. Mapping Provision: The Provision of and Participation in Further Education by Students with Learning Difficulties and/or Disabilities: A Report to the Learning Difficulties and/or Disabilities Committee*, London, HMSO, 1996

14. J. Bradley, L. Dee and F. Wilenius *Students with Disabilities and/or Learning Difficulties in Further Education; A Review of Research Carried out by the National Foundation for Educational Research*, Slough, NFER, 1994, p. 27

Chapter 12: Quality Initiative – The Development of Staff and Organisations

In this chapter, the committee makes the case for a national quality initiative aimed at assisting colleges to implement the recommendations in the report, and describes the three main elements and intended outcomes of the initiative.

THE ISSUES

1. the role of the Council in encouraging colleges to adopt a strategic approach to implementing the committee's recommendations
2. developing and delivering a centrally-managed and co-ordinated strategy to improve the quality and relevance of teacher education and staff development for teachers working with students with learning difficulties and/or disabilities
3. ensuring that the committee's thinking about inclusive learning is integrated into any new teacher education or staff development initiatives.

THE QUALITY INITIATIVE

12.1 The committee has made three types of recommendation in this report:

- those which could be implemented through the Council's funding methodology, strategic planning framework, inspection arrangements and data collection and audit arrangements
- those that are concerned with the activities of other agencies, where the Council could seek to exert influence or expect agencies to take the initiative themselves
- those which could be implemented by colleges, some of which may require external support.

12.2 The quality initiative is concerned primarily with encouraging and supporting change in colleges. Colleges will be better able to adopt the committee's recommendations if they receive some external support. This support should be managed and co-ordinated at a national level in order to ensure: the best use of resources; outcomes which are directly linked to the committee's recommendations, and the dissemination and sharing of good practice. The quality initiative which we propose has three elements:

- funds to encourage colleges to adopt a strategic approach to implementing the committee's recommendations, encouraged by the Council
- a central co-ordinating and advisory body, with links to the Further Education Staff Development Forum, the Further Education Development Agency (FEDA), the Teacher Training Agency, universities, institutes of higher education, awarding bodies and other organisations concerned with general teacher education and continuous professional development in the sector
- a centrally-managed and co-ordinated programme of staff development linked to the committee's thinking about inclusive learning.

This chapter addresses each of these elements.

THE COMMITTEE'S PRINCIPLES

12.3 The committee has adopted four principles in designing the quality initiative:

- high levels of knowledge, skills, experience and confidence on the part of staff are essential if the further education sector is to become more inclusive
- if our recommendations are to work, senior managers must understand the implications they have for their own strategic role
- a strategic, nationally co-ordinated approach is required to bring about the changes the committee wants to see in colleges
- the initiative must link with other initiatives in teacher education, staff development or curriculum development work in colleges.

WHAT WE MEAN BY TEACHER EDUCATION AND STAFF DEVELOPMENT

12.4 Teacher education and staff development are separate types of activity, although the distinctions are not always clear cut in further education:

- *teacher education;* sometimes known as teacher training, is systematic, planned training which is accredited by a university or a national awarding body and which takes place over a period of time; it has well-defined progression routes and leads to accreditation which has national currency
- *initial teacher training*; either full or part time, and leads to a first professional teaching qualification
- *continuing professional development;* leads to a further professional teaching or managerial qualification and may be delivered by a university, a college or other body and accredited through a national awarding body or through a university
- *staff development;* may be through a variety of formal and informal activities:
  - formal activities are planned, usually in the form of short programmes or single events, delivered in and by the college or a local, regional or national agency and do not generally lead to formal accreditation; they usually have no intended progression routes or national currency; they may be used to gain credits toward accreditation through assessment and accreditation of prior learning; and may be used as credits towards a national vocational qualification or, for example, a qualification in the use of British Sign Language; non-teaching staff may take part in these activities

- informal activities are usually *ad hoc* or incidental to other events, such as advice sessions with colleagues, team-teaching or support teaching.

12.5 The activities of the newly formed Further Education Staff Development Forum will bring about significant changes in teacher education and staff development, including management training, perhaps by drawing the two areas closer together.

Characteristics of good teaching and management

12.6 Students in the workshop series told us that good teachers:

- understood how the students' disability or learning difficulty might affect their learning and participation in college life
- identified the support that a student required and made sure it was available at the right time
- understood how students learnt best and used materials and teaching styles which matched their learning requirements
- recognised and recorded students' progress in learning and gave students clear and helpful information on their progress
- know students individually and have the skills to listen to, and take account of their views.[1]

12.7 In chapter 10, we described the influence that managers have on the quality of provision. The inspectorate told us unequivocally that:

- the quality of provision is good where senior managers and governors are knowledgeable about the work and are actively involved in its development[2]
- the quality of provision is generally high where appropriately qualified and trained teachers are employed
- teachers are given insufficient opportunity to undertake specialist training, especially for work with students with complex difficulties
- teachers need staff development training in: the use of information technology; assessment techniques and using the outcomes of assessment to devise and implement individual programmes of learning; using a variety of methods for giving students information; designing learning materials; and in breaking down learning into small steps.

12.8 Over 50% of respondents providing evidence for the committee referred to the importance of good management. They indicated that the quality of college management was a crucial factor in ensuring improvement in the quality of learning for students with learning difficulties and/or disabilities. Much of the evidence pointed to the need for managers to be well informed and confident about this area of work, for them to give it the same priority in terms of strategic planning and quality assurance as the rest of the college's provision. We explored this in more detail in chapter 10.

12.9 Funding for staff development was another issue raised frequently by respondents. Many colleges regretted the loss of ear-marked funding through the grant for educational support and training (GEST). GEST ceased to exist as a separate funding initiative in 1992-93; the money formerly allocated to GEST was included in the main allocations to colleges under the new funding methodology. We were advised that the sum transferred to the Council from LEAs was about £8 million. Funding for special needs training was a small but important percentage of this amount. As a consequence of these new arrangements, many college co-ordinators found it difficult to bid successfully for resources for specific and highly-specialised training or staff development.[3]

12.10 The importance of links between the quality of staff and the quality of their training was raised by the respondents to the call for evidence, who commented that students achieve more if their teacher is properly qualified to teach students with learning difficulties and/or disabilities.[4]

12.11 Colleges which took part in the exercise to test the committee's thinking about learning were asked to indicate what might prevent or support their progress in adopting our recommendations. They indicated that:

- the positive attitudes, understanding and skills of managers are important to their successful adoption
- colleges' strategic and operational plans should give priority to the committee's recommendations
- raising the levels of staff awareness, confidence and skill in working with students with learning difficulties and/or disabilities is essential if colleges are to provide for more of these learners successfully
- staff development is essential for teachers to help them: identify learning styles; undertake assessment; review and record learning goals; match teaching to learning styles; and provide learning environments which promote inclusiveness.[5]

The link between training and the quality of teaching

12.12 We spent some time considering evidence from earlier enquiries and surveys, to examine further the link between training and the quality of teaching. We also wanted to confirm or refute our opinion that existing staff development was of varying quality and sometimes of little relevance for the changing roles of staff. We wanted to identify the strengths and weaknesses identified through earlier enquiries and surveys in order to learn from them.

12.13 Three earlier reports by Her Majesty's Inspectorate indicated that good-quality staff development and training leads to improvement in the quality of provision. The reports, produced over a period of three years, trace a continuing need for accredited, high-quality training and for a national initiative which would co-ordinate and develop what was already available.[6] In particular, the reports indicated:

- the importance of ear-marking monies for training if colleges are to recruit and meet the requirements of new groups of students with learning difficulties and/or disabilities
- a need for national validation for staff development in this area
- senior staff in some colleges did not consider that they needed training and some had insufficient knowledge and understanding of the criteria for quality to discharge their management functions properly
- there was a need for in-service education and training amongst college staff generally as well as those specialising in this work
- specialist staff were often isolated in colleges and not involved in college staff development programmes
- the lack of training for many part-time staff had an adverse effect on the quality of their work.

12.14 The committee found the outcomes of a recent national survey of particular relevance. According to the findings of this survey, colleges were developing a more co-ordinated approach to staff development, though training did not match the needs of all staff. Action was needed to ensure:

- successful integration of students with learning difficulties and/or disabilities into mainstream provision
- management support for the co-ordinator responsible for provision of these students

- the requirements of students with complex disabilities, mental health difficulties, behavioural difficulties and dyslexia were met
- learning styles and systems of learning support are properly evaluated and monitored
- students are provided with a suitable range of assessment methods and that their achievements are accredited.[7]

12.15 Over half the colleges in the survey said that they gave priority to issues related to students with learning difficulties and/or disabilities in staff development programmes. However, much of the work served only to raise the awareness of staff of these issues. The specialist team played an important role in co-ordinating and delivering staff training. There was concern that GEST funding had come to an end. GEST funding had been used to provide training in, amongst other areas, Brailling, deaf awareness, assessment and profiling, national vocational qualifications and their implications for students with learning difficulties, information technology and sign language.

12.16 A variety of training programmes and events are used by colleges. These include non-accredited in-house programmes, sometimes provided by external organisations such as the educational psychology or speech therapy service; short courses provided by external bodies or voluntary organisations and networks. In some instances, the local education authority provided short programmes or events.

12.17 The survey found that 3% of all staff in the sector were totally engaged in making provision for students with learning difficulties and/or disabilities. There were proportionally fewer of these staff on senior lecturer or management grades. In addition to teaching, they often undertook management and liaison work for which they were rarely trained.[8]

12.18 The committee considers it essential that its recommendations are relevant to the priorities of the sector as a whole, if they are to be implemented by colleges and influence the whole of their activities. A recent report[9] spelt out some of these priorities. Although it makes no specific references to students with learning difficulties and/or disabilities, the report identifies some key changes in the teacher's role. The report states that these changes are:

- *from subject knowledge to curriculum knowledge; that is, how general or non-subject specific learning, for example, core skills, can be achieved through a subject and related to other areas of learning*
- *from teacher-centred pedagogic knowledge to learner-centred pedagogic knowledge; that is, that teachers will need to be experts in the management of learning and in how to enable their students to become managers of their own learning*
- *intra-professional knowledge to inter-professional knowledge; that is teachers will need to know about other sources of expertise, for example, in the use of technology, and how students can access them*
- *from classroom knowledge to organisational knowledge; that is, teachers will need to develop teamwork, negotiating and collaborative skills and to develop organisational skills that enable them to link their specialist role to the wider aims of the college*
- *from insular to connective knowledge; that is, teachers need to be able to help students to connect their past, present and future learning and not restrict their professional knowledge to what happens when a student is in college.*[10]

Teacher education in further education

12.19 There is no mandatory requirement for teachers in further education to be professionally qualified, unlike schools where all teachers must gain qualified teacher status. Over 60% of full-time staff teaching in further education have a recognised teaching qualification. However, over half the lecturers in colleges are recruited without teaching qualifications and subsequently gain them through part-time study. Approximately 20% of staff are part time. Colleges recruit many staff who have industrial or business experience but no teaching qualifications, and some specialist staff who combine teaching with the practice of their specialism, for example, in the arts and crafts. Many staff begin teaching in further education on a part-time basis or begin their careers as school teachers.

12.20 The diversity of qualifications available to those teaching in further education reflects the diversity of the sector itself and the entrepreneurial nature of the awarding bodies. The major teaching qualification that has been recognised for a mandatory grant by the Department for Education and Employment is the Certificate of Education, though a significant minority of staff have a Post Graduate Certificate of Education, which may or may not have a further education focus. Courses leading to these certificates will rarely include anything on students with learning difficulties and/or disabilities.

12.21 We found that the various routes into further education teaching and lack of co-ordination of training mean that:

- provision for teacher education for further education is fragmented
- teachers frequently begin their careers in further education with no experience of or training for working with students with learning difficulties and/or disabilities.

The Council's expectations

12.22 The Council has indicated in its guidance on staff development and strategic planning (November 1993) that it wishes to see the integration of staff development and training with a college's strategic objectives. In particular, the Council expects a college to make sure that its staff have the necessary skills to implement the college's strategic plan.

Staff development in colleges

12.23 A college is responsible for deciding upon its own staff development priorities which must be funded from within its overall budget. The Council took an early decision to include funding previously ear-marked for GEST in its main allocation to colleges. Expenditure on staff development varies between colleges. A recent survey found that colleges in the London area allocate between 1.5% and 4% of the total college budget to staff development. The main priorities for staff development were related to GNVQ/NVQ assessor training and management training. There is some evidence that the number of joint training initiatives between colleges and other services and schools has declined since 1992.[11]

Qualifications of staff in colleges of further education

12.24 Details drawn from the Council's staff individualised record (SIR) of the highest qualification levels attained by staff in colleges within the further education sector 1994 show that:

- just under 46.7% of staff whose primary role involved teaching and learning hold a professional teaching qualification
- just under a fifth (19.2%) of staff whose primary role involved supporting teaching and learning hold a professional qualification
- those engaged in supporting teaching and learning officially hold lower levels of qualification than those staff primarily engaged in teaching and learning
- 50% of part-time staff either had no formal qualifications or their qualifications were not known.[12]

Specialist training for teachers in further education colleges

12.25 The SIR provides information about staff who have received some kind of training to teach students with learning difficulties and/or disabilities. Details based on provisional information drawn from the SIR in November 1994 indicate that:

- 5% of staff (5,000) whose primary role involved teaching and learning had received training relating to students with learning difficulties and/or disabilities
- a further 2% of staff (400) involved in supporting teaching and learning had received training
- on the basis of these data, 38% of staff (41,700) whose primary role involved teaching and learning and 16% of staff (2,700) who supported teaching and learning have not received training but considered training to be applicable to them
- 18% of staff (20,000) whose primary role involves teaching and learning were not considered to require training.

The 'other support' category in the SIR includes the majority of middle and senior managers. It is of concern to the committee, that only 1% of staff (500) have received training.[13]

12.26 However, the SIR does not indicate:

- the length or level of training
- whether it was accredited
- anything about its quality or relevance to the member of staff's current role
- whether training was focused on further education or schools
- whether it was teacher education, continuous professional development or staff development.

12.27 The SIR does not cover specialist colleges for students with learning difficulties and/or disabilities and so it is not possible to estimate the level and relevance of training in those colleges. The Council's inspectorate does, however, comment on training in its reports on provision funded by the Council at these establishments.

Some characteristics of specialist training and development in further education

12.28 Staff in further education follow a wide variety of accredited training and staff development programmes. It is difficult to ascertain how many staff are registered for each type of accredited course, although some statistics are available; for example, there were 8,917 staff registered for City and Guilds courses relating to disability and learning difficulties or to learning support in 1994-95. Evidence indicated that staff development in this area tends:

- to be isolated from the college's main staff development programme
- not to be integrated into the college's strategic, operational and development plans
- to concentrate on specific disabilities and in this respect is 'needs-led'
- to be voluntary in attendance
- to rely on the college co-ordinator for provision for these students and their team for planning and delivery
- not to be provided for managers.[14]

Training and development in the school sector

12.29 We drew some comparisons with training in the schools sector where:

- standards for training are set and monitored centrally
- accreditation and progression routes to higher levels of training are readily available
- there are ear-marked funds for a national programme of specialist training.

12.30 The Teacher Training Agency (TTA) was established in September 1994 and is responsible for the supply of trained teachers to the schools sector. The TTA is the lead body for teacher training in schools and is responsible for applying standards set by the secretary of state. All teachers in schools are required to achieve qualified teacher status (QTS) by following a recognised course. The quality of training is monitored by OFSTED.

12.31 Specialist training for teachers of pupils with special educational needs is part-funded through the Grant for Educational Support and Training (GEST) which includes a local education authority contribution. Under this scheme, teachers with some classroom experience are eligible for recognised accredited training. Local education authorities bid for training monies against certain criteria. In previous years, funds were ear-marked for a number of teachers to receive training each year in the specialisms of visual impairment, hearing impairment and severe learning difficulties. In 1994-95, these areas were covered by a general special educational needs grant for particular specialisms, the development of school policies and the partnerships with parents scheme. In 1995-96, the grant is £10.5 million, in 1996-97, it will be £10.4 million. Training of educational psychologists is funded separately.

12.32 Staff development in schools is part-funded through GEST and LEA central funds. In addition, schools may choose to top up funding from their own budgets. There are priority areas against which LEAs bid after consultation with their schools. Priorities include school effectiveness, truancy and disaffected pupils. Staff development may be designed and delivered by an LEA, consortium or individual school. School co-ordinators, peripatetic teachers, educational psychologists, advisory teachers, advisers and inspectors are likely to be involved in the design and delivery of programmes of staff development for special schools. The LEA or a consortium of schools or LEAs may choose to purchase a programme of staff development from an institute of higher education or other provider; attendance may then be accredited or be used as a credit towards full accreditation.

Specialist training of teachers in schools

12.33 Statistics supplied by the Department for Education and Employment indicate that out of a total of 424,195 full- and part-time teachers, 8,334 have received accredited training in special educational needs teaching (just under 2% of teachers). However, there is a danger in drawing a direct comparison with the picture in further education where 5% of staff, whose primary role involved teaching and learning, have received some form of specialist training. The latter figure gives no indication of the extent and level of the training, whether it was accredited, or related to schools or further education.

A Special Professionalism: A report of the Further Education Special Needs Training Group (1987)

12.34 *A Special Professionalism*[15] marked a significant step forward in thinking about training in this area of work. The Further Education Special Needs Training Group was established by the-then Department for Education and Science in February 1986, following the publication in 1984 of advice to the secretaries of state on teacher training and special educational needs from the Advisory Committee on the Supply and Education of Teachers (ACSET). The group was set up to:

- examine the recommendations for the further education sector made by ACSET in its report
- consider how far a basis already existed for the development of a further education system of general awareness training and specialist training to the extent recommended by ACSET
- suggest how the most effective use might be made of existing resources of staff and materials for these purposes

and what developments were desirable to reinforce these resources.

12.35 The report recommended that:

- a national, co-ordinated framework for staff development and teacher training should be established
- the framework should be based on eight levels of staff development needs and each level would be determined by the extent of responsibility held by staff for students with learning difficulties and/or disabilities
- within this framework, staff development for senior and middle managers would be given priority
- three levels of accredited continuous professional development or teacher training for teachers with substantial responsibility for the teaching and learning of students with learning difficulties and/or disabilities, or who co-ordinated college provision should be established
- staff development should be accredited and enable staff to progress to higher level qualifications.[16]

Changes in the further education sector

12.36 Significant changes have taken place in the further education sector since *A Special Professionalism* was published. These include:

- incorporation of colleges
- the specific reference in the *Further and Higher Education Act 1992* to students with learning difficulties and/or disabilities
- the placing of particular responsibilities on the Council for these students
- the transfer of further education from local education authorities with, very often, the loss of the co-ordinated framework for development and training provided by the best of these
- colleges taking responsibility for staff development and continuous professional development
- changes in the curriculum offered by colleges
- changes in the nature of the student population
- changes in teachers' conditions of service and a more extensive use of part-time staff
- increased employment of staff, such as those responsible for student services, who have considerable contact with students but who may not be teachers.

12.37 The evidence received by the committee, for example, from the National Institute of Adult and Continuing Education, indicates that because colleges are competing with one another and with other providers of education and training, they are reluctant to enter into joint or collaborative initiatives on staff development which would enable staff from different organisations to share and discuss their ideas. Changes in the internal organisation of other services, such as health and social services, have contributed to a decline in joint training activities.

12.38 When *A Special Professionalism* was published, GEST funds were available to colleges of further education; and 'special needs' was an identified national priority area. GEST funds played an important part in helping colleges to develop and improve provision. In some instances, colleges made provision for certain groups of learners, such as students with emotional and behavioural difficulties or severe learning difficulties, because managers knew that GEST funding was available to facilitate training for the staff who would teach these students. Although the report's recommendations were not implemented, there was at the time of its publication, funds available through GEST and elsewhere for them to be acted upon.

Strategy for implementing the committee's recommendations for colleges

12.39 It is commonly accepted that change is necessary in three areas for educational organisations to effect systematic improvement. These areas are the curriculum, organisation and management, and staff development. Change is likely to be most effectively introduced and managed where it is reinforced and supported by development in each area. The committee has gone some way to accepting this analysis by giving attention to each area in its recommendations for a quality initiative.

12.40 The committee wishes to see a co-ordinated strategy for implementing its recommendations for colleges. This will bring together three elements: teacher education, staff development and a pump-priming fund for colleges. We begin by considering teacher education and staff development.

Teacher education and staff development

12.41 The evidence we received indicated that the quality of provision for students with learning difficulties and/or disabilities is good, and its extent may be considerable, when:

- senior managers are well informed about the provision and are involved in its implementation
- staff have received good-quality training and have participated in relevant staff development activities.

The evidence also indicated that:

- the changes the committee wishes to see can only be brought about if staff in colleges are well trained and properly skilled in meeting the needs of students with learning difficulties and/or disabilities
- many staff are not trained and much training has been poor with features that the committee does not wish to see perpetuated; for example:
  - –lack of co-ordination
  - –lack of accreditation and progression routes to higher levels of training
  - –a negative focus on disability rather than on the implications of some disabilities and learning difficulties for an individual's learning
  - –varying quality
  - –insufficient focus on the changing roles and responsibilities of teachers, managers and governors
  - –little involvement of senior managers
  - –little or no relation to the college's strategic plan or other staff development activities.

12.42 The way in which staff in colleges think about their work with students with learning difficulties and/or disabilities has changed in the last three or four years. The *Further and Higher Education Act 1992*, the priority given to these students by the Council, and the committee's own activities have contributed to a raised awareness in colleges both of the nature and importance of good-quality provision and the developmental and training needs of staff at all levels. Changing social attitudes as represented, for example, in the *Disability Act 1995,* and the increased expectations of people with disabilities and/or learning difficulties play an important part in our understanding of how the priorities for training are changing.

Knowledge, skills and understanding required by staff

12.43 The committee has identified some of the broad areas of knowledge, skills and understanding required by college staff if its vision of an inclusive further education sector is to be realised. These include:

For managers:

About the legal framework:

- understanding what colleges are required to do in law, including their duties under the *Further and Higher Education Act 1992* and the *Disability Act 1995*
- understanding the Council's legal duties toward students with learning difficulties and/or disabilities and what the Council requires colleges to do in respect of them
- awareness of broader debate on learning difficulties and/or disabilities within the context of equal opportunities.

About funding and strategic planning in relation to provision for students with learning difficulties and/or disabilities:

- understanding the Council's funding methodology as it applies to these students, and other sources of funding, including joint funding
- understanding the importance of developing a systematic planned approach to provision for these students
- skills in seeking and making use of information about the local community and its needs, other providers, local employment markets, etc.

About quality:

- understanding the implications of the committee's ideas about inclusive learning for their college
- skills in developing and applying performance indicators to this area of work
- leadership skills in developing and extending opportunities for participation, progression and achievement
- knowledge and skills to develop and implement policy and practice on learning support
- awareness of the importance of physical access and the physical environment and how these affect the participation and achievement of students.

For teachers and co-ordinators:

About learning:

- knowledge and understanding of various disabilities and learning difficulties and how these may affect the ways students learn
- recognising and understanding individual approaches to learning
- skills in matching these with the right teaching methods for individual students
- skills in devising learning environments that match the students' requirements
- skills in diagnostic assessment
- skills in assisting students to identify their learning goals
- skills in identifying, assessing and recording progress
- skills in developing and implementing individual learning programmes
- skills in developing learning materials which suit a range of abilities
- skills in assisting students to take responsibility for their own learning.

About support:

- knowledge, understanding and skills in managing and providing learning support
- knowledge of funding methodology and skills in managing resources
- skills in the use of information technology as a support for learning
- knowledge of specialist equipment and its uses to support learning
- knowledge and understanding of the general scope of courses in the sector
- staff development skills.

About management and collaboration:

- management skills
- skills in liaison and collaboration with others

- knowledge and understanding of the structures, systems and priorities of other services and education and training providers
- knowledge of the local community's educational and training needs
- knowledge and awareness of how issues concerning people with learning difficulties and/or disabilities are part of broader equal opportunities issues.

These areas of knowledge, skills and understanding would form the basis of a curriculum for training.

SUMMARY OF MAIN FINDINGS

12.44 When we compared what we found with the principles set out above, we concluded that the main weakness is in the lack of a co-ordinated and centrally-measured strategy to improve the quality of teaching and learning in colleges, supported by the Council.

ADDRESSING WEAKNESSES AND BUILDING ON STRENGTHS

Teacher education and staff development to support the committee's recommendations

12.45 In keeping with its views on inclusive learning, the committee wishes all teacher education and staff development to include information and guidance on students with learning difficulties and/or disabilities. In addition, it wishes training to be:

- inclusive, in that issues concerning students with learning difficulties and/or disabilities are integrated into all teacher education and staff development
- placed within the context of equal opportunities issues
- concerned with the way disability or learning difficulties may affect how students learn
- concerned with the match that the teacher should aim to achieve between a student's learning style, learning goals and learning environment
- influenced by current thinking and developments on learning support
- concerned with the roles of governors and senior managers in ensuring that provision for students with learning difficulties and/or disabilities is properly co-ordinated across the college.

Furthermore, the committee wishes such training to be:

- designed to enable progression to higher levels of training
- accredited by a nationally-recognised awarding body or count toward accreditation.

Contributing to the sector's priorities

12.46 The committee believes its recommendations have fundamental implications for colleges. In particular, our emphasis will encourage colleges to:

- improve teachers' skills in recognising and meeting a wide variety of individual learning styles and requirements
- help students to work more independently
- improve the quality of learning support for all students
- improve teachers' skills in assessing and recording students' progress and performance.

An advisory body for accredited training concerning students with learning difficulties and/or disabilities

12.47 The varying quality and fragmentation of existing training is sufficient justification, in our view, for the establishment, for a fixed period of time, of a central advisory and co-ordinating body for accredited teacher education concerning students with learning difficulties and/or disabilities. The body's main aims would be to ensure the committee's recommendations on training are met and to advise on specialist training. It might have similar functions for further education as the Special Educational Needs Training Consortium for schools, established in 1994 under the auspices of the Council for Disabled Children. The consortium monitors and develops professional development opportunities for teachers of pupils with special educational needs.

12.48 Such an advisory body would need to establish early links with the Further Education Staff Development Forum, but it is vital that the impetus of this report is not lost as the Forum gets to grips with its challenging task. Links must also be made with the Teacher Training Agency in order to ensure some continuity between training in the school and further education sectors.

Programme of staff development

12.49 There was considerable evidence from colleges, the inspectorate and others that a centrally co-ordinated programme of staff development would be required to assist colleges to implement the committee's recommendations. It will be important to involve the full range of interested groups, including colleges, universities, institutes of higher education, voluntary organisations, professional and college associations and others. A consortium of colleges, providers and others could be established, perhaps co-ordinated and managed by FEDA. Training should be accredited or contribute to accreditation.

12.50 Some preliminary work and costings on the programme have been undertaken. The first stages would include creating a framework, a needs analysis with colleges, further work on the knowledge, skills and understanding required by staff at different levels, devising a training curriculum, the production of high-quality training materials and making arrangements for accreditation. Estimates suggest it will cost £5 million over three years to train some 4,500 staff.

Funds to encourage colleges to adopt the committee's recommendations

12.51 It is important that the Council give clear signals to colleges of its support for the committee's recommendations. It can best do this in the adjustments it makes to its funding, inspection, strategic planning and data collection activities. In addition, funds for this purpose were seen as essential by colleges in the testing exercise. The funds would be used to support the staff development programme. They would be managed by FEDA on behalf of the consortium described in paragraph 12.49. The committee has undertaken preliminary work on this element of the initiative. Initial stages are likely to include devising objectives which reflect the committee's recommendations, agreeing action plans with colleges, and making arrangements for monitoring their implementation. It is estimated that all this will cost £3 million over three years.

12.52 Total estimated costs for the quality initiative are £8 million over three years.

RECOMMENDATIONS

12.53 The committee makes the following recommendations to the Council. It should:

- work with the Department for Education and Employment, the Teacher Training Agency, the Further Education Staff Development Forum, universities, institutes of higher education, awarding bodies, college and professional associations and others to establish a central co-ordinating and advisory body for accredited teacher education concerning students with learning difficulties and/or disabilities
- provide funds for a centrally co-ordinated programme of staff

development to be provided over three years, supported by a consortium of interested bodies but centrally managed. The programme would have objectives that are linked directly to the committee's recommendations on learning and learning environments, assessment, collaboration, support for learning, organisation and management

- make available funds for a period of three years in order to assist colleges to implement the committee's recommendations.

12

References

1. SCPR *Student Voices: The Views of Further Education Students with Learning Difficulties and/or Disabilities: Findings From a Series of Student Workshops Commissioned by the Learning Difficulties and/or Disabilities Committee,* London, Skill: National Bureau for Students with Disabilities, 1996

2. Evidence from the FEFC inspectorate, (unpublished)

3. Responses to the call for evidence, (unpublished)

4. Responses to the call for evidence from ALBSU and presentation of evidence by the Special Education Training Needs Consortium, 26 January 1996

5. Responses to the testing exercise, (unpublished)

6. HMI *'Students with Special Needs in Further Education', Education Observed 9,* London, DES, 1989; HMI *'Special Needs Issues' Education Observed,* London, HMSO/DES, 1990; HMI *Access to Secondary and Further Education for those with Learning Difficulties and/or Disabilities*, London, DES 1992

7. *Learning Difficulties and Disabilities: A Report of a Survey of Post-16 Provision Carried out During 1992;* London, NATFHE, 1993; Report on a conference held in 1993, the University and College Lecturers' Union NATFHE, 1993

8. *Ibid.*

9. Michael Young, Norman Lucas, Graham Sharp, Brian Cunningham *Teacher Education for the Further Education Sector: Training the Lecturer of the Future*, London, Institute of Education, London University, 1995

10. *Ibid.*

11. *Ibid.*

12. Staff Individualised Record, November 1994

13. *Ibid.*

14. Special Educational Needs Training Consortium and Skill Further and Higher Education Monitoring Group

15. D.V. Stafford *A Special Professionalism: Report of the Further Education Special Needs Teacher Training Working Groups*, London, HMSO, 1987

16. Special Educational Needs Training Consortium and Skill Further and Higher Education Monitoring Group

ANNEXES

Annex A: The Council's Duties Under the Further and Higher Education Act 1992

The Further Education Funding Council (the Council) was set up under the *Further and Higher Education Act 1992* (the Act) to ensure that there are sufficient and adequate further education facilities throughout England. It does so mainly by allocating funds to further education colleges and sixth form colleges which make up the English further education sector. It also funds universities and external institutions outside the sector which provide further education. It also funds places for individual students with learning difficulties and/or disabilities at specialist colleges outside the sector where a sector college cannot meet their educational requirements. The range and type of institutions and courses which the Council may fund are limited to those specified in the Act.

The Council's principal legal duties under the *Further and Higher Education Act 1992* are:

- to secure the provision of sufficient full-time further education facilities suitable to the requirements of 16 to 18 year olds
- to secure adequate further education facilities for all other students, including part-time facilities for 16 to 18 year olds, for courses which fall within the scope of schedule 2 to the Act
- to have regard to the requirements of students with learning difficulties and/or disabilities
- to make the most effective use of resources and, in particular, to avoid disproportionate expenditure
- to ensure that the quality of further education is assessed.

The Council's duties extend only to England.

Annex B: Terms of Reference and Membership of the Committee

THE COMMITTEE'S TERMS OF REFERENCE

Having regard to the Council's responsibilities towards students with learning difficulties and/or disabilities, to review the range and type of further education provision available, and to make recommendations as to how, within the resources likely to be available to it, the Further Education Funding Council can, by working with colleges and others, best fulfil its responsibilities towards these students under the Further and Higher Education Act 1992.

B

MEMBERSHIP OF THE COMMITTEE

Chair:

Professor John Tomlinson CBE, Director, Institute of Education, University of Warwick

Members:

Toni Beck	Head of the School of Learning Support, Oaklands College
Deborah Cooper	Director, Skill: National Bureau for Students with Disabilities
Gwynneth Flower	Chief Executive, CENTEC (from March 1995)
Mike Hanson	Former Chief Executive, South Thames TEC (until September 1994)
David Kendall	Principal, Derwen College
Lynn Lee	Principal, St Vincent College, Gosport
Peter Moseley	Principal, Hull College
Margaret Murdin	Principal, Wigan and Leigh College
Jill Murkin	Training Manager, Marks and Spencer (until July 1994)
Peter Raine	Former Executive Director of Social Services, London Borough of Brent
Jo Stephens	Chief Education Officer, Oxfordshire County Council
Sharon Welch	Former Director of Public Affairs, an international children's charity
Mike Young	Personnel Manager, Organisational Effectiveness, Personal Communications Division, British Telecom (from March 1996)

Assessors:

Eddie Brittain	Further, Higher and Youth Training Directorate, Department for Education and Employment
David Tansley	Training, Enterprise and Education Directorate, Department for Education and Employment (until December 1995)
Eric Galvin	Department for Education and Employment (alternate representative)

Observer:

Richard Hart	Further Education Funding Council for Wales

FEFC staff team:

Elizabeth Maddison	Education programmes division and secretary to the committee
Pat Hood	Adviser to the committee
Peter Lavender	Adviser to the committee
Merillie Vaughan Huxley	Inspectorate
Lisa Young	Clerk and administrator to the committee
Beverley Mulvey	Administrative assistant

Annex C: International Visits

The committee wanted to be able to learn from aspects of further education in other countries. Accordingly, committee members made visits to Scotland, the United States of America and Canada.

Objectives for the visits

Each visit had the same broad objectives. These were:

a. to identify aspects of arrangements for students with learning difficulties and/or disabilities in further education in these countries which differ from those in England, focusing on 10 areas:

   i. values and beliefs

   ii. legislation

   iii. policy

   iv. funding arrangements

   v. qualifications framework

   vi. research and development

   vii. teacher training

   viii. quality assurance

   ix college practice

   x. arrangements for collaboration at national, regional and local levels;

b. to identify aspects of these arrangements which are considered to work well and which the committee might wish to use as a contribution to its thinking for use in England;

c. to report back to the committee on the outcomes of each visit.

Scotland, 20–24 November 1995

The visit aimed to produce an informed impression of what worked well in the Scottish system and which factors contributed to success for students. Visits and meetings included: staff at the Scottish Office with responsibility for developing and implementing national policy on funding, inspection and the national qualifications framework; key figures in academic research, research and development and teacher training; visits to two colleges to meet specialist staff, senior managers and finance officers; informal discussions about higher education and the role of the Scottish Higher Education Funding Council.

Main findings of the visit included:

a. the development of provision for students with learning difficulties and/or disabilities appears to take place within an 'inclusive intellectual democracy', where the educational process is valued and where all learners are entitled to have their achievements recognised within a national framework;

b. the management of change appears to be based on a thorough diagnosis of need, both of society and of the individual; time is spent reaching a consensus of opinion on what is wrong and how it can be put right; the views of practitioners are crucial at each stage of policy development and implementation;

C

c. implementation appears to be carefully co-ordinated and managed centrally by a single government authority; the sector's views on how and when it can best adopt a new initiative are taken seriously. This unified approach appears to contribute to the development of partnerships between further education and health and social services at local level;

d. the education profession would appear to be held in relatively high esteem and trusted to get things right; teaching and learning is considered by HMI to be generally good. The system is perceived to be less obviously regulatory with, for example, a 'broader brush' funding methodology equivalent to additional support, an inspection framework which emphasises the developmental aspects of inspection and, as yet, no published inspection reports; at present there is no explicit link between funding allocations and the assessment of the quality of a college's provision;

e. for funding purposes, no distinction is made between learning which leads to qualifications or progression to other programmes of study, and other kinds of learning; there is no equivalent to the requirements of schedule 2 in England. The Scottish Funding Unit allocates funds according to the volume of a college's work, not by type of programme;

f. an inclusive national system of qualifications is being developed, which will enable the achievements of all learners to be recognised within the same broad framework;

g. the development and implementation of policy for students with learning difficulties and/or disabilities is closely supported by research and development work which contributes to a theoretical foundation for policy and provides practical assistance to practitioners;

h. there is no tradition of independent specialist colleges in Scotland; the concept of an extended curriculum does not appear to be widely recognised;

i. there appears to be less emphasis than in England on the achievement of accreditation as the main outcome of learning, and more interest in how a student's experience of further education translates into benefits in later life. However, there was little current evidence about students with learning difficulties and/or disabilities once they left college.

Canada, 20–29 March 1996

The visit had two aims. First, to examine the extent to which the Canadian system matched what students required. Second, to see to what extent colleges meet a wide variety of individual requirements as part of their everyday activities. Visits were made to three community colleges in two provinces (Humber College, Toronto; George Brown College, Toronto; Camosun College, Victoria), Burnaby Skills Centre and Burnaby Open Learning Agency. Meetings were held with representatives of Canada's National Institute for the study of Public Policy Affecting Persons with Intellectual Impairment and Other Disabilities (Roeher Institute) and with the Human Resources Development Ministry, Hull.

Main findings of the visit included:

a. education in Canada is the responsibility of the 12 individual provinces, each of which has separate legislative arrangements. There is little national education legislation;

b. the national and provincial governments promote a policy of equality and inclusiveness for people with a 'mental or physical disability'. In practice, this work concentrates on accommodating those with physical disabilities. There appears to be an absence of provision for people with learning difficulties. Colleges do not consider it their job to offer support to such learners;

c. entry to college is based upon a strict academic standard. As most courses are over-subscribed, there is no pressure to change these requirements. It is argued that lowering academic goals for some students would debase college standards;

d. students with learning difficulties and/or disabilities can stay in high school until age 21. High school courses tend not to be filled. Students are accepted only if tutors consider they can move on to employment;

e. colleges are allocated funding for changes to the learning environment, much of which is used for staffing and staff development.

United States of America, 10–16 April 1996

The visit aimed to identify the impact on post-compulsory education of anti-discrimination legislation; to examine the extent to which the system in the USA matches what is required by students and how colleges meet a variety of individual requirements.

The visit included meetings with officials at the Department for Education; the Department of Labor; the American Association of Community Colleges; Rockville and Montgomery Community Colleges; and the Chimes sheltered workshop and training programme.

Main findings of the visit included:

a. individual states are responsible for their own education systems;

b. there seems to be a contrast between education law for schools, which gives access to education for all, and the legislative framework for colleges, which requires colleges to make 'reasonable accommodations' in response to requests from students. This legislative framework appears to place responsibility on students to articulate the 'accommodations' they need. The emphasis appears to be on facilitating access to an existing curriculum often through the support of a college programme outside the classroom. There was no evidence during the visit of significant activity aimed at changing classroom practice or the range of courses available;

c. colleges are concerned with providing 'reasonable accommodation' and support but do not readily go beyond this;

d. people with severe or profound and multiple learning difficulties do not appear to attend community colleges;

e. there is no inspection system and no tradition of inspection;

f. there do not appear to be ready links between the staff working with students with learning difficulties and/or disabilities and general teaching staff, for example, in order to develop classroom practice.

Annex D: Testing the Committee's Thinking about Inclusive Learning with Colleges

Introduction

1 The committee tested its thinking about inclusive learning in a number of ways:

- seminars for representatives of the disability movement, parents and others
- presentations and workshops at national and regional events run by other organisations[1]
- discussion and debate with Council staff
- visits to colleges[2]
- testing exercise with 20 colleges.

2 This annex describes the exercise with colleges and the appendix includes the 'audit instrument used'.

Testing the thinking with colleges

3 The committee tested the thinking with 20 colleges in June 1995. An audit instrument[3] was devised that enabled colleges to assess the extent to which they were already able to offer inclusive learning. The instrument asked how far a college could recruit and meet the requirements of a wide variety of learners. The exercise concentrated on learners with disabilities and/or learning difficulties but colleges were also asked about the possible benefits of the committee's thinking for other students.

4 Each college was asked to scrutinise its mission, strategic and operational plans, policies, structures and practices against three criteria for assessing the extent to which learning is inclusive. These were:

- the extent to which the college is proactive in recruiting a wide variety of learners
- how far teaching and learning promotes and supports inclusiveness
- the extent to which individual learning environments are provided which promote and support inclusiveness.

5 Colleges were invited to identify:

- the extent to which they considered themselves to be inclusive already
- the internal changes that would be required if they were to adopt the committee's thinking and some approximate costings anticipated by these colleges
- what the Council might do to promote the successful adoption of the committee's thinking
- the extent to which its adoption would benefit students with learning difficulties and/or disabilities
- the mechanisms which might be used to monitor the participation of such students and to safeguard resources.

D

Outcomes

6 Eighteen out of 20 colleges warmly welcomed the focus on inclusive learning and wished to see its adoption supported by the Council. Two colleges expressed reservations about whether current attitudes amongst managers and staff would make it possible for inclusive learning to be adopted. The most supportive colleges reported that everything in their internal and external environments was supporting a greater focus on individual learners. They considered that an individual approach was the key for all students. All the colleges considered that inclusive learning, if properly implemented and supported, would benefit students with learning difficulties and/or disabilities. However, it was vital that resources for students with learning difficulties and/or disabilities were not diluted. Mechanisms for monitoring levels of participation and the quality of the student's learning experience would need to be strengthened. Otherwise, the temptation would be to assume that all was well just because colleges were thinking about their provision in a different way. Funding arrangements for additional support were seen by all the colleges to be a powerful tool to promote inclusive learning. It was important that these arrangements were understood and used to their full potential.

7 All the colleges, and other groups with which the committee discussed its thinking, emphasised the importance of staff training and the understanding and attitudes of senior managers.

8 Colleges raised other issues which have helped to inform the committee's recommendations, including:

a. *recruiting a wide variety of learners*

Some colleges do not see it as their mission to recruit a wide variety of learners. They told the committee that they aim to recruit students who could benefit from a carefully-defined curriculum offer;

b. *a strategic approach to change*

The committee's thinking about inclusive learning could only be adopted over a period of time. It would require a strategic approach from colleges. However, regardless of their present stage of development, colleges provided detailed analyses of how they could move forward. Some colleges considered that they were already well on the way to providing inclusive learning. This was where the philosophy and practice had been enthusiastically espoused at all levels of the college, including governors, senior managers, teachers, finance and accommodation officers and other non-teaching staff;

c. *importance of senior managers*

The colleges reported that learning and participation could only be inclusive where senior managers are committed and fully involved. These staff would be crucial to the success of the approach;

d. *the skills and attitudes of teachers*

Colleges reported that the skills, experience and confidence of their teaching and other staff would be key resources for a college which wishes to promote inclusive learning. Teachers need to have an understanding of models of learning, the skills to observe and assess learners and to draw conclusions about their preferred methods of learning; and the skills and experience to help learners identify relevant learning goals. Teachers would need increased management and co-ordination skills to draw together elements of a learning environment and to evaluate the extent to which it matches a learner's requirements. A focus on inclusive learning would require teachers to respond to individual requirements with a variety of teaching strategies and materials. There are implications

D

for other college staff. They will need to develop new skills, for example, in conducting and making use of the outcomes of local needs analysis, in targeting marketing materials, in costing learning support and other elements of a learning environment and in devising accessible information. Staff attitudes will be crucial. Teachers and other staff will need help to understand how a focus on inclusive learning contributes to their general professional effectiveness. The focus is not relevant simply to their relationships with students with learning difficulties and/or disabilities. Colleges told us that effective staff training would be needed to dispel anxiety, raise confidence and challenge unhelpful assumptions about students with learning difficulties and/or disabilities;

e. *resource-based learning*

Some colleges misunderstood the focus of inclusive learning, believing it to be concerned primarily with resource-based or workshop learning. Colleges will need more help to understand that, whilst workshop learning might be one component of a student's individual learning environment, nearly all students want and need to learn in groups for at least part of the time. An individualised approach to learning does not mean that learners necessarily learn on their own. However, it does mean that even when they work in groups, students will be working in ways and on tasks that match their individual learning styles and learning goals;

f. *'pump-priming' funds*

Colleges emphasised that the Council should take a lead in indicating the value it places on inclusive learning by allocating funds for a pump-priming initiative. However, colleges did not want the Council to underwrite all of the development work that would be required, recognising that any development monies would be held back from the general funds allocated to the sector;

g. *a quality initiative*

The colleges indicated that a centrally co-ordinated and managed initiative would be required to tackle some of the complex issues raised in their responses. A national quality initiative, co-ordinated and supported centrally but involving colleges and other interested bodies directly in its design and delivery would be essential.

References

1 Presentation by chairman to the Skill John Baillie Memorial Conference, Forte Crest Hotel, 29 November 1994; Presentation by chairman and members to the North West Post-16 Regional Network Conference, Manchester Conference Centre (UMIST), 24 May 1995

2 Series of visits to colleges as part of committee's testing exercise (see annex F)

3 Audit instrument for testing exercise (see the appendix to this annex)

Appendix to Annex D: Testing the Committee's Approach to Inclusiveness

AUDIT INSTRUMENT FOR COLLEGES: EDITED VERSION

CONTENTS

Section E: How inclusive is your college now? *Page 15*

Question 14: based on your responses to the questionnaire, what would be an estimate of the extent of your college's inclusiveness now?

Question 15: how inclusive could you be within a year?

Question 16: how relevant to your college's present and future plans is the committee's approach to inclusiveness?

Question 17: in your view, what incentives or mechanisms might encourage colleges to adopt the committee's approach if it were finally recommended to the Council?

Question 18: are there any initiatives in your college which the committee might find it helpful to know about?

GUIDE TO USING THE AUDIT INSTRUMENT

Introduction

1 The Council's learning difficulties and/or disabilities committee wishes to test its emerging approach to inclusiveness with a small representative group of colleges. The testing exercise seeks to find out how much and in which ways colleges would need to change if its approach were adopted by the Council. The committee also wishes to know what some of the implications of its approach might be for the Council and for colleges.

The Committee's Approach to Inclusiveness

2 You will receive a briefing on the committee's emerging approach to inclusiveness at the May seminar. The field workers will be able to provide further information. The main elements of the emerging approach are set out here very briefly. They should be used as fundamental guide when your college assesses its own inclusiveness through the use of the audit instrument.

3 By inclusiveness, the committee means a movement away from labelling or defining individuals as having a deficit or as requiring something additional to access and participate in further education towards defining a further education service that is in itself inclusive. By using the approach, colleges would meet the requirements of a wide variety of learners as part of their every day activities.

4 The committee has developed three criteria for assessing inclusiveness. These are:

- the college is proactive in recruiting a wide variety of learners
- teaching and learning promote and support inclusiveness

- individual learning environments are provided which promote and support inclusiveness.

5 The committee considers that inclusiveness can be brought about by concentrating on four main elements: individual approaches to learning, learning goals, learning environments and the match or fit between each of these elements, through which progression and achievement take place. The approach requires that:

- each learner has an individual approach to learning, regardless of disability or learning difficulty and this should be identified and built on
- each learner should have their individual learning goals identified; these may be short, medium or long term
- each learner should be provided with an individual learning environment
- each learner should be provided with a match or fit between each of these three elements.

6 The committee considers that a learning environment consists of the following components:

- individual learning programme
- a curriculum which supports progress in learning
- entry and exit procedures
- opportunities to negotiate and manage own learning
- procedures for assessing, recording and accrediting achievement
- effective teaching
- trained staff
- learning materials/resources
- technology
- guidance and counselling
- learning support services, including external services
- learner support services
- the physical environment.

7 The audit instrument takes the three criteria for inclusiveness described in paragraph 4 and examines their most important factors through a series of questions.

8 The committee recognises that, whilst its approach must concentrate on students with disabilities and/or learning difficulties, it may be relevant to other students. The instrument therefore invites you to indicate your views on whether the approach might benefit other students in a commentary or in notes on particular sections.

The Exercise

9 This exercise invites your college to 'audit' its own degree of inclusiveness, using the criteria developed by the committee. You are then asked to analyse the outcomes and decide what changes could be brought about to make your college more inclusive. Once you have prioritised these in an action plan you are then asked to estimate what the costs of the plan might be and what staff training and development it would involve. You are also asked to give your college's views on possible implications for the Council's activities in order to help the committee form its recommendations. In summary, the testing exercise has seven steps:

- *audit* – how inclusive is your college now?
- *analyse* – what changes could your college make to become more inclusive?
- *prioritise* – what would you do short/medium/long term?
- *action plan* – using the outcomes of the questionnaire to draw up an action plan for your college
- *cost the plan* – what are the resource implications?
- *identify the plan's implications* – under the headings given in the instrument
- *report* – to the field workers.

10 This is not a developmental project. You are not asked to implement your plan, though your college may wish to do so once the activity for the committee has finished. It is hoped that the exercise itself will be of benefit to the college and fit well with its developmental and strategic planning processes.

The Audit Instrument

11 The audit instrument has been developed after discussions with a small group of colleges. It involves an assessment by the college itself: it is not an external evaluation.

12 Section E of the instrument invites your college to give an overall assessment of its present stage of inclusiveness, against its current aspirations.

Management of the Exercise

13 Your college will be assisted by two field workers commissioned by the Council on behalf of the committee to undertake this work. The two workers, Sally Faraday and Stella Dixon will be supervised by Pat Hood, adviser to the committee, who will report to the reference group.

Briefing Seminar

14 Your college should identify one person to co-ordinate the exercise and who should act as named contact for the field workers. You may also wish to set up a small working party or reference group of key people to help co-ordinate the work. The named person should be responsible for the completion of the college's report.

15 There will be an initial briefing seminar for the 20 participating colleges on 15 May. The committee's emerging approach to inclusiveness will be more fully explained at the seminar. Colleges attending the seminar will also receive a progress report on the committee's work.

Schedule

16 The exercise has a tight time schedule designed to allow the committee to make full use of its findings when it considers the contents of its final report in July 1995. Given the time available, you may choose to audit all or part of your provision, for example, a single campus or two faculties.

The schedule is as follows:

15 May 1995	• briefing seminar for colleges
	• schedule of visits by field workers arranged with colleges
	• first meeting of reference group
	• work under way in colleges
	• audits completed
By 19 June	• college reports completed
	• college reports analysed at second meeting of reference group
By 10 July 1995	• final report to committee.

The main period of activity for colleges will be from mid-May to late June.

Outcomes

17 The college's report should be completed by 19 June 1995. It should consist of the completed instrument plus any additional commentary your college may wish to make. The college's report will be treated confidentially and will be used only by the committee. The committee particularly welcomes your views on what incentives might encourage colleges to adopt the committee's approach to learning and learning environments.

18 The committee wishes to produce final recommendations for the Council that will enable all colleges to become more inclusive. It needs to know if the approach represented in the audit instrument will improve provision for students and can be developed across the sector. The committee recognises that colleges are at different stages in their development and this means that its recommendations must be realistic. It hopes to use colleges' reports to decide whether its criteria for inclusiveness are the right ones or whether they require amendment or additions. The committee will also use the reports to answer six questions:

- is its approach likely to be feasible in the majority of colleges?
- does it benefit students with disabilities and/or learning difficulties?
- can these students still be adequately protected?
- what are the implications for the Council and colleges of its approach?
- what are the implications for staff training and development?
- what are the likely costs in a range of colleges?

19 The committee is particularly interested in initiatives that have already been successful in developing a more inclusive approach in a college. You may wish to provide brief details of any initiatives in your college in section E of the instrument.

20 The committee would like to thank you and your college for supporting its work by taking part in the exercise.

COMPLETING THE AUDIT

D

Colleges taking part in the exercise were asked to complete the numbered questions 1 to 18, given on pages 5 to 15. Of these, questions 1 to 9 asked the college to identify changes it might make to help it become more inclusive. For each change it identified, the college was then asked to apply the following questions:

What might prevent you making these changes?

a. *internal* – in order of importance;

b. *external* – in order of importance.

What might support these changes?

a. *internal* – in order of importance;

b. *external* – in order of importance.

Please give an outline of the main implications for staff development and training of the changes you have identified. Please include support staff in your considerations.

What would be the priorities for staff development and training?

Please give an outline of the main implications for the management and organisation of the college of the changes you have identified.

What would be the approximate costs to the college of such changes?

Please give an outline of the main implications for the Council's activities of such changes:

a. the funding methodology;

b. inspection framework;

c. strategic planning framework;

d. data collection;

e. other.

D

SECTION A: THE COLLEGE IS PROACTIVE IN RECRUITING A WIDE VARIETY OF LEARNERS

QUESTION 1

Does the college actively seek to recruit traditionally under-represented groups or learners for whom provision might be considered 'difficult' or 'expensive'?

		YES	NO
a.	college mission and policy	❑	❑
b.	college policy and strategies in operational plan	❑	❑
c.	in some faculties/ departments/schools/ sections	❑	❑
d.	in some programmes	❑	❑
e.	college does not seek to accommodate all learners	❑	❑

Sources of evidence might include:

- college mission addresses the issue
- college has undertaken profile of its student population and compared it with profile of local community, identified gaps in its provision and taken steps to remedy them
- college strategic and operational plans identify strategies for recruiting certain groups of learners
- faculties/departments/schools/sections have recruitment targets for certain groups of learners
- resources are identified for outreach/flexible recruitment
- link/in-fill arrangements for certain learners
- planning meetings and collaboration with other local providers and services
- marketing/publicity material is accessible to people with learning difficulties or disabilities and is available in appropriate locations
- college prospectus welcomes people with disabilities/learning difficulties by providing details of provision, core entitlement and other possible support arrangements; photographs show a wide variety of learners
- information is easily available about the possible progression routes students might follow.

Please indicate what changes the college could make to become more effective in recruiting certain learners

a. short term (within three months);

b. medium term (within six months);

c. long term (a year or more);

d. what would be the priority?

(*please also answer the questions on page 4 in relation to this question*)

QUESTION 2

Does the college train and support staff in meeting the requirements of a wide variety of learners?

		YES	NO
a.	college policy on staff development	❑	❑
b.	policy and strategies for implementation on staff development for all teachers and non-teaching staff, including senior managers	❑	❑
c.	in some faculties/ departments/schools/ sections	❑	❑
d.	in some programmes	❑	❑
e.	certain teachers only	❑	❑

Sources of evidence might include:

- college policy and programme of implementation on staff development that prioritises teaching and learning strategies
- links between staff appraisal/review and individual staff development

- arrangements for co-teaching/paired teaching/mentoring
- regular training sessions/advice sessions/'clinics' offered by specialist staff
- sufficient time/resources allocated to cross-college co-ordinator's function
- use of external specialists to deliver staff training
- joint training with health/social services/schools
- training/awareness sessions provided by people with learning difficulties or disabilities
- appropriate involvement of parents through clubs/support sessions/OU courses
- training targeted at non-teaching staff
- joint training for teachers and non-teaching staff
- use of specialist team to design and deliver training
- senior managers participate in training.

Please indicate what changes the college could make to train and support its staff more effectively to meet the requirements of a wider variety of learners

a. short term (within three months);

b. medium term (within six months);

c. long term (a year or more);

d. what would be the priority?

(*please also answer the questions on page 4 in relation to this question*)

D

SECTION B: TEACHING AND LEARNING PROMOTE AND SUPPORT INCLUSIVENESS

QUESTION 3

Are students' individual learning styles and approaches identified?

		YES	NO
a.	college policy	❑	❑
b.	policy and implementation strategies across college by all teachers	❑	❑
c.	in some faculties/ departments/schools/ sections	❑	❑
d.	in some programmes	❑	❑
e.	in some subject areas	❑	❑
f.	by some teachers	❑	❑

Sources of evidence might include:

- whole college policy on learning
- policy and practice on initial or diagnostic assessment
- policy and practice on the assessment of prior learning
- policy and practice on gathering information on previous education and training
- policy and practice with students that enable them to give their views on how they learn best
- policy and practice on induction and assessment that enables students to test out different ways of learning
- training for staff in identifying different styles of learning.

Please indicate what changes the college could make to become more effective in identifying individual learning styles and approaches

a. short term (within three months);

b. medium term (within six months);

c. long term (a year or more);

d. what would be the priority?

(*please also answer the questions on page 4 in relation to this question*)

D

QUESTION 4

Are students' individual learning goals identified, regularly assessed, reviewed and recorded?

		YES	NO
a.	college policy	❑	❑
b.	policy and implementation across the college in all subjects in all programmes	❑	❑
c.	in some faculties/schools/ departments/sections	❑	❑
d.	in some programmes	❑	❑
e.	in some subject areas	❑	❑
f.	by some teachers	❑	❑

Sources of evidence might include:

- whole college policy on learning
- student learning contracts
- policy and practice on review and assessment
- policy and practice on use of tutorial time
- policy and practice on regular record-keeping
- policy and practice on student self-assessment
- policy and practice on student negotiation of learning
- policy and practice on analysing what students need to learn in order to progress to another course or to join a first course
- policy and practice in analysing the conceptual and practical requirements of a programme of learning and in turning these into individual learning goals for students
- college information system systematically produces relevant data which is used to monitor and improve.

Please indicate what changes the college could make to become more effective in identifying, assessing, reviewing and recording individual learning goals

a. short term (within three months);

b. medium term (within six months);

c. long term (a year or more);

d. what would be the priority?

(*please also answer the questions on page 4 in relation to this question*)

QUESTION 5

Do teachers match the individual learning styles of a wide variety of students in their use of teaching strategies, materials, aids, technology, groupings of students, pace and variety of approach?

		YES	NO
a.	college policy	❑	❑
b.	policy and implementation across the college by all or most teachers	❑	❑
c.	in some faculties/ departments/schools /sections	❑	❑
d.	in some programmes	❑	❑
e.	in some subject areas	❑	❑
f.	by some teachers	❑	❑

Sources of evidence might include:

- variety of student activities within a class
- variety of ways of reporting and recording learning
- students negotiating and managing their own learning, easy access to materials, choosing assignments, devising own ways of recording activities
- students working individually, in pairs or groups on different topics geared to their interests and abilities
- opportunities for students to work at own pace

- use of technology as an aid to learning
- students understand how the present activity relates to earlier activities and to the next learning activity
- students understand how their work is to be assessed and what criteria will be used
- teachers ask open-ended, supportive questions, promote dialogue and participation by valuing students' contributions
- teachers' effectiveness is assessed using explicit criteria.

Please indicate what changes the college could make to enable teachers to be more effective in matching the individual learning styles of students

a. short term (within three months);

b. medium term (within six months);

c. long term (a year or more);

d. what would be the priority?

(*please also answer the questions on page 4 in relation to this question*)

SECTION C: INDIVIDUAL LEARNING ENVIRONMENTS ARE PROVIDED WHICH PROMOTE AND SUPPORT INCLUSIVENESS

D

QUESTION 6

Does the college identify the components of an individual learning environment for each student?

		YES	NO
a.	college policy	❑	❑
b.	policy and procedures for implementation across the college for all students	❑	❑
c.	in some faculties/ departments/schools/ sections	❑	❑
d.	in some programmes	❑	❑
e.	for some students	❑	❑

Sources of evidence might include:

- strategic/operational plans address the issues
- individual learning contract that describes each component
- individual learning programme
- individual learning support plan/contract
- individual tutorial contract/plan/agreement
- use of management information systems to record relevant data
- statement for individual student about physical environment in which learning is to take place, for example, provision of loop, ramps, adapted work surfaces, part of main campus
- contract or record of individual arrangements for technological support
- contract or record of individual arrangements for learner support services, for example, creche, counselling

D

- contract/record of individual arrangements for use of library, open-learning workshops, other learning resource areas
- contract/record of individual arrangements for learning and other support from external agencies, for example, social work support, Brailling, psychiatric support, benefits assistance, signer
- contract/record of individual arrangements for assessing progress and achievement
- contract/record of individual arrangements for accreditation, for example, amanuensis, additional time, signer
- use of a variety of forms of accreditation that match the learning goals of individual students.

Please indicate what changes the college could make to become more effective in identifying the components of an individual learning environment for each student

a. short term (within three months);

b. medium term (within six months);

c. long term (a year or more);

d. what would be the priority?

(*please also answer the questions on page 4 in relation to this question*)

QUESTION 7

Does the college guarantee to provide the components of an individual learning environment for students?

		YES	NO
a.	for all students through a policy of entitlement and/or through co-ordinated cross-college services	❑	❑
b.	some components guaranteed and their availability made known to all students on pre-entry and on entry	❑	❑
c.	up to a certain level of cost and variation	❑	❑
d.	each student's requirements identified and costed individually each time	❑	❑
e.	some components guaranteed	❑	❑

Sources of evidence might include:

- policy on entitlement
- strategic and operational plans that includes entitlement
- core entitlement identified, costed and delivered
- core entitlement described in student information material
- co-ordinated cross-college learner and learning support services
- resourcing arrangements.

Please indicate what changes the college could make to guarantee a wider variety and larger number of components of an individual learning environment to a greater number and range of students

a. short term (within three months);

b. medium term (within six months);

c. long term (a year or more);

d. what would be the priority?

(*please also answer the questions on page 4 in relation to this question*)

QUESTION 8

Does the college ensure that learning environments match the individual requirements of students?

		YES	NO
a.	college policy	❑	❑
b.	policy and strategies for implementation across the college for all students	❑	❑
c.	in some faculties/ departments/schools/ sections	❑	❑
d.	in some programmes	❑	❑
e.	for some students	❑	❑

Sources of evidence might include:

- whole college policy on student reviews
- policy and practice on use of tutorial time
- policy and practice on regular assessment
- policy and practice on seeking students' views
- students participating in design of part/all of a learning programme
- regular course/programme reviews
- monitoring of levels of achievement and use of data to decide and implement strategy
- monitoring of levels of retention and use of data to decide and implement strategy
- monitoring of progression from one programme to another and use of data to decide and implement strategy
- monitoring of individual student progress and use of data to decide and implement strategy
- consultation with other relevant agencies, for example, health/social services, voluntary organisations, advocacy/self-advocacy groups
- monitoring of use by programme area of college facilities and learning resource areas.

Please indicate what changes the college could make to become more effective in monitoring the match between the learner's requirements and the learning environment

a. short term (within three months);

b. medium term (within six months);

c. long term (a year or more);

d. what would be the priority?

(*please also answer the questions on page 4 in relation to this question*)

QUESTION 9

Does the college collect, collate, monitor and use information about learner requirements and the way in which it is meeting them?

		YES	NO
a.	by college policy	❑	❑
b.	by college policy and strategies for implementation for all students	❑	❑
c.	in some faculties/ departments/schools/ sections	❑	❑
d.	in some programmes	❑	❑
e.	for some students	❑	❑

Sources of evidence might include:

- use of management information systems to collect and collate data on student requirements and the college's response to them
- use of individual student records to collect and collate data on student requirements and the college's response to them
- use, monitoring and review of records of achievement
- use, monitoring and review of student profiles/personal portfolios
- use, monitoring and review of student contracts
- use, monitoring and review of learning agreements
- use, monitoring and review of tutorial files/records
- monitoring and review of individual learning programmes
- use of data gained by any of the above to systematically improve the college's response to learner requirements
- strategies to seek students' views and systematic use of this information to improve the college's response
- outreach work/links with community and/or other providers used to collect advance information about student requirements

D

- arrangements to make use of students' transition plans to identify and meet student requirements.

Please indicate what changes the college could make to become more effective in collecting, collating, monitoring and using information about learner requirements and the way in which it is meeting them

a. short term (within three months);

b. medium term (within six months);

c. long term (a year or more);

d. what would be the priority?

(*please also answer the questions on page 4 in relation to this question*)

SECTION D: BENEFITS TO STUDENTS WITH LEARNING DIFFICULTIES AND/OR DISABILITIES

This section invites you to give your college's views on some of the implications of the committee's approach for students.

QUESTION 10

How might the access and participation of students with learning difficulties and/or disabilities be monitored if the committee's approach were adopted?

QUESTION 11

How might resources be protected for certain learners?

QUESTION 12

Would the committee's approach benefit students with learning difficulties and/or disabilities?

QUESTION 13

Would the committee's approach benefit students generally?

SECTION E: HOW INCLUSIVE IS YOUR COLLEGE NOW?

This section invites you to comment on your college's degree of inclusiveness.

QUESTION 14

Based on your responses to the questionnaire, what would be an estimate of the extent of your college's inclusiveness now?

On a scale of 1–10

1 = fully inclusive, mission, policy, strategic and operational plans, college seeks, recruits and retains wide variety of learners and meets their individual requirements effectively.

2 = whole college implementation well under way, college able to retain a wide variety of learners and meet their individual requirements.

3 = whole college policy and implementation developed; action plan in place and work under way.

4 = college has undertaken systematic needs analysis, is aware of gaps in its provision, has recognised need for change.

5 = individual schools/faculties/departments identifying need for changes, devising own local needs analysis and strategies.

6 = external pressure for change; college asked to meet needs of wider variety of students (local schools, community, health and social services, TEC, inspection).

7 = some programme areas meet individual requirements of a wide variety of learners.

8 = some programme areas attempting to meet requirements of a variety of learners.

9 = college has policy of meeting requirements of certain groups of learners only.

10= college meets requirements of certain groups of learners only.

QUESTION 15

How inclusive could you be within a year? Please comment.

QUESTION 16

How relevant to your college's present and future plans is the committee's approach to inclusiveness? Please comment.

QUESTION 17

In your view, what incentives or mechanisms might encourage colleges to adopt the committee's approach if it were finally recommended to the Council? Please comment.

QUESTION 18

Are there any initiatives in your college which the committee might find helpful to know about? Please give details.

Annex E: A Brief History of Provision for Students with Learning Difficulties and/or Disabilities

INTRODUCTION

1 This annex is intended to place the committee's analysis of the strengths and weaknesses of existing arrangements and its consequent recommendations in the context of the evolution of thinking about provision of further education for students with learning difficulties and/or disabilities.

Legislation for students with learning difficulties and/or disabilities

2 In 1893 it became compulsory for school authorities to make provision up to the age of 16 in their own or other schools for blind and deaf children.[1] Until then, these children could be given total or partial exemption from school from the age of 11. Allowing deaf and blind children to stay on at school was a significant recognition of the value and purpose of education for disabled young people.

3 The *Education Act 1944* had established the right to remain in education beyond 16, for all those children that were considered 'educable'.[2] The local education authorities were given a duty to decide which children required special educational treatment and hence which did not or 'would not benefit'. Children not thought capable of being educated in schools were to be reported to the local authority for the purposes of the *Mental Deficiency Act 1913*.[3]

4 Some shift in this division of children into the 'educable' and 'non-educable' took place following the *Mental Health Act 1959*.[4] This Act allowed appeals by parents against decisions that their child was incapable of being educated in school.

5 The *Education (Handicapped Children) Act 1970* removed jurisdiction for children with severe learning difficulties ('the mentally deficient') from health authorities and transferred responsibilities to the education service.[5] The staffing and buildings of 'junior training centres' became part of the education service at that point. This meant that some 24,000 children in these centres and special care units, and 8,000 in about 100 hospitals, ceased to be regarded as 'mentally deficient' and became entitled to special education. They were now to be regarded as 'severely educationally sub-normal'.

6 The *Education Act 1976* required local education authorities to arrange for the special education of all 'handicapped' pupils to be given in county and voluntary schools where practicable, or, if not, in special schools, or, with the secretary of state's approval, in independent schools.

7 The *Education Act 1981*[6], following the Warnock Report[7] determined that all children were to be considered to be 'educable'. Those with 'special educational needs' had to have their needs assessed, specified and met within ordinary local schools where practicable, or special schools, or independent schools.

8 The *Children Act 1989* defined 'children' as being up to and including the age of 18.[8] Whilst the Act is not concerned primarily with education, it is relevant in its emphasis on the importance of collaboration and the responsibilities of different agencies including parents. The Act recognised the importance of listening to the views of children and young people themselves.

9 The *National Health Service and Community Care Act 1989*[9] gave local authorities the duty to assess social care needs in relation to adults with a disability who requested it, and a duty to publish community care plans and to collaborate. However, local authorities were not required to assess educational needs, though many have chosen to do so.

10 The *Further and Higher Education Act 1992* placed particular responsibilities for students with learning difficulties and/or disabilities upon the Further Education Funding Council. The Act used definitions of disability similar to those used in the *Education Act 1981*. These definitions concentrate on what individual learners can and cannot do by comparison with others. The letter of guidance from the secretary of state to the Council emphasised that the Council should ensure that adequate arrangements exist for assessing the needs of students with learning difficulties and/or disabilities and identifying appropriate provision within further education. The Council must take account in its distribution of funds to colleges of the additional costs of making provision for such students, including any additional support required to enable individuals to have access to the curriculum.

11 The *Education Act 1993*[10] required the secretary of state to issue a code of practice to offer practical guidance to local education authorities on their responsibilities towards 'children with special educational needs (SEN)'. The earlier terminology was retained. The Act acknowledged the importance of the transition from school by requiring that each young person should have a transition plan which would serve to draw together the different agencies involved with them.

The development of further education opportunities for students with learning difficulties and/or disabilities

12 Provision on any scale in further education for students with disabilities and/or learning difficulties was first made in the later 1970s and early 80s as part of the development of pre-vocational work. Early provision was developed as an *ad hoc* response to the growing expectations and demands of parents, professionals and students who wished to see post-statutory education made available to all young people. The commitment and expertise of individual college staff often determined what provision was made.

13 Students from special schools tended to arrive in college with a 'label' derived from the kind of school they had attended. For example, young people were referred to as 'ESN(S) educationally sub-normal – severe students' or 'ESN(M) educationally sub-normal – moderate students' or 'EBD emotional and behavioural students'. Generally, young people were placed on courses which were separate and designed specifically for them. This was because:

- students were not always considered by everyone in the college to be 'full' members of the student body with the right to participate in the life of the college
- with a few exceptions, local education authorities provided weighted funding only for discrete/separate provision and not for individuals

- it was usually only possible to secure favourable student: teacher ratios, classroom and support assistants, classrooms and other facilities if students with similar types of disability or learning difficulty were grouped together
- colleges were still unsure of the curricula they should be offering to students with learning difficulties and/or disabilities and to some extent teachers continued with the approaches developed in special schools.

14 A report in 1987 found a number of weaknesses in provision.[11] Many of the teachers who established this college provision had begun their careers in schools. They sometimes were unaware of the further education curriculum or its organisational and funding structures. Often they taught only students with learning difficulties and/or disabilities. Senior managers frequently knew little about this area of work and were sometimes slow to become involved or to support staff. There was sometimes a misunderstanding or failure of communication between 'specialist' staff and managers about the aims of the work and the requirements of the students. The lack of understanding served to widen the gap between this provision, which was growing rapidly, and the rest of the college's provision. The work was considered generally to have low status compared to vocational and academic work. The work's status was often reflected in the poor quality of its accommodation and the training opportunities available to staff. Most importantly, provision was often not evaluated as rigorously as other work in the college.

15 It is only within the last 10 years or so that staff responsible for the co-ordination of discrete provision or learning support have been allocated senior manager posts. For example, at the time of the survey into provision undertaken by the National Bureau for Handicapped Students in 1987, there were few staff on senior lecturer grade in this area of work.[12] Previously, the operation of the 'bar' on salary levels for staff engaged in so-called 'lower level' work which included all pre-vocational provision, meant that they were also paid less than many of their colleagues. The consequent low status of this work contributed to the difficulty experienced by staff attempting to bring about closer links with the rest of the college's provision.[13]

16 A lack of clearly-defined progression routes from 'discrete', separate provision into other courses affected student opportunities. Another limiting factor was the expectation in a college that the responsibility for meeting the requirements of students with learning difficulties and/or disabilities lay almost entirely with the specialist team. This expectation sometimes corresponded with a lack of interest or evident anxiety from other staff about being involved with these students.

17 Because of the way provision was funded and planned, it was often difficult to provide support for students who progressed beyond their discrete provision, for example, onto the Youth Opportunity Programme (YOP) and later the Certificate of Pre-vocational Experience (CPVE). However, if support could be provided, there was a variety of pre-vocational courses which prepared students for a vocational or academic course. These pre-vocational courses were often developed by the college in response to local demand and were generally not accredited.[14]

18 Much pioneering and innovative work was undertaken by specialist and non-specialist teachers who devised new curricula and assessment regimes and developed new teaching strategies for these new further education learners. As a result, further education became more generally available to students with learning difficulties and/or disabilities. However, the existence of provision still depended on the confidence, commitment and expertise of individual staff. The availability of transport, local funding arrangements and the nature of a student's disability or learning difficulty all played a

part in deciding whether an individual took part in further education.[15] Where senior college managers and local education authority officers supported the work, pride was often taken in the size and range of a college's discrete provision.

19 Access to general further education colleges for students with sensory or physical disabilities depended again on the attitudes, confidence and skills of individual lecturers. The support of the local education authority and senior managers to secure resources was essential. In addition, many of these students attended independent residential establishments, some of which were colleges, some schools and communities, which catered for particular disabilities or learning difficulties. As well as intensive specialist support to assist students following vocational and academic programmes, the residential colleges also provided opportunities for students to learn independence skills away from home.

20 Some colleges of agriculture and horticulture established provision for students with learning difficulties and/or disabilities as part of the diversification of their activities in the 1980s. The real life learning environments provided by the colleges together with their long experience in breaking down learning into small steps made them well suited for such students.

21 Sixth form colleges were established as part of LEA secondary education policies in the late 1960s or 70s. Their aim was to provide a full-time continuing general education for students aged between 16 and 19. Many colleges benefited from close links with their LEA and were integral to the implementation of an authority-wide special needs strategy where one existed. However, many sixth form colleges were restricted in the courses they were able to offer. Past history and location, for example on the site of a former grammar school, could limit the nature of the curriculum on offer. Some colleges were established with a specifically academic focus, with the local further education college resourced for other work. These factors made it difficult for some sixth form colleges to meet the requirements of students with learning difficulties.

22 Since incorporation, some of the sixth form colleges have embraced GNVQ and adult work, and have recruited a wider variety of learners. A number have developed particular expertise in identifying and meeting the requirements of students with specific learning difficulties (dyslexia) by, for example, building on existing strategies to improve study skills.

23 The Warnock Report, the *Education Act 1981* and the ideas of *adult status*[16] and *'an ordinary life'*[17] had a profound effect on the shape of further education for students with learning difficulties and/or disabilities. Further education was expected to provide opportunities for learners to develop skills that would equip them for greater autonomy and independence and for possible employment, and to assist them to take on new roles in the community and in their families. People with learning difficulties and/or disabilities wanted to enjoy the same variety and richness of human experience as other people. Further education was expected to provide the same levels of support and opportunities for integration that many pupils were beginning to experience in schools. The growing self-advocacy movement and the increased capacity and eagerness of people with disabilities and/or learning difficulties to articulate what they required from further education also encouraged practitioners and planners to rethink provision.

24 The introduction of the national curriculum in 1988 and the rethinking of the role of the special school as a partner with mainstream schools, exemplified in the recommendations of the Fish Report [18] contributed to this re-shaping.

25 From the mid 1980s, there has been a growing emphasis on the concept of adult status for people with learning difficulties and/or disabilities. The part played by financial independence and employment in

E

the development and support of adult status has been widely recognised in western countries through the work of the Organisation for Economic Co-operation and Development and national organisations. In the UK, colleges made considerable efforts to provide courses at level 1 of the national vocational qualification as part of a growing concern that these students should have equal opportunities to develop skills for employment. Many colleges responded by devising strategies to support individual learners on academic and vocational courses. Some LEAs devised funding mechanisms that made it easier for students to receive individualised support. Some senior managers and practitioners worked closely together to devise structures for resourcing individual students, sometimes developing considerable expertise in deploying staff and equipment, using external support agencies and changing staff attitudes and practice.[19]

26 The development of strategies to provide individual support for a student's learning encouraged closer liaison between specialists and other staff. Some of the barriers to student progression began to break down. Successful learning support depended upon colleges adopting an approach that extended across the range of provision. This whole college approach was most effectively co-ordinated at a senior level.[20]

27 The Further Education Unit (FEU) and HMI played a leading role in the development of the concept of learning support. There was a growing interest from senior managers in the concept as they began to understand its applicability to other learners. The expertise of good teachers working with students with learning difficulties and/or disabilities was viewed increasingly as a resource for the whole college. These teachers' skills included an understanding of the process of learning, the capacity to meet the requirements of a variety of learners, expertise in devising tailor-made materials and knowledge of assessment techniques. The function of learning support in assisting colleges to attract and retain new groups of learners was increasingly recognised.

28 Adult education has a long tradition of meeting a wide variety of individual requirements. Many institutions made extensive provision for adults with learning difficulties, people with mental health difficulties, deaf students and others, as part of their effort to meet community needs. As in colleges, the emphasis was on establishing provision for a wider variety of students. However, provision was often in separate courses with few opportunities for progression or accreditation. Sometimes students continued in classes and programmes for a number of years with few recognised or clear outcomes or measures of their progress in learning. Many classes provided valuable learning opportunities for adults, some of whom were too old to have experienced education in schools. There were examples of pioneering work, for example, under the REPLAN scheme for unemployed adult learners or as part of LEA developments in literacy or basic education work. Stimulus and practical support were provided by national organisations such as the National Institute for Adult and Continuing Education and the Adult Literacy Agency (later the Basic Skills Agency) and the Advisory Council on Adult Continuing Education. Key reports such as the Russell Report[21] and *The Disadvantaged Adult*[22] played an important part in focusing attention on adult learners with learning difficulties and/or disabilities.

29 The impetus for change in provision for adults with disabilities and/or learning difficulties stemmed from the influence of the advocacy movement and the fundamental shifts in attitudes which led to the formulation of the concept of 'an ordinary life'. The closure of long-stay hospitals and the policy of care in the community which became more formalised in 1981 were significant consequences of that change.[23]

30 The requirement upon social services to undertake individual assessments and devise individual care plans for adult clients has been matched to some extent by the development of individual learning plans for adult learners. In the best practice, these plans attempt to take into account the aims and objectives of the individual's care plan. For adults with learning difficulties or mental health difficulties, the curriculum often aims to develop new skills needed to take up new roles in the community, including the potential for employment.[24]

31 The Further Education Funding Council's funding arrangements for students with learning difficulties and/or disabilities have built on and strengthened the movement toward integration and the provision of learning support by allocating weighted funding to colleges based on the requirements of individual students. The arrangements also acknowledge that some students may require a course which is specifically designed for them or a placement at a specialist college outside the sector for at least some of their time in further education.

References

1. *Elementary Education (Blind and Deaf Children) Act 1893*

2. *Education Act 1944*, London, HMSO

3. *Mental Deficiency Act 1913*, London, HMSO

4. *Mental Health Act 1959*, London, HMSO

5. *Education (Handicapped Children) Act 1970*, London, HMSO

6. *Education Act 1981*, London, HMSO

7. HMSO *Special Educational Needs. Report of the Committee of Enquiry into the Education of Handicapped Children and Young People,* (Warnock Report), London, HMSO, Cmnd 7212, 1978

8. *Children Act 1989*, London, HMSO

9. *National Health Service and Community Care Act 1989*, London, HMSO

10. *Education Act 1993*, London, HMSO

11. FEU/NFER, *Perceptions of Special Needs in Further Education*, London, HMSO, 1990

12. R. Stowell *Catching Up? Provision for Students with Special Educational Needs in Further and Higher Education,* London, NBHS/DES, 1987

13. Her Majesty's Inspectorate *'Students with Special Needs in Further Education': Education Observed 9,* London, DES, 1989

14. *NVQs and Learners with Special Needs*, FEU, 1990

15. Written evidence from FEU to enquiry into 16 to 19 education by parliamentary standing committee on education, 1992

16. *Disabled Youth: The Right to Adult Status,* OECD-CERI, Paris, 1988

17. *An Ordinary Life; An Ordinary Working Life*, King's Fund Centre.

18. *Educational Opportunities for All?* Report for the committee reviewing provision to meet special educational needs, ILEA, London, 1985

19. Her Majesty's Inspectorate *'Students with Special Needs in Further Education': Education Observed 9,* London, DES, 1989

20. Supporting Learning: *Part 1 A Model For Colleges; Part 2 Practical Guidance For Colleges; Part 3 Assessing Learning Support Needs*, FEU, London, 1992, 1993, 1994

21. *Adult Education: A Plan for Development* Report of a committee of enquiry appointed by the secretary of state for education and science under the chairmanship of Sir Lionel Russell CBE, London, HMSO, 1973

22. Peter Clyne, *The Disadvantaged Adult: Educational and Social Needs of Minority Groups*, Harlow, Longman, 1972

23. Care in the community: a consultative document DHSS 1981, London also Community Care: Agenda for Action (the Griffiths Report) 1988, London.

24. A New Life: Transition Learning Programmes for People with Severe Learning Difficulties Moving from Long Stay Hospitals into the Community, FEU, London, 1992

Annex F: Contributors to the Work of the Committee

The committee would like to offer its thanks to the following individuals, organisations, college staff and students who have contributed to its work.

Aitchison, Jill	College of North West London
Apsis, Simone	British Council of Organisations for Disabled People
Ariel, Ed	Human Resources Development, Canada
Ashton, Dr Elizabeth	Camosun College, British Colombia, Canada
Atkinson, Sue	Portland College
Bagolt, Andrew	student, Hinwick Hall College
Baldwin, Anne	Newham Sixth Form College
Banbury, Maureen	HMI/Office for Standards in Education
Barnes, Bob	Office of Population Census and Surveys
Barton, Prof. Len	University of Sheffield
Berry, Chris	The Association of National Specialist Colleges/Toynton and Weelsby Hall Further Education College
Black, Charles	William Morris House
Blair, Susan	Croydon College
Bolton, John	Blackburn College
Boulton, Alison	MENCAP/Lufton Manor College
Bradley, Dr Judy	National Foundation for Educational Research
Bradshaw, Wendy	Royal National Institute for Deaf People
Bradshaw, Jill	College of Speech Therapists
Braithwaite, Nancy	Schools Curriculum and Assessment Authority (Dearing review of 16 to 19 qualifications)
Brenchley, Janet	Oldham LEA
Bright, Andrew	People First
Brookes, David	The Association for Colleges
Brough, Margaret	Blackburn College
Brown, Graham	Tyneside Open College Federation
Buckridge, Anthea	United States Embassy
Bullock, John	Salford College
Burnette, Jenny	FEFC (finance)
Bynner, Prof. John	City University
Caskie, Helen	The Staff College
Chalk, Daphne	North Nottinghamshire College
Child, Derek	The Open University
Clare, Mariette	Mid-Warwickshire College, project co-ordinator, student workshop series
Clarke, Dr Nick	Kirklees Metropolitan Council
Clifford, Carmella	student, Henshaws Society for the Blind
Clifford, Alan	Kirby College
Closs, Alison	Moray House Institute, Scotland
Collins, Ian	SSCI ASSIST/Hereford & Worcester LEA
Connell, Kevin	RNIB Vocational College

Cookson, Nancy	Gateshead College
Cowan, Sue	Little Plumstead Hospital, Norfolk LEA
Cox, Alison	Stevenson College
Craft, Madeline	Association of Principals of Sixth Form Colleges
Crowley, Mary	Waltham Forest LEA
Crowne, Stephen	Further Education Development Agency
Crozier, John	Shropshire LEA
Curtis, John	Skill
Dalamangas, Pola	Delphi International, USA
Davis, Peter	The Association of National Specialist Colleges
Davis, Terry	Joint Forum for the GCSE and GCE: Standing Committee For Examination Candidates with Special Requirements
De Vries, Dr Peter	Economic and Social Research Council
Dee, Lesley	University of Cambridge, Institute of Education
Denham, Jane	Scottish Higher Education Funding Council
Dent, Susannah	Henshaws Society for the Blind
Dickinson, David	Basingstoke College of Technology
Dicks, Elsa	National Council for Vocational Qualifications
Dixon, Martha	Learning and Literacy, Government of Canada
Dixon, Dr Stella	Further Education Development Agency
Donkin, Joan	Bradford and Ilkley Community College
Dotson, Mary	Delphi International, USA
Dryden, Gordon	Royal National Institute for the Blind
Dumbleton, Paul	Scottish Further Education Unit
Duckitt, Keith	FEFC (information systems)
Edmonds, Cate	Queen Mary's College, Hampshire
Ellis, Mark	Ideas in Motion, University of Liverpool
Ennals, Paul	Royal National Institute for the Blind
Egron-Polak, Eva	Association of Universities and Colleges of Canada
Evans, Pauline	student, Oaklands College
Ewing, Sheena	Blackburn College
Faraday, Sally	Further Education Development Agency
Ferris-Taylor, Rita	Brent Social Services
Fish, John	consultant, Organisation for Economic Co-operation and Development, CERI, Paris
Fletcher, Karen	Nash House Further Education Centre
Forshaw, Barbara	Manchester College of Arts and Technology
Foster, Elridge	Department for Education
Galambos, Dianne	Sheridan College, Ontario, Canada
Garrad, Helen	National Union of Students
Gilbert, David	The Association of National Specialist Colleges (NATSPEC)
Giles, Joan	HMI/Office for Standards in Education
Gizzi, Julian	Beachcroft Stanleys, solicitors
Goodacre, John	Hereward College of Further Education/National Federation of Access Centres
Goodey, Christopher	Newham Parents' Support Network
Gordon, Dr Robert	Humber College, Ontario, Canada
Green, Brian	Dudley College of Technology
Griffiths, Jane	FEFC (analyst, responses to the call for evidence)
Griffiths, Matthew	FEFC (inspectorate)
Harper, Stephanie	East Birmingham College
Harrison, Joyce	Association of Educational Psychology, University of Southampton
Harvey, David	Somerset College of Arts and Technology
Henderson, John	Scottish Office
Henry, Charlie	Educational Psychology Services, Norfolk LEA
Hersov, John	Hersov Associates
Hitt, Mary	Stevenson College
Hook, Dr Richard	Humber College, Ontario, Canada

F

Holloway, Tony	FEFC (finance)
Horrex, Elizabeth	MENCAP Amersham and Cheshire
Horrocks, Christiana	Social Services Inspectorate
Hutchinson, David	North Nottinghamshire College
Jeffrey, Tom	Department for Education
Jenkins, Tricia	Ideas in Motion, University of Liverpool
Jones, Lynne	Skelmersdale College
Jones, Todd	Economics and Education Opportunities Committee, House of Representatives USA
Jones, William E	American Association of University Affiliated Programmes for Persons with Developmental Disabilities
Johns, Chris	Social Services Inspectorate
Keeley, Tony	Higher Still Development Agency
Kempner, Caroline	FEFC (research and statistics)
Kingsford, Margaret	Blackburn College
Klein, Cynthia	Southwark College, Language & Literacy Unit
Lawton, John	MENCAP/Action 19+
Laycock, David	Computer Centre for Disabled People/National Federation of Access Centres
Layer, Lynn	North West Post-16 Regional Network
Legard, Robin	Social and Community Planning Resarch
Leggatt, Joe	Guildford College
Leonard, Joan	ASSET
Lloyd Smith, Mel	University of Warwick, Institute of Education
Lones, Dr Jane	Lord Mayor Treloar College/The Association of National Specialist Colleges (NATSPEC)
Longdon, Elaine	Portland College
Low, Colin	City University
Lynch, Paul	Sheffield College
Lynne-Jones, Mary	Lewisham College
Macadam, Margaret	Norah Fry Research Centre
MacLeod, Donald	Human Resources Development, Canada
Macqueen, Lynn	FEFC (education programmes, East Midlands)
Maddern, Phil	Home Farm Trust
Mahony, James	American Association of Community Colleges
Malach, Alyson	Liverpool College
Malone, Catherine	student, Oaklands College
Maychell, Karen	consultant, National Foundation for Educational Research
McClure, Roger	FEFC (finance)
McDowell, Alan	Enable/Birmingham Adult Dyslexic Self-Help Group
McGill, Rosemary	The Spastics Society (now SCOPE)
McGinty, Jean	consultant, Royal National Institute for the Blind/The Association of National Specialist Colleges (NATSPEC)
McGivney, Veronica	National Institute of Adult and Continuing Education
McKeown, Sally	National Council for Educational Technology
Meager, Nigel	Institute for Employment Studies
Melia, Dr Terry	FEFC (inspectorate)
Mitchell, Debbie	Association of Blind and Partially Sighted Teachers and Students
Moore, Robin	Office of International Visitors, US Information Agency
Morgan, Ellen	University of North West London
Mullen, Brenda	Derby College for Deaf People/National Association of Tertiary Education for Deaf People
Nadin, Philip	Birmingham Adult Dyslexic Self-Help Group
Nelson, Steve	Oaklands College
Neville, Mandy	Circles Network
O'Hara, Min	Educational Psychology Service, Salford LEA
Palmer, Margaret	Hertfordshire Careers Service

F

Palmer, Wendy	East Midlands Further Education Council
Panitch, Melanie	Roeher Institute, Canada
Parsons, Maggie	Handsworth Careers Service
Perry, Brian	Hereford and Worcester LEA
Pettit, Aiden	Further Education Development Agency
Pointon, Ann	consultant, Channel 4
Polack, Mrs M	MENCAP Wolverhampton
Preedy, Sue	Umbrella
Quirke, John	FEFC (research and statistics)
Qureshi, Dr Hazel	University of York
Read, Alison	Scottish Further Education Unit
Reeves, Mike	Surrey Careers Service
Riddell, Professor Sheila	Stirling University
Ringer, Lawrence	United States Department of Education
Rioux, Marcia	Roeher Institute, Canada
Ritchie, Jane	Social and Community Planning Research
Robertshaw, Sylvia	Henshaws Society for the Blind
Robertson, Pat	HMI Scotland
Robertson, Patricia	Association of Blind and Patially Sighted Teachers and Students
Robinson, Ed	North Nottinghamshire College
Robinson, Heather Jane	The Canadian Teachers Federation
Robinson, Lois	People First
Rolph, Sheena	Little Plumstead Hospital, Norfolk LEA
Rogers, Joan	North West Post-16 Regional Network
Rourke, Anna	ACE Access Centre
Roy, Dr Walter	Plumstead Hospital Parents' Group
Russell, Phillipa	Council for Disabled Children
Schostack, Dr John	University of East Anglia, Centre for Applied Research in Education
Searle, Valerie	Hinwick Hall College
Siemasko, Ruth	Department of Social Security
Simpson, Brian	North Warwickshire College
Simpson, Paul	Royal Association for Disability and Rehabilitation (RADAR)
Slaney, Ann	Hertford Regional College
Smallwood, John	Portland College
Smith, Dr Michael	The Association of National Specialist Colleges (NATSPEC)
Smith, Felicity	College of Occupational Therapists
Smith, Frank	National Association of Disabled Students, Canada
Stanton, Geoff	Further Education Unit
Stockton, Barry	Lancashire LEA
Stokes, Gordon	North Warwickshire College
Susini, Sheila	Humber College, Canada
Sutcliffe, Jeannie	National Institute of Adult and Continuing Education
Sutherland, Dawn	Camosun College, Canada
Swindells, David	University of Huddersfield, School of Education
Taubman, Dan	National Association of Teachers in Further and Higher Education
Tench, Karen	Ontario Association for Community Living, Canada
Tennyson, Carol	FEFC (inspectorate)
Thew, Michelle	National Deaf Children's Society
Thomas, Andrew	Social and Community Planning Research
Thomas, Derek	National Development Team
Thomson, Dr George	University of Edinburgh, Education Department
Thomson, Jackie	Lambeth College
Thrane, Emily	FEFC (education programmes)
Tingle, Myra	Centre for Micro-Assisted Communication
Tompkins, Carole	Dunstable College
Topping, Janet	Breakspeare School Parents' Group
Tuckett, Alan	National Institute of Adult and Continuing Education

Turner, Gay	Association of Metropolitan Authorities
Vincent, Professor Tom	Open University
Walker, Colin	Business and Technology Education Council
Wallace, John	Thurrock College
Walmsley, Jan	Open University
Ward, Mike	United States Department of Education
Wedell, Prof. Klaus	University of London, Institute of Education
Weinstock, Anne	Rathbone C.I.
West, Bob	National Federation of Access Centres/Hereward College Access Centre
Whitbread, David	Association of County Councils
Whittaker, Andrea	Kings Fund Centre
Whittlesea, Cecilia	SELECT Training Consultants
Wilenius, Fred	FEFC (analyst, responses to the call for evidence)
Wilkins, John	Department for Education and Employment
Williams, Jane	United States Department of Education
Wilson, Diane	Beachcroft Stanleys, solicitors
Wilson, Peter	Open College Network
Winter, Ronald C	Maryland State Department of Education, USA
Yeo, Alan	Beaumont College
York, Debra	Staffordshire ASSIST
Zein, Peter	student, Portland College

The committee would like to offer its grateful thanks to the 300 students who participated in the workshop series, held in 1995, and to the staff of the following organisations for their help with the series:

Brunel College, Bristol

Lewisham College

Skill: National Bureau for Students with Disabilities, London

Moller Centre, Cambridge

Hereward College of Further Education

Loughborough University

Bolton CE Services

Salford College

Playhouse Theatre, Leeds

Gateshead College

Visits by committee/working group members and advisers:

Bilston Community College	John Tomlinson, Margaret Murdin, Lisa Young
Bournville College	Eldridge Foster, David Kendall, Peter Moseley
Baltimore City	John Tomlinson, Community College Deborah Cooper, Elizabeth Maddison
Burnaby Community	Skills Centre, Canada Peter Moseley, Sharon Welch
Carmel College	Pat Hood
Camosun College, Canada	Peter Moseley, Sharon Welch
Catsonville Community College, USA	John Tomlinson, Deborah Cooper, Elizabeth Maddison
Derwen College	Lynn Lee, Toni Beck, David Kendall, Margaret Murdin, Sharon Welch, Elizabeth Maddison, Pat Hood, Lisa Young
East Birmingham College	John Tomlinson, David Kendall, Pat Hood

Herefordshire College Art and Design	John Tomlinson, of Elizabeth Maddison
Hinwick Hall College	Lynn Lee, Toni Beck, David Kendall, Sharon Welch, Pat Hood, Lisa Young
Hull College	Peter Lavender, Lisa Young
Humber College, Ontario, Canada	Peter Moseley, Sharon Welch
James Watt College, Scotland	Pat Hood, Elizabeth Maddison
Joseph Priestley College	David Kendall, Peter Raine, Pat Hood, Lisa Young
Kingsway College	Deborah Cooper, Peter Raine, Jill Murkin
Little Plumstead Hospital	David Kendall, Peter Raine
Luton Sixth Form College	Deborah Cooper, Toni Beck
Manchester College of Art and Technology	Toni Beck
Marlborough School, Woodstock	John Tomlinson, Elizabeth Maddison, Peter Raine, Gwynneth Flower
Montgomery Community College, Rockville Campus, USA	John Tomlinson, Deborah Cooper, Elizabeth Maddison
North Nottinghamshire College	Technology seminar
Ormerod School, Oxford	John Tomlinson, Elizabeth Maddison, Peter Raine
Portland College	Lynn Lee, Toni Beck, David Kendall, Sharon Welch, Pat Hood, Lisa Young
Royal National College for the Blind, Herefordshire	John Tomlinson, Elizabeth Maddison, Gwynneth Flower
RNIB Vocational College, Loughborough	Lynn Lee, Toni Beck, David Kendall, Elizabeth Maddison, Pat Hood, Lisa Young
Skelmersdale College	Pat Hood
South Thames College	Sharon Welch, Toni Beck, Peter Moseley, Jill Murkin
Southwark College	Jo Stephens, Deborah Cooper, Mike Hanson
St Vincent College, Gosport	Toni Beck, David Kendall, Pat Hood
Stevenson College, Scotland	Pat Hood

Colleges which took part in testing the committee's thinking about inclusive learning:

Blackburn College

Brooksby College

East Birmingham College

Eastleigh College

Gateshead College

Hull College

Kidderminster College

Lewisham College

Long Road Sixth Form College, Cambridge

Manchester College of Arts and Technology (MANCAT)

Oaklands College

Oxford College of Further Education

Park Lane College

Skelmersdale College

St Vincent College, Gosport

St Austell College

Tamworth College

Trowbridge College

Wigan and Leigh College

Wyggeston and Queen Elizabeth I College

Appendix 1 to Annex F: Responses to the Call for Evidence

Responses from organisations

Organisation	Surname	First name
16 Plus	Heal	Louise
19+ Action Group	Judge	Paul
19+ special needs	Patterson	Judith
A Cause for Concern	Levell	Peter
Accrington & Rossendale College	Harford	Lindsay
ACE/Access Centre	Broadbent	Steven
Acorn F E Centre at Rampton Hospital	Oxley	Rachel
Acquired Aphasia Unit	Cooper	Jayne
Action For ME	Colby	Jane
Adult Basic Education Service	Dartnell	Vivienne
Adult Dyslexic Organisation	Soloman	Ruth
Adult Vocational and Educational Support Services	White	Paul
Airedale and Wharfedale college	Greenwood	N D
Albert Place Centre & Meadowside Centre, Trafford Social Services		
Adult Literacy and Basic Skills Unit	Wells	Alan
Alton College	Rumble	Michael
Amersham & Wycombe College, FE Corporation	Leman	Patricia
Aquinas College	Moore	Eddie
Arnold and Carlton College		
Arts Council of England (The)	Semple	Maggie
Ashworth Adult Education Department	Thomas	R
Assets Disability	Carter	Ken
Association for Colleges	Brookes	David
Association for Residential Care	Churchill	James
Association for Stammerers	Cartwright	Peter
Association of Camphill Communities of Great Britain	Luxford	Michael
Association of Colleges in the Eastern Region	Young	Andrew
Association of County Councils	Campbell	Stephen
Association of Educational Psychologists	Harrison	Joyce
Association of National Specialist Colleges, The	McGinty	Jean
Association of Workers for Children with Emotional and Behavioural Difficulties	Rimmer	Alan
ATLA	Chalmers	Roz
	Hunter	Penelope
	Mitchinson	Freda
	Newton	H
	Poole	Christina

ATLA	Rallings	Philippa
	Smith	June
	Uren	Jackie
	Zysblat	J
	Plail	Gillian
	Gamage Mr and Mrs (students)	
	Hatton	Joan (student)
	Love	Elsie (student)
	McDouall	Kenneth (student)
	McDouall	Joan (student)
	Parker	Joyce V
Avalon Trust	Phillips	Helen
Avon Coalition of Disabled People	Pickersgill	Ruth
Avon Community Education	Allan	Yvonne
Avon County Council	Crook	Maggy
Award Scheme Development and Accreditation Network (ASDAN)	Harper	Steve
	Swaffield	Karen
Aylesbury College	Lawson	Don
Aylesbury Society for Mentally Handicapped Children and Adults	Richardson	K
Aylesbury Vale Community Healthcare NHS Trust	Kuzmanov	Cilla
Barking College	Brunyee	David
Barking and Dagenham LEA	Hillsden	S
Barnados/Cheshire Social Services	Thornton	Mair
	Howe	John
Barnados/Ian Tetley F. E. P.	Pickup	Chris
Barnet College	Crennell	Margaret
Barnsley College	Pickett	Norman G
Basic Skills/Learning (Drop in Centre)	Gray	Terence
	Martin	Frank
Basildon College	Woodrow	S J
Basingstoke College of Technology	Bird	Kay
	Parker	J
Beckton School	Angele	Maggie
Bede College	Wakefield	J M
Bedford College	Reece	D J
Bedford College	Learning Support Team	
Bedford Spastic Society Residential Centre, The	Cunningham	John
Bedfordshire County Council	Alexander	C A
Bedfordshire Guidance Services	Alexander	C A
Bedfordshire Society Working with Autism	Jones	David
Berkshire Social Services	Valdez	Maureen
Berkshire Working Group on Deafness in Post-16 Education and Training	Carter	Ken
Beverley College	Tuckey	Sue
	Anstess	John
Bicester Adult Continuing Education Centre	Hutchins	Laura
Bilston Community College	Self-advocacy Group	
Birkdale Further Education Direct Support (BFEDS)	Loxham	E

F

Birkenhead Sixth Form College	Tomlinson	Barbara
Birmingham Adult Dyslexic Self Help Group		
Birmingham City Council	Edwards	Gwenn
Birmingham College of Food, Tourism and Creative Studies	Davies	Clive
Birmingham TEC	Giles	Elaine
Bishop Burton College	Davies	A J
Blackburn College	Ewing	Sheena M
Blackpool and the Fylde College	McAllister	Michael J
Blenheim Centre, Continuing Education, Leeds City Council	Aveyard	Margaret
	Wallis	Margaret
	Frankland	Anthony
BMS, Bexley College	Elgar	Carolyn
Bolton Bury TEC	Bain	Sue
Bolton College	Wilson	Jean
Bolton Community Education Service	Foster	Liz
Bolton Institute	Clift-Harris	Jenny
	Whittaker	J
Boston College	Simpson/Adams	
Bourne Social Education Centre	Maclachlan	Gail
Bournemouth and Poole College of FE, The	Roger	Simons
	Scott	Alison
Bournville College of Further Education	MacHattie	Carrie L
	Burton	Paula L
Boys and Girls Welfare Society	Liston	Judy
Bracknell College	Marston	Dianne
Bradford Eduction Advice Centre	Sutcliffe	Godfrey
Bradford & Ilkley Community College	Chambers	Peter
	Donkin	Joan
	Neal	Les
	O'Connor	Lynette
Braintree College	Greenard	S L
Breakspeare SLD School, parents' group	Topping	Janet
Breakthrough Deaf-Hearing Integration	Jarrett	Dawn L
Bridge College	Preece	Sue
	Ridgeway	Andrea
Bridgeway Centre, The	Cronin	Gaynor
Brighton College of Technology	Brownhill	M
Brighton, Hove & Sussex Sixth Form College	Blyth	Margaret
British Association of Teachers of the Deaf	Shaw	John F
	Underwood	Ann
British Dyslexia Association	Cann	Paul
British Epilepsy Association	Harnor	Mike
Broadview Further Education Centre	Walker	Angela
Brockenhurst College	Snell	M J
Bromley Health	Edmonds	Janet
Brooklands College	Copas	P J
Brooksby College	Clohesy	John Mark
Broomfield College	Wilkinson	Anne
Broxtowe College	Lewis	J N

Brunel College of Arts and Technology	Bevan	W I
Buckinghamshire Adult Continuing Education	Scott	Peter
Buckinghamshire Social Services	Young	Stan
Bury Health Care NHS Trust	Bacon	P
Bury People First	Pearce	Sharon
Bury Resource Centre	Williams	Deborah
	Delves	Ian
	Coatham	Lynn
	Wakeling	Ian
Business and Technology Education Council	Billam	Diane
Calderdale College	Sunderland	Val
Calderdale Healthcare NHS Trust	Ellis	Linda
Cambridge City Council	Cracknell	Tim
Cambridge Regional College	Coulthard	Margaret
Cambridge and Huntingdon Health Commission	Williams	Stephen
Cambridgeshire County Council	Forbes	Martin
Camden and Islington Health Authority	Tinsley	Peter J
Camphill Blair Drummond	Bruhn	Michael
Canterbury College	Manser	Edward
Capel Manor Horticultural and Environmental Centre	Adams	C R
Capers (Starbright Group)	Falkingham	Beryl
	Pencavel	Marian
Careers Service West, Bristol	Fryer	Ian
Carers National Association, Newham Branch	Watts	Mary
Carlisle College	Johnson	Andrew
Carmel College	Conwell	Kathy
Carshalton College	Watkins	David
Castlebeck Care (Teesdale) Ltd	Betton	Michelle
Cathedral Centre	Haskins	Mary
	Topham	Richard
Catholic Caring Services	Bolton	Donna
	Clarkson	John
	Jordan	Susan
	Sadiq	Faryaz
CAVE	O'Malley	John
CELFACS Community Learning Disabilities Team	Ackroyd	Carol
CENMAC	Tingle	Myra
	Becke	Gil
CENTRA (FE Centre of NW Regional Association of LEAs)	Young	Barbara H
Central Middlesex Spastics Society Skills Development Centre	Harrison	Marie
Chadsworth School	Main	M W
Charles Keene College	Gray	Linda
Chelmsford College	Walden	Phil
Cheshire Careers Service	Smith	Jean
Cheshire County Council	Donnely	Verity
Cheshire Merseyside & West Lancashire District Workers' Educational Association	Hall	Dorothea
Chesterfield College	Spilman	Liz
Chichester College of Arts, Science & Technology	Fairbank	Sandie

F

Organisation	Surname	First name
'Choices' Work Placement Programme	Buckley	Eileen
	Rogers	Avril
City and Guilds of London Institute	Butcher	Murray
City and Islington College	McLoughlin	Frank
City College Manchester	Farrell	Sheila
City College Norwich	Debbell	Diane
	Brannen	Richard
City College Norwich	Turner	Richard
City Lit Support Unit, The	Morton	Denise
City Literary Institute, The	Cooper-Hammond	John
	Davey	C
	Fearnley	Clare
	McKenna	Stewart
City of Bath College	Clayton	Brenda
City of Leeds College of Music	Equal Opportunities Officer	
City of Liverpool Community College	Malach	Alyson
City of Liverpool Education Directorate	Roberts	Ken
City of Salford Social Services Department	Hewitt	Peter
City of Westminster College	Leavy	I (and students)
	Miles	Carol
	Woollacombe	Nick
Clarendon House	Ives	Cheryl Margaret
Cleveland County Council, Adult Education Service	Kenrick	Julie
Cleveland Social Services Department	Lauerman	M
Coalition of Advocacy Groups (Sheffield), The	Naylor	Graham
Colcheser Institute	Winder	Enid
Coleg Elidyr Parents' Association	Cowie	Noeline
College of North East London	Harries	Waveney
	Prince	E
	Self-advocacy Group	
	LDD section	
	Robinson	Ian
College of North West London, The	Smith	Reg
College of Occupational Therapists	Hall	Michael
Community and Social Services Department, Wakefield	Raynor	Mervyn
Community Team for people with learning difficulties, Wiltshire	Simpson	Helen
Community Team for people with learning disabilitites, Bucks	Hatfield	Christine
Computer Centre for People with Disabilities/National Federation of Access Centres	Laycock	David
Connect	Peggs	S E
Cornwall College	Allsop	Trish
	Stanhope	Alan
Cornwall County Audiology Service	Dwight	D W
Cornwall Deaf Childrens Society	Sweet	Elaine
Cornwell Business College	Cornwell	J
Council for Disabled Children	Russell	Philippa
Council for the Advancement of Communication with Deaf People	Simpson	T Stewart
Countersthorpe College	Centre 88	
County Transition Advisory Group, Lancashire	Howarth	I R

Coventry City Council Community Education – N W Area	Selby	Ann
Coventry Education Department	Galliers	D
Coventry Social Services Department	Summerfield	Jenny
Coventry Technical College	Eastman	Jessica
	Lee	Ann
Craven College	Walton	Jennifer
Crawley Hard of Hearing Club	Annells	Sheila
Cricklade College	Bevan	Eva Mavis
	Browning	Peter
Croydon College	Brett	Terry
Cumbria Careers Ltd	Ludlow	Peggy
Cumbria Deaf Association	Verney	Ann
Cumbria LEA	Slater	Harry
C.D.T. Linc	Angel	Stella
Darlington College of Technology	Hollis	George
Denbigh Education Centre	Wilson	Lesley
Department of Health	Cooper	E D
Derby College	Ashman	Susan
Derby College for Deaf People	Iqbal	A
Derbyshire Careers Services	Miln	Beverley
Derbyshire County Council Community Education Service	Rae	Donald
Derbyshire County Council	Adair	Lin
Derwentside College	Menzies	Bos
Devon Careers, Exeter	Moran	Cathy
Devon Careers, Plymouth	Fortey	John
Devon County Council – Education Department	Jenkin	S W G
Dewsbury College	Coleman	Margaret
Dilston College of Further Education		
Disability West Midlands	McCorkindale	Susan
Disabled Living Foundation	Bennett	Susan
Doncaster Careers Service	Kime	M A
Doncaster College	Calloway	Neil
Doncaster College for the Deaf	Dickson	R B
	Evans	J B D
	Emmott	T K
Dorset Social Services Department	Kippax	Chris
Down's Syndrome Association	Campbell	Bridget
Doyle Centre (Devon County Council)	Folland	M M
Dudley College	Roper	S C
Dundee Careers Service, Special Needs Advisory Group	Grant	John
Dyslexia Institute, The	Brooks	E J
	McCormack	Eileen
	Patterson	Felicity
	White	S
Ealing Tertiary College	Nind	M N
East Berkshire College	Berisford	S
East Berkshire Community Health	Smith	Karen
East Berkshire NHS Trust	Gilbert	Jan
East Birmingham College	Harper	Stephanie

F

East Devon College	Lucas	Alison
East Gloucestershire NHS Trust	Fretwell	B
East London & City Health Authority	West	Sylvia
East Midlands Further Education Council (EMFEC)	Ainscough	Roy
East Surrey College	Dunlop	Bob
East Sussex Careers Services	Davey	Barbara
East Sussex County Council	Penney	Trish
East Sussex County Council Social Services	Anstey	M
East Warwickshire College	Collins	Elizabeth
	Pawsey	Tracy
East Yorkshire College	principal	
Eastbourne College of Arts and Technology	Williams	John A
Eastleigh College	Higgins	Marlene
	Preston	Jo
	Roberts	A
ECSTRA (support service for deaf people in further education)	Tansell	Peter
Education Department, Hertfordshire County Council	Roberts	Mark
Elizabeth Fitzroy Homes	Eastwood	J
Elms School	Bacon	J M
Emscote Centre	Emscote Users Council	
Enfield College	Holm	Barbara
ENTERnet	Blair	Sue
Epsom Hard of Hearing Group	Birtwell	Betty
Essex Careers and Business Partnership	McMellon	Bill
Evesham College of Further Education	Powell	Heather
	Blades	David
Exeter College	Barnard	Pam
Fairdeal	Bodsworth	Jo
Fairfield Opportunity Farm	Hester	B A K
Farnborough College of Technology	Hasted	Ron
FE College	Holloway	Jeanne
Further Education Unit (evidence subsequently published by FEU)	Stanton	Geoff
Filton College	Coles	Jonathon
First Community Health	Thomas	C
Firth Park Advice Centre	Morris	Pauline
Former Librarian Royal National College for the Blind	Greenall	Elizabeth C E
Fortune Centre of Riding Therapy	Johnson	L
Foxfield School	Richardson	Robert
Franklin College	Parratt	E
Frimley Special Courses (MENCAP)	Wright	Marilyn
Furness College	Plant	Fay
Gabalfa Community Workshop	Shiers	Barry
Gateshead College	Bell	Susan
Gateway Sixth Form College	Challacombe	M S
Gillingham Adult Education Centre	Hargrave	Roberta
Gloucestershire College of Arts & Technology	Escolme	Richard
Gloucestershire County Council, Education Department	Haworth	D J
Gloucestershire Social Services	Friar	Jeremy
Grantham College	Design for living course	

Grantham College	New directives course	
	Saville	M D
Greater London Association of Disabled People	Hasler	Frances
Greenhead College	Conway	Kevin
Greenhill College	Acilman	Brian
Greenwich Learning Disability Services	Sandean	Danny
Grimsby College	Lowden	Celia
Guildford College of Further and Higher Education	Leggett	Joe
	Hayes	Jean
Hackney Social Services	McMahon	Margaret
Halesowen College	Couless	Michael
	Couless	Susan
	Godfrey	Andrea
	Huynh	Phan Tuyet
	Langford	Faye
	Smith	Mark James
	Stockton	Rebecca Louise
	Swansborough	Steven John
Hammersmith & West London College	Flatley	Christine
Hard of Hearing Club (Camborne)	Ripsher	A J
	Ripsher	M
Haringey Association for Independent Living	Mann	Polly
Haringey Housing & Social Services	Keston Centre	
Harrogate College	Clarke	Ian
Hartpury College	Brookham	John
Havering College of Further & Higher Education	Morgan	Penny
Haywards Heath Sixth Form College	Derbyshire	Brian
Health & Disability Team Dorchester Social Services	Whitfield	Ann
	Jackson	Shirley
Hearing Impaired Service, Humberside County Council	Garnett	Michael
	Underwood	Ann
Hearing Impaired Service, Knutsford, Cheshire	Wilson	William
Heltwate Special School	Smith	D R
Hendon College	Kiestos	Thomas
	Leigh	Ben
	Miller	Michelle
	Patel	Sheila
	Phillips	Steven
	Runswick	Elaine
	Watson	Stuart
	John	Scott
Henley College, The	Kimbell	M D
Hereford and Worcester Careers Service	Little	Roger
Hereford & Worcester County Council	O'Toole	Anne
Herefordshire College of Technology	Purser	Chrissie
Herefordshire College of Art & Design	MacIntre	Louise
Hereward College of Further Education	Firminger	Janice
Hertford Regional College	Slaney	Ann

F

Hertfordshire Careers Service	Palmer	Margaret
Hertfordshire County Council	Green	Colin
Hertfordshire Transition Support Group	Palmer	Margaret
Hertfordshire Social Care (Day Services, North Hertfordshire)	Parker	Bob
	Gates	Jan
High Peak College	Martin	Nicola
Highbury College	Winter	B
Hills Road Sixth Form College	Greenhalgh	Colin
Holy Cross Sixth Form College	Mafi	Helena C
Home Farm Trust	Madden	Philip
	Gadd	Michael
Hopwood Hall College		
Horizon House Day Centre (Rugby MIND)	Amos	H
	Geehan	J
	Herbert	Margaret Rose
	Kempton	Philip
	Robson	P
	Taylor	Susan
	centre co-ordinators	
Horizon House Day Centre, East Warwickshire College	Baldwin	Iris
Horizon NHS Trust	Sherratt	David
Huddersfield New College	Morris	Ruth
	Woodrow	Christine
Huddersfield NHS Trust	Lambert	E M
Hull College	Eastwood	A (parent)
	Holian	Thelma
	Kettener	Alan (student)
	White	Derek (student)
	Andrew	Phillip (student)
	Bentley	Susan (student)
	Waldon	Joanne
	Wheatley	Barrie
	Wragg	T
	visually-impaired students	
Humberside Adult Education Service, Boothferry/Scunthorpe Area	Garner	Susan
	Cole	Margaret
Humberside Education Services	Thomas	Trevor
Humberside Hearing Impaired Service	Wolsey	Lesley
Huntingdonshire Regional College	Elias	K
Ian Tetley Memorial School	Cairns	Paul
Initiative on Communication Aids for Children (ICAC)	Bernadt	Ann
Institute of Careers Guidance	Bereznicki	C
Institute of Educational Technology	Vincent	Tom
Integrate Ltd	Trustam	Rosemary
Isle of Wight College	Burgess	Sue
Islington Careers Service	Davis	S J
Islington Council	Davis	Steve
Itchen College	Savage	N
Jack Drum Arts and Entertainment	Ward	Julie

John Procter Education & Training	Procter	John
John Ruskin College	Kennedy	Mandy
Joint Group (physical and sensory handicap), Wakefield	Turner	David
Joseph Rowntree Foundation		
Josiah Mason College	Greenhough	M M
Keighley College	Packham	Graham
Kensington & Chelsea College	Howard	Ursula
Kent Adult Education Service	Jenkins	Angela
Kent County Council, Physical and Sensory Service	Rousseau	Lindsey
King Edward VI College	Cotton	Ann Josephine
King George V College	Collier	P
Kingsway College	Maudslay	Liz
Kirby College of Further Education	Smith	Margaret
Kirkley Hall College	Pike	C J
Knowsley Community College	Lane	Susan
	Walker	Linda
Lackham College	Sumner	Hazel
Lambeth Accord	Green	Wanda
Lambeth College	Milbourne	Linda
Lancashire Adult Education Service	Hooper	R C
Lancashire County Council	Carter	Philip A
	Rowbottom	Don
Lancashire LEA	Howarth	I R
Lancaster University	Preece	J
Lancaster & Morecambe College	Piggott	J
Lancasterian School	Rashid	Shazia
Language & Literacy Unit, Southwark College	Klein	Cynthia
LEAP in Teesdale ABE	Lee	Jenny
Learning Disability Team, Exeter	Hodgson	Ray
LEE Services (Heritage Care)	Gutman	Toni
Leeds College of Technology	Piercy	David
Leek College of Further Education and School of Art	Smith	Val
Leicester South Fields College	Khanna	Neelam
	Rayfield	Susan
Leicestershire LEA	Swan	Julia
Leonard Cheshire Foundation/Adult Basic Education	Fiddes	Susan
Lewes Tertiary College	Hayes	Barbara
Lewisham College	Holman	Judy
	Swabey	Alison
	Silver	Ruth
Lewisham Community Team for Adults with Learning Disabilities	Bradshaw	J
	O'Connor	S
Library Association, The	Clayton	Carl
	Fraser	Veronica
Lifespan Healthcare NHS Trust	Mackenzie	Graham
Lincoln College	Rux-Burton	John
Link into Learning/Wigston College	Chappell	Doreen
Linkage Community Trust	Berry	Chris
Local Education Authority's Forum for the Education of Adults		

F

(LEAFEA)	Tuckett	Alan
London Borough of Croydon Social Services Department	Lyons	Sharon
London Borough of Richmond upon Thames Education Department	Dickinson	Phil
London Borough of Sutton, Housing & Social Services	McIntosh	Barbara
London Borough of Waltham Forest	Crowley	Mary
London Chamber of Commerce and Industry Examinations Board	Lysons	Kenneth
London Learning Disability Forum	Cox	Brian E
London Region TVEI Network	Dee	Lesley
	Hill	Mary
	Maudslay	Liz
Long Road Sixth Form College	Robinson	Peter
Longlands College	Dyce	Tom
Loughborough College of Art & Design	Bunkum	Alan
Ludlow College	Pafford	David
Luton Sixth Form College	Bennett	Sue
Macclesfield College	Summers	Judith
Macintyre Care	Lock	Chris
Mackworth College, Derby	Pickering	Malcolm
Making Space	Lyne	David
Manchester Adult Education Service	Corbridge	R L
	Chadwick	Janet
Manchester College of Arts and Technology	Kirby	Pat
Margaret Danyers College	Parker	Margaret A
Marshfields School	Berryman	B
Matthew Boulton College, Student Forum	Mason	Lynn
Meadowside Centre	Advocacy Group	
Meanwood Park Hospital	Beckett	Claire
	Buchan	Terry
Meldreth Manor School	The Spastics Society	
MENCAP	Heddell	Fred
MENCAP, District Office, Berkshire/Buckinghamshire/Oxfordshire	Tan	Elizabeth
MENCAP, Northern Division	Parkin	John
MENCAP, Pathway Employment Service, Rotherham	Bostwick	Fiona
MENCAP, E/I Support Group	Edington	O M
MENCAP, Amersham and Cheshire	Horrex	K Elizabeth
MENCAP, Bedford	Scargill	Veronica
MENCAP, Bristol	Hannam	Pam
MENCAP, Dunstable	Mercier	Wendy
MENCAP, High Wycombe	Billington	J
	Sterry	Molly
MENCAP, Maidenhead	Johnson	Jean H
MENCAP, New Forest	Pepper	Sue
MENCAP, Nottingham	Bramhall	Debra
MENCAP, Southampton	Labon	Kay
Meridans Student Council, Resource and Activity Centre	Petrie	Moira
Merton Sixth Form College	Fairless	Hilary
	Fairweather	J
Merton Sixth Form College	Lake	Ruth
	Jackson	Joann

F

Metropolitan Borough of Stockport	Cross	Arthur
Metropolitan Borough of Wirral, Local Education Authority	Griffiths	David
Mid-Cheshire College	Ellingham	R
Mid-Staffordshire Health Authority	Sorual	Imad
Mid Warwickshire College	Critchley	H
Middlesex LEA, Psychology Service	Phillips	P
Millfields S.E.C. (social services)	Robinson	John
Milton Keynes College	Bedlington	Jane
	Jarvis	Linda
Molly Cope Court	Cope	Richard
Monks Park School	Dent	Alan William
Monkwearmouth College	Upright	Richard
Morley College	Craven	Judy
	Van de Water	Mary Ellen
	1993 Student Executive Committee	
Morningside Further Education Centre	Taylor	Eric
	Holmes	Linda
Myerscough College	Morwood	Alistair W
National Association for Tertiary Education for Deaf People (NATED)	Mullen	Brenda
NATFHE, the University & College Lecturers Union	Taubman	Daniel
National Association for Special Educational Needs, The	Hawkins	Jean
National Association for the Care and Resettlement of Offenders	Hraboweckyj	Anna
National Association of Principal Educational Psychologists	O'Hara	Min
National Association of Teachers of English & Community Languages To Adults	Siudek	Margaret
National Autistic Society	Collins	Michael
National Deaf Childrens Society	Laurenzi	Carlo
National Development Team	Platts	Helen
National Extension College	daSalvo	Anna
	Pinchbeck	Amanda
National Federation of Access Centres	Firminger	Janice
	West	Bob
	Williams	Rees
	Goodacre	John
National Mencap Homes Foundation	Baker	Colin
National Schizophrenia Fellowship	Took	Mike
National Youth Agency	Hand	Jenny
National Association for the Education and Guidance of Offenders		
NCT Parent Ability, The National Childbirth Trust	O'Farrell	Jo
NEDRDA	Hill	Sue
Nelson & Colne College	Gilchrist	Helen
New College, Durham	Harrison	Barbara
NEW College, Pontefract	Machin	David
New Tunmarsh Centre	Mistry	Rajendrakumar
Newark & Sherwood College	Towner	Peter
Newbury College	Bickell	Kerrie
	Worsley	Enid

F

Organisation	Surname	First name
Newcastle-Under-Lyme College	Ayres	R F
	Granter	J
Newcastle College	Bagshaw	John
	Farquharson	Lynne
Newcastle Education Department	Flynn	Pam
Newcastle Further Education (NCFE)	Sutcliffe	Isabel M
Newcastle & District Hard of Hearing Club	Harrison	S C
Newham College of Further Education	Davies	Rachel
Newham Council, Social Services Department	Constable	Gill
Newham Learning Support Service	Lowe	Mary
Newham Parent's Support Network	Goodey	Christopher
Newham Sixth Form College		
National Institute for Adult Continuing Education (NIACE) (evidence subsequently published by NIACE)	Tuckett	Alan
Norfolk Adult Education Service, lip-reading tutor	Peck	Doris
Norfolk Careers Service	Holt	Tim
Norfolk College	Dockney	B C
	Porter	S M
Norfolk County Council, Careers Service	Wedsell	Colin
Norfolk County Council Education	Godding	Bernard
Norfolk Network 81	Brickley	Pat
North Birmingham College	Eyre	J
North Cumbria Health Authority	Macleod	R A
North Derbyshire Tertiary College	Kavanagh-Coyne	J
North East Worcestershire College	Gamble	Jon
	Welsher	Linda M
North Hertfordshire College	Armstrong	Eileen
North Hertfordshire People First	Hitchin Group	
North Lincolnshire College	Plunkett	Barbara
North London TEC	Wood	Simon
North Trafford College	Robinson	T
North Warwickshire College	Jones	Stephanie
North Warwickshire NHS Trust	Moulin	Lawrence
North Yorkshire LEA	Allgood	G B
North Yorkshire Careers Guidance Services Ltd	Robinson	Jacky
North Yorkshire County Council, Learning Opportunities	Goring	Anne
North Yorkshire County Council, Social Services Department	Rhodes	Cynthia M
North Yorkshire Health Authority	Griffin	Leigh
Northampton College	Hays	Catherine
	Quilter	Ruth
Northamptonshire Adult Education Service	Dodds	C R
Northamptonshire County Council	Goulding	Kerstin
Northamptonshire Further Education Group for Students with Disabilities & Learning Difficulties	Matthews	Graham
Northamptonshire Social Services Department	Hugman	Ian
	Pounder	Tony
Northbrook College	Reglar	Peter
Northgate Further Education (NHS Trust)	Bewick	Janet M
Northgate Hospital, Further Education Department		
Northumberland College of Arts & Technology		

Northumberland Training & Enterprise Council Ltd	Cook	Maureen
Norton Radstock College	Salter	T S
Norwich Road Community Resource	Vanhinsburgh	Julie
Nottingham Community Health, NHS Trust	McGuirk	Elizabeth
NSF	Ives	Christopher
Nuneaton Adult Team, Social Services Department	Smith	S
Nuneaton Social Education Centre		
NWA healthcare	Hughes	G
N.M.C. (Neuromuscular Centre)	Kelly	Sarah
Oak Lodge School	East	Anne
Oaklands Centre, The	Glenn	M J
Oaklands College	Nelson	Steven
	Woods	Rosemary
	Learning Difficulties Co-ordination Group	
Office for Standards in Education (OFSTED)	Chorley	D H
Office of Public Management	Brown	Helen
Oldham College	McHugh	Wendy
Oldham LEA	Edwards	Kathleen
Oldham NHS Trust	Ryan	John
	Steward	John
Open University, The	Peters	G
	Walmsley	J
Opportunities and Networks in Southwark	Dunn	Susan
	Honess	Julia
Optimum Health Service	Auty	Patricia M
Orchard Trust, The	Gordan-Smith	George
Oxford Brookes University, School of Education	Bines	Hazel
Oxford College of Further Education	Otley	Noel
Oxfordshire County Council	Brayton	Howard
Pace Enterprise and Employment Services	Bottomley	John
Parents and Carers Group, WALCAT	Cornell	Angela
Park Lane College	Brown	Jonathon
Paston Sixth Form College	Downes	Barbara
Peggy Edwards Centre	Richards	Rowena
Penn Fields School	Hodgson	R
Pennine Camphill Community, parents of students	Gosling	J B
Peter Symonds College	Samways	Angela
Peterborough Regional College	Fisk	Stephen
Peterborough Regional College	Stapleford	Keith
Peterlee College	Goodrum	Val
PHAB	Hope	Paul
Phoenix NHS Trust	Le-Pine	Lesley
Phillips Resource Centre	Weare	Lynda
Plymouth College of Art & Design	Farrow-Jones	Sue
Plymouth College of Further Education	Rospigliosi	G
	Baxter	Marion
	Lloyd	Barry
	Lile	Sheila

F

Plymouth College of Further Education	skills development programme	
	Stone	Vivienne E
	Stutridge	Marianne
PMLD Link, Editorial Board	Boucher	Joan
Portland College	Davies	P S
Portsmouth College	Westbury	Richard
Portsmouth & Havant Post-16 Forum	Baker	John
	Foster	Andrew
Priory School	Mummery	Frances
Prison Education Consultant	West	Tessa
Queen Elizabeth Sixth Form College	Woods	Peter
R E T C	Fidler	Lynda Mary
	Hayes	Jane
Rathbone Society, The	Gould	Alison
Ravenswood	Hart	David
	Brier	Norma
Reading Adult College	Westbrook	Joan
Redbridge College	McGrath	J A
Redbridge Health Care	Kelly	Alex
	Rosen	Alison
Reigate College	Walters	Sarah
Richard Collyer in Horsham, The College of	Clarke	Paul
Richard Huish College	Stokes	Barbara
Richmond Adult & Community College	Evans	Mary
Richmond upon Thames College	Vallance	Jenny
Ridge College, The	Lyon	Ann
RNIB Redhill College	Stockley	Jennifer
RNID Court Grange College	Whitehead	Graham
Romsey and Waterside Locality Planning Teams Adult Education Subgroup	Evans	Anne
Rose Cottage Further Education Unit (Glyne Gap School)	Baker	Steve
Rotherham College of Arts & Technology	Sheehy	Sue
Rotherham Further Education Partnership on students with learning difficulties and disabilities	Richards	Colin
Rotherham Social Services Department	Chester	David
Royal Association for Disability & Rehabilitation, The	Simpson	Paul
Royal College for the Blind, The	Housby-Smith	C
Royal College of Nursing	Hancock	Christine
	Sines	David
Royal Cornwall Hospitals Trust	Voyce	M A
Royal Hospital NHS Trust, The	Francis	Dennis
Royal London Society for the Blind, The	Spittle	Barbara
Royal National Institute for the Blind (RNIB)	Dryden	G
Royal National Institute for the Deaf (RNID)	Alker	Doug
	Gaines	Adam
Royal School for the Deaf	Hedges	Joyce
Royal School for the Deaf	Shaw	John F
Runshaw College	Wales	Janet
Rutland Sixth Form College	Firmin	Catherine

F

Salford Careers Service	Loader	Kay
Saltash College (part of St Austell College)	Wright	Malcolm
Salvation Army Social Services	Robinson	John
Sandwell Strategic Forum for Education and Training, The	Holding	Gordon
School Leaver Liaison Group, SRT, Stockport	Whiteley	Viv
SCSI-ASSIST	York	Debra
	Perry	B T
South East Derbyshire College, Ilkeston	Jones	Judith
South East Regional Association for the Deaf	Holt	S John
South East Regional Group of Special Needs Careers Officers	Glover	Sharon
	Higgins	Gillian
Second Chance, Bridgenorth College Campus	Cooper	Lynn
Second Chance, Shrewsbury College of Art & Technology	Fricker	Angela
	Matthews	Pam
SENSE: The National Deaf Blind and Rubella Association	Boothroyd	Eileen
Sensory Impairment Service, Oxfordshire	Moore	Edward
Service for Visually Impaired Children, Coventry	Wright	R A
Shaftesbury Education	Burnham	Michael
Sharing Care, Leeds	Walton	Bill
Sheffield College, The	Lynch	Paul R
	Martin	Christine
Sheffield Family & Community Services	Jones	Glenys
Shelley School	Parker	Heather
	Thomas	Jillian P
Shena Simon College	Young	Glyn
Shrewbury College of Arts & Technology	Conrad	Patrick
	Rudd	Chris
Shrewsbury Sixth Form College	Francis	Sally
Shropshire Social Services	Painter	Roger
Sidestep Training Ltd	Laycock	Deborah
SIMS Education Services	Carr-Archer	H
Sixth Form College, Farnborough, The	Harris	Marilyn
Skelmersdale College	Farmer	Ian
Skill, Mental Health Working Party	Chirico	Margaret
Skill (Yorkshire and Humberside Regional Group)/Yorkshire and	Swindells	David
Humberside Association for Further and Higher Education	Hills	Graham
Skill (North West) Region	Johnstone	David
Skill: National Bureau for Students with Disabilities (evidence subsequently published by Skill)	Cooper	Deborah
Skill (Yorkshire and Humberside Branch)	Swindells	David
Slough Family & Child Guidance Service	Brockless	J
Social services, Northallerton, North Yorkshire	Pudney	Juliet
Social Services, Bedfordshire	O'Sullivan	J
Social Services, Hertford	Woolrych	Richard
Social Services Adults with Learning Difficulties, South Wirral	Jones	Harry
Social Services Department, Lowestoft, Suffolk	Gibbons	Sheila
Social Services Department, Bury St Edmonds, Suffolk	Goodenough	Teresa
Social Services Department, Cheshire County Council	Sargeant	Helen
Social Services Department, Wolverhampton	Gray	Ken

F

Social Services, Walsall	Phillips	Don
Social Sevices	Dunkerley	Dinah
Solihull Careers Service	Taylor	D E
Solihull College	Lowe	Vicky
Somerset College of Arts & Technology	Davies	Bryn
Somerset College of Arts & Technology	Lloyd-Jones	Nicole
	Tacageni	Christopher
Somerset County Council	Mayor	George
Somerset County Council, Learning Difficulties Strategic	Barwood	Ann
Planning Team	Harvey	David
Somerset Social Services	Singleton	Sue
	Bale	Fleur
South Birmingham College	Cooper	Maureen
South Bolton Sixth Form College		
South Bristol College	Taylor	Prue
South Cheshire College	Briscoe	S C
South Devon College	Lupson	J F
South Downs College of Further Education	May	Fran
South East Derbyshire College	Jones	Judith
South East Essex College of Arts & Technology, The	Pitcher	A
South East Essex Sixth Form College	Dennis	L J
South East Region Special Educational Needs Network	MacLeod	Vicki
South Humberside LEA	Hayward	Anne
South Kent College	Berry	Christina
South Park Sixth Form College	Walker	Muriel
South Thames College	Vigurs	Annette
South Tyneside College	Piddington	Pauline
South Tyneside LEA	Reid	I L
South West Association Further Education & Training	Blythe	Penni
Southampton Technical College	Grenier	Anne
Southampton Day Services	Lillywhite	Ross
Southampton Health Commission	East	K
Southend Community College	Warnes	Jill
Southgate College	Dowrick	Jill
Southport College	Hobson	Margaret
Southwark College	Foster	John
	Held	Madeleine
	Rose	Judith
Southwark Day Care Forum	Rose	Judith
	Hurley	Irene
Spastics Society, The (now SCOPE)	Gilbert	David
	McGill	Rosemarie
Special Adult Learning Programmes, Bedfordshire Adult and Continuing Education	Harris	Meryl
Special Comunication Needs Ltd (SCN)	Hugh	Stefanie
Special Education Needs Training Consortium	Dee	Lesley
Specialised Courses Offering Purposeful Eduction (SCOPE)	Adams	B
Speech and Language Therapists, The College of	Beer	Marcia
Speech & Language Therapist for the Deaf, Royal Berks Hospital	Crawford	Rachel

Spelthorne College	Lewis	Anne
Springfield School	Lewis	D
St Ann's School		
St Charles Catholic Sixth Form College	O'Shea	Paul
St Dominic's Sixth Form College	Lipscomb	John L
St Georges Healthcare (NHS) Trust	Way	Andrew M
St Helens College	O'Brien	Derek
St John Ambulance Brigade	Davison	Edward Richard
St John's School for the Hearing Impaired	Ellis	Angela
St Mary's NHS Trust Hospital	Ajayi-obe	Abiola
Staff College, The	Toogood	Pippa
Staffordshire ASSIST	Garner	Malcolm W
Staffordshire County Council	Hunter	P J
Stanmore College	Wise	J
Stanton Vale School	Ormerod	P N
Stockport College	Marley	Joyce
Stockport Health Authority Trust, Education, Social Services - Multi-Agency	Whiteley	Vivien
Stockton and Billingham College of Further Education	Larry	A E
Stoke-on-Trent College	Bradbury	Kathryn
	Powell	R T
Stoke-on-Trent Sixth Form College	Richardson	J
Stourbridge College	Pugh	Vivienne
Stratford Upon Avon College	Sheils	D P
Stroud College of Further Education	Critchley	Zena
Suffolk College	Serritiello	Carmine Renato
Suffolk County Council Day Services, Unit 9 Business Services	Service users	
Suffolk County Council Community Education Service	Hopkins	Annie
Suffolk Social Services Department	Kent	Simon S
Sunderland Social Services	Hepplewhite	Ian
	Marsden	John
Surrey Adult & Continuing Education Service	Jackson	Irene
Surrey Hearing Impaired Service	Barton	Liz
Surrey Training & Enterprise Council	Essex	Mike
Sutton Coldfield College of Further Education	Turner	Gwen
Sutton College of Liberal Arts	Hebden	Kate
Swalcliffe Park School Trust	Cooling	Maurice
Swindon College	Budd	Patricia
S.C.A.T.	Newton	Eric John
S.C.A.T./ Six Acres Day Centre	Veysey	Ginny
	Freeney	Mike
	Furey (student)	Michelle
	Young (student)	Gillian
Taking Part	Bryant	Caia
Tameside College of Technology	Burgess	Barbara
	Luckock	Ann

F

Tamworth College	Boughton	G
	Hendy	Alan
Coventry Education Service, Task Group for Developing Work with Adults with Learning Difficulties	Newbold	Alan
TEC National Council	Muir CBE	Peter J
Telford College of Arts & Technology	Glazier	John
Templehill Community Ltd	Keys	Richard
Tendring Adult Community College	Garlick	Cynthia
	Mathieson	Michael
Thanet College	Morgan	Cheryl
Thomas Danby College	Dugan	Theresa
Thomas Rotherham College	Briggs	Nigel
Thurrock College	Wallace	John
Tile Hill College	Harris	Steve
	Galliers	M
Totton College	Joiner	Susan
	Joiner	Michael
	Hiscock	Jill
	Evans	Anne
Tower Hamlets College	Zera	Annette
Trowbridge College	Bright	George
	Maddocks	Alun
Truro College	Burnett	Jonathon
	Stansfield	P J
Turnshaws Special School/What Next	Staves	L
TVEI Regional SEN Network (Yorkshire and Humberside)	Broadhurst	Marion
Tynemouth College	Sunderland	Maureen
Umbrella	Preedy	Susan
University of East London	Corbett	Jenny
University of Huddersfield, School of Education	Swindells	David
University of Leeds	Chamberlain	Anne
University of Liverpool	Haworth	Sarah
University of London Institute of Education	Dee	Lesley
University of Newcastle	Dyson	Alan
University of the West of England, Training & Research Associates	Woodward	Elizabeth
Users Forum, Kempston Centre, Bedfordshire	Doyle	Barbara
Visual Impairment Support Team, Special Needs Teaching Service	Weaver	Bridgid
Wakefield College	Constantine	Anne
Waldon Association, The	Beard	Peter
Walsall Community Health Trust, St Margarets Hospital	Jones	Lorraine
Waltham Forest College	Henderson	Carrie
Wandsworth Adult College	Watson	Elizabeth
Warminster & District Society for Mentally Handicapped Children and Adults	Burden	Veronica
Warrington Collegiate Institute	Drewe	Sylvia
	Harthill	A M
Warrington Community Care	Halliwell	David D
Warrington Day Centre	Lockwood	Ena
Warrington MIND	Kerrigan	A T

Warwickshire Careers Service	Morgan	Jean
Warwickshire Social Services	King	Margaret
WCC Social Services Department	Sarson	P
Welcome Ear Club, Affliated to Hearing Concern	Baxter	Evelyn
West Berkshire Priority Care Service, NHS Trust	Hutchinson	Josephine
West Cheshire College	Maynard	Carol
West Cumbria College	Craine	Lynn
West Hertfordshire College	Evans	Tim
West Hertfordshire College		
West Kent College	Meadows	Danny
West London Healthcare NHS Trust	Sherwood	S
West Midlands Autistic Society Ltd	Morgan	Hugh
	Edwards	Gwenn
West Midlands Autistic Society/Oakfield House Autistic Community	Morgan	Hugh
West Pennine Health Authority	Elton	Peter J
West Suffolk College of Further Education	Carmichael	Andy
	Lally	Ann
	Pederson	Wendy
West Thames College	Gibbons	Susan
Westminster College	Burgess	Carol
Weymouth College	Buckley	Trevor
Whitby Community College	Gwinnell-Smith	Gary
Wigan and Leigh College	Corner	Roy
	Johnson	Barry
	Saldanha	Jane
	Scapens	Dianne
	Turner	H P
Wightlink IOW Ferries Ltd	Williams	M
Wigston College, Link into Learning	Fieldsend	Judith
Wilberforce College	Howard	P
William Morris House	Wooding	Thomas Thorten
Wiltshire Careers Guidance Services	Curbishley	Lesley
Wiltshire LEA	Harper	T J
Wirral Metropolitan College	Shackleton	Jenny
	Welch	Anne
West Midlands Access Federation, University of Wolverhampton	Donnelly	Enda
Woking Sixth Form College	Nevett	Brenda
Wolverhampton Health Care	Girach	M H
Wolverhampton LEA	Phillips	Ian
Wolverhampton Mencap	Polack	Margaret
Wolverley NHS Trust	Close	Ann
Woodhouse Sixth Form College	Drescher	Gillian
Woodlands School	Forde	S J
Worcester College of Technology	Wilkins	C D
Worcester Sixth Form College		
Workers Educational Association	Munby	Zoe
	Hall	Dorothea M

F

Wulfrun College	Mothersdale	G K
	Tomlinson	Wayne
Wyke Sixth Form College	Rodmell	Jo
Yearsley Bridge Centre	Members Council	
Yeovil College	Chiffers	Andrew
York College of Further Education and Higher Education	Smedley	Jane
Young Enterprise	Hallwood	Gretl

Responses from individuals

Allen Barbara	parent(s)
Allen William	person with learning difficulty/disability,
Robert Callard	lipreading tutor
Allerton Juliet	lip-reading tutor
Allibone Frederick George	person with learning difficulty/disability
Anderson H R A	parent(s)
Anderson I	parent(s)
Appleton Janet	parent(s)
Atkinson Lyn	parent(s)
Bainbridge	parent(s)
Baines Christine Linda	person with learning difficulty/disability
Baker Magnus Alistair	person with learning difficulty/disability
Barrett Patricia	person with learning difficulty/disability
Baruch Lucy R	person with learning difficulty/disability
Bennet Avril	person with learning difficulty/disability
Bentley Barbara	person with learning difficulty/disability
Boast Roy S	person with learning difficulty/disability
Bonney May/Michael	parent(s)
Bonser Jonathan Andrew	student teacher
Bowles Reginald	person with learning difficulty/disability
Bradshaw J	parent(s)
Bramble Anna	support tutor for dyslexic students
Brooks Beryl	person with learning difficulty/disability
Bubb Elizabeth	person with learning difficulty/disability
Bullock Ernest Paul Charles	person with learning difficulty/disability
Burnett Sarah	trainer
Button Joanne	parent(s)
Charters Frances	PGCE student
Clark C A	parent(s)
Clissold Shirley Ann	person with learning difficulty/disability
Collie Madeleine	person with learning difficulty/disability
Comtois Fernand	parent(s)
Corcoran Leo	retired lecturer
Cordery Joan	person with learning difficulty/disability
Cowley Madeleine	parent(s)
Cox Simon	person with learning difficulty/disability
Crees Diana Christine	person with learning difficulty/disability, retired teacher
Croft A	person with learning difficulty/disability
Crossland Ann	parent(s)
Davey Gillian/Godfrey	parent(s)
Davies Margaret Ann	parent(s)
Davies T V	person with learning difficulty/disability
Dawe S	parent(s)
Dawson J	parent(s)
Eagland Elizabeth	person with learning difficulty/disability
Ehsansullah Lillian	person with learning difficulty/disability, advocate
Evans Pauline	person with learning difficulty/disability, parent(s)
Farrington Gail Mary Ann	student
Fisher Anne	parent(s)
Forward T	parent(s)
Gentle Chris/Marion	parent(s)
Gilbert James Ernest	person with learning difficulty/disability
Gillam E	carer
Grieves James, Lamdie	parent(s)

F

Griffiths	lipreading tutor
Grove John S	
Haigh Hanson	person with learning difficulty/disability
Haigh Irene	person with learning difficulty/disability
Harkness Stuart	person with learning difficulty/disability
Harvey Majorie	person with learning difficulty/disability
Hayes Ivan	person with learning difficulty/disability, carer
Hazlett Robert and Patricia	parent(s)
Heapy Dorothy	person with learning difficulty/disability
Hefferman Olive	person with learning difficulty/disability
Henley Jane	parent(s)
Henry Charlie	
Heys F	retired special needs teacher
Hill A E F	
Holme Helen Michelle	person with learning difficulty/disability
Holroyde Mary	person with learning difficulty/disability
Hopkins Veronica	parent(s)
Horrex David	person with learning difficulty/disability
Howe Pauline Hazel	person with learning difficulty/disability
Hulbert J	parent(s)
Hutt Ralph	person with learning difficulty/disability
Johnson A C	professional
Johnson Margaret H	retired college principal
Jones Edward Charles	person with learning difficulty/disability
Jones Stephen	
Jordan Linda/Mark	parent(s)
Josephs Rosalina	lipreading tutor
Knapman David	consultant educational psychologist
Leeming David	parent(s)
Lemer Miriam	parent(s)
Lewis Christopher Martin	educational psychologist
Lomas Sheila	person with learning difficulty/disability
Mackie Ada	parent(s)
Marsh Carol & John	parent(s)
Massey Jack	person with learning difficulty/disability
McGechan Colin & Joyce	parent(s)
Merriott Pamela/Torben	parent(s)
Montgomery Eileen	person with learning difficulty/disability
Moore Beryl	adult placement carer
Morris Carl Allen William	person with learning difficulty/disability
Morris Rachel Josephine	carer
Mumtaz Adeeba	parent(s)
Neal M A	person with learning difficulty/disability
Newby Walter David	person with learning difficulty/disability
Newby/Smith Michael/Claire	person with learning difficulty/disability, parent(s)
Nicholas Jill Margaret	parent(s)
Nurse Mary Elizabeth	person with learning difficulty/disability
Oakes B	person with learning difficulty/disability
Paintin Ivy N	person with learning difficulty/disability
Pearson Ethel E	person with learning difficulty/disability
Perks Michael Anthony	person with learning difficulty/disability
Polack Margaret/R A	parent(s)
Portal Kate	
Powell Michael Brian	person with learning difficulty/disability
Priddle Annette Diane	person with learning difficulty/disability
Prince David	person with learning difficulty/disability
Prince Valerie Joan	parent(s), schoolteacher
Rees Alan	carer

F

Ripley Joseph Raymond	person with learning difficulty/disability
Ritchie Angela	parent(s)
Rixter Penny	head of support unit
Roberts Graham	person with learning difficulty/disability
Roberts Keith	person with learning difficulty/disability
Roberts Peter	person with learning difficulty/disability
Robinson Lesley	parent(s)
Rogers Roy	person with learning difficulty/disability, freelance researcher
Scaife Leslie, William	parent(s)
Sellman Ingrid	lipreading tutor
Sheen Raymond/Carole	parent(s)
Shrubshall Bernadette	
Slowey Paul	person with learning difficulty/disability
Smith J A	person with learning difficulty/disability
Spedding Helen	lipreading teacher
Stone Henry William	person with learning difficulty/disability
Summers Mark	person with learning difficulty/disability
Sutton E	parent(s)
Sutton Malcolm	parent(s)
Swallow Candice, Jade	person with learning difficulty/disability
Symes P J	other
TerryShirley	person with learning difficulty/disability
Thompson Jean	person with learning difficulty/disability
Thompson Merry	lipreading tutor
Thomson T A	person with learning difficulty/disability
Tombs Anne	person with learning difficulty/disability
Tomkins A	carer
Trenchard P J	parent(s)
Turner J	parent(s)
Veall Roger M	person with learning difficulty/disability
Vernon Mary	
Waine Judith	special needs educator, SLD team leader
Warne Brian	person with learning difficulty/disability
Watkins Dorothy	person with learning difficulty/disability
Watson F M	person with learning difficulty/disability
Watts Colin James	person with learning difficulty/disability
Watts Sarah	person with learning difficulty/disability
WheeldonJean	person with learning difficulty/disability
Whitehead Christine Elizabeth	lipreading tutor
Woodger John Page	person with learning difficulty/disability
Wooding Vera Mary	parent(s)
Wright K C	person with learning difficulty/disability
Wring Sheralun	person with learning difficulty/disability
Yarnell Joan	person with learning difficulty/disability, student
Young Hilary Anne	person with learning difficulty/disability
Young S E	parent(s)
Younger Sadie McW	person with learning difficulty/disability

Appendix 2 to Annex F: Outline of Evidence Strategy

Introduction

1 The committee gathered evidence in seven ways:

- its call for evidence
- commissioning research, including a review of previous research and a survey of provision
- commissioning a series of workshops for students with learning difficulties and/or disabilities
- attending conferences and workshops and holding seminars for particular groups
- establishing short-life working groups to consider particular issues
- visiting colleges and other organisations, in England and elsewhere
- inviting individuals and representatives of organisations to give oral evidence.

2 The committee also took the decision to publish some of its work during its three-year life. These publications are listed at the end of this appendix.

The call for evidence

3 The committee's call for evidence was sent to over 6,000 recipients. The evidence received in response took a variety of forms, including video-tapes, reports, research, students' work, personal letters and official statements. Most of this evidence was received by September 1994. Responses to the call for evidence were received from the following:

- individuals with learning difficulties and/or disabilities
- their parents/carers and/or advocates
- further education colleges
- LEA maintained schools
- specialist establishments for those with learning difficulties and/or disabilities
- local education authorities
- local authority social service departments
- careers services
- health authorities
- Training and Enterprise Councils
- voluntary organisations
- training and rehabilitation organisations
- other individuals concerned about the provision of further education for students with learning difficulties and/or disabilities.

4 The 1,091 responses were analysed by two consultants who reported their findings to the committee. Figure 1 at the end of this appendix shows the number of responses focusing on each of the issues raised and figure 2 the number of responses according to the type of respondent. The call for evidence asked for information about: what 'disability and/or learning difficulty' means; assessment; the extent to which colleges cater for students' needs and the needs of communities; funding arrangements and their impact; specialist support services; the role of health and local authorities and joint working; and on the quality of provision and of students' experiences.

5 The 10 main issues raised by the respondents were:

i. *funding support;* (mentioned by 17% of all respondents). Concerns included the Council's additional support funding mechanism and funds for external and specialist support;

ii. *funding methodology;* (mentioned by 26% of all respondents). Concerns included funding for support; the link between funding and accreditation; time-limited funding; and guidance for advisers, teachers and co-ordinators;

iii. *assessment;* (mentioned by 35% of all respondents). Concerns included the costs and funding of assessment; the importance of focusing on individuals rather than the demands of the curriculum or available resources; the role of specialists, such as educational psychologists; and the importance of ensuring effective transition into further education and beyond;

iv. *assessing achievement;* (mentioned by 36% of all respondents). Concerns included the links between achievement and funding; the focus on accreditation; and the development of nationally-recognised accreditation schemes that offer real progression;

v. *college provision and management;* (mentioned by 31% of all respondents). Concerns included structures which best ensure good-quality further education provision; integrating and managing progression; gaps in provision, especially for: students with profound and complex learning difficulties, adults with learning difficulties and/or disabilities, students with sensory impairment, students with dyslexia or specific learning difficulties; and how to manage teaching, learning and curriculum development;

vi. *training and staff development;* (mentioned by 14% of all respondents). Concerns included the need for staff development and disability awareness training;

vii. *definitions;* (mentioned by 22% of all respondents). Concerns included differences in the definitions used by different agencies and assistance in applying them; and concerns about labelling and categorising students;

viii. *links with other agencies;* (mentioned by 21% of all respondents). Concerns included uncertainty about the responsibilities of various agencies involved in further education and support for students, especially for those over the age of 19;

ix. *provision at specialist colleges;* (mentioned by 8% of all respondents). Concerns included the Council's procedures for funding places;

x. *provision for students aged over 19;* (mentioned by 9% of all respondents). Concerns included uncertainty about the criteria for inclusion of programmes within the scope of schedule 2 to the *Further and Higher Education Act 1992*.

New research, including a review of research and survey of provision

6 As its first task, the committee commissioned an overview of research from the National Foundation for Educational Research (NFER). The review covers national and international research, definitions, provision, assessment, funding, support systems, quality and achievement, transition and inter-agency working. The review examines nine key questions and includes a full bibliography. It found many gaps in the research and offers suggestions of where further research is needed. The report has been published and a copy sent to every college. The full report is available from NFER.

7 The mapping exercise, commissioned by the committee from the Institute for Employment Studies (IES) following

F

competitive tender, set out to find the extent of the need for further education and the current provision for students. The committee commissioned the survey because there was no up-to-date national information. The aim of the project was to:

- estimate from existing information the number of people aged 16 and over (in each region) in England with learning difficulties and/or disabilities
- estimate the extent of their participation in further education
- identify the factors which influence their participation, and
- estimate any unmet educational need.

8 The project began with a review of national research on the numbers of people with disabilities or learning difficulties, identifying existing and significant national data sets and analysing each of them to form some general figures relating to the incidence of disability within the general population. However, much of the data overlapped. Much of it also used different definitions. It was therefore not possible to deduce the likely need in the general population, a proportion of whom might reasonably be thought to require further education. The second part of the research surveyed the provision made in colleges through a national questionnaire. It involved a pilot survey undertaken in 20 colleges in Spring 1995 and a postal questionnaire piloted with a sample of 100 sector colleges in the summer term 1995.

9 The main survey itself was launched in October 1995 and concluded by mid-March 1996. It covered all sector colleges and a sample of external institutions and related to all students enrolled on 1 November 1995. The response rate was just over 60% (274 colleges). The distribution of responses by type of college and region was statistically representative of the sector as a whole, but higher response rates were achieved from larger colleges. The committee drew heavily on this research in its report, particularly in the chapter 4. The research is published as a companion volume. The IES also completed for the committee a preliminary project on how further education participation could be measured and what is already known about what influences that participation by people with learning difficulties and/or disabilities. At the time of publication of this report, work was under way to develop a practical guide for colleges. It will help them to better assess needs in their local community and to monitor participation more accurately. This work is being funded by the Council on behalf of the committee and the widening participation committee.

Seminars and workshops for people with disabilities and/or learning difficulties

10 The views of further education students with disabilities and/or learning difficulties were sought through a series of workshops commissioned from Skill: The National Bureau for Students with Disabilities following competitive tender. Skill worked in partnership with several agencies, including Social and Community Planning Research (SCPR) which wrote the report. From a careful sifting of around 2,000 applications, 266 personally invited students took part in 10 workshops at venues around the country. Students told the researchers that they wanted:

- more opportunities to give their views about their experiences of further education
- more opportunities to develop self-advocacy skills in order to have a say at college
- to feel valued and welcomed at colleges
- not to be labelled as having a disability or learning difficulty, though recognised the value of this when resources were required
- recognition that they attended college for the same reason as other students – for experience, skills and qualifications

- teachers to listen to their aspirations and take them seriously
- to find out more about their course before they came to college
- to know when assessment was taking place, and its purpose
- additional support and specialist equipment to be in place straight away and for it not to make them feel different from other students
- teachers to know about their disability or learning difficulty and to understand how it might influence their learning
- teachers to use a variety of approaches in their teaching, to give regular constructive feedback and to get to know them well
- opportunities to learn alongside other students
- to get into and move around college with the same ease and freedom as other students; and to travel to college and between sites quickly and effectively.

11 The full report has been sent to every college. Copies are available from Skill.

Attendance at conferences and workshops, and holding seminars for particular groups

12 Seminars, conferences, workshops and meetings attended by committee members, the staff team and the chairman allowed more evidence to be taken from particular groups and for work done by the committee to be shared with others. These events included regional and colleges' seminars; national conferences and events organised by voluntary organisations.

13 The committee held seminars to obtain the views of particular groups of people. These included:

- a seminar for representatives of the research community to consider how to map provision and participation (February 1994)
- a seminar on assessment in sector colleges (February 1994)
- two meetings for organisations providing and receiving support services (February 1994, January 1995)
- a meeting for voluntary organisations on the kind of evidence that they might submit to the committee (May 1994)
- a seminar on assessment for placements in specialist establishments (May 1994)
- a seminar for parents of students with a learning difficulty and/or disability and parents' organisations (July 1995)
- a seminar with colleges to test the committee's approach (July 1995)
- a meeting for advocates and self-advocates working in or involved in further education (September 1995)
- a seminar for those using and managing enabling technology (February 1996)
- a seminar on legal issues (March 1996).

Short-life working groups to consider particular issues

14 At its early meetings the committee established working groups, co-opting individuals with particular expertise and knowledge. The groups reported to the committee through written reports. Working groups considered:

- assessment of individual needs, assessment of students' learning and achievements
- assessment to offer advice to the Council's tariff advisory committee on aspects of the funding methodology
- support systems and support services for students
- inter-agency collaboration, including the role of local authorities and health services
- definitions, including what 'disability and/or learning difficulty' means.

F

Visits to colleges and other organisations, both in England and elsewhere

15 A full list of visits undertaken by the committee, its staff and the chairman is given at annex F. A summary of the findings of visits to other countries is given at annex C.

Individuals and representatives of organisations invited to give oral evidence

16 The committee sought oral evidence from a number of organisations. The Council offered advice on:

- the quality of further education provision for students with learning difficulties and/or disabilities in sector and specialist colleges
- funding arrangements for students with learning difficulties and/or disabilities
- the recurrent funding methodology, 1995-96 consultation
- funding allocation issues
- placement of students in independent colleges
- strategic planning
- the role of its regional committees
- mapping provision and participation in further education for students with learning difficulties and/or disabilities.

17 Evidence from other organisations included advice on:

- the further education curriculum, from Geoff Stanton, Further Education Unit
- the *Education Act 1993*; schools matters and implications for the work of the committee, from the Department for Education and Employment
- the committee's thinking about inclusive learning, from people involved in the disability movement
- international evidence, from Mr John Fish, consultant (formerly OECD)
- specialist colleges, from the NATSPEC advisory committee, students at specialist colleges and their tutors
- employment, training and careers guidance, from the DfEE, together with the chief executive, Rathbone C.I.
- disability, learning difficulty and adult learning, from the chief executive and research and development colleagues, National Institute of Adult Continuing Education; and from the principal and colleagues, North Warwickshire College
- curricular, organisational, managerial and staff development, from the chief executive together with the development officer, Further Education Development Agency
- college strategic planning, from the principal and colleagues, Blackburn College
- the implications of the committee's work for teacher education and staff development, from the SENTC/Skill further and higher education monitoring group
- OFSTED and the new schools inspection system, and findings from inspection related to provision for adults and young people, from HMI.

Evidence to working groups included:

- findings of the NFER survey on collaboration, from Karen Maychell, NFER
- the local management of transition, from Barry Stockton, consultant to FEU
- definitions of learning difficulty/disability from social care and training perspectives, from Stella Dixon, FEU and John Curtis, Skill
- the accreditation of achievement, from Elsa Dicks, NCVQ; Colin Walker, BTEC; Terry Davis, the Associated Examining Board; and Nancy Braithwaite, SCAA (Sir Ron Dearing's review of the 16 to 19 qualifications).

Figure 1. Number of responses to the call for evidence by issue raised

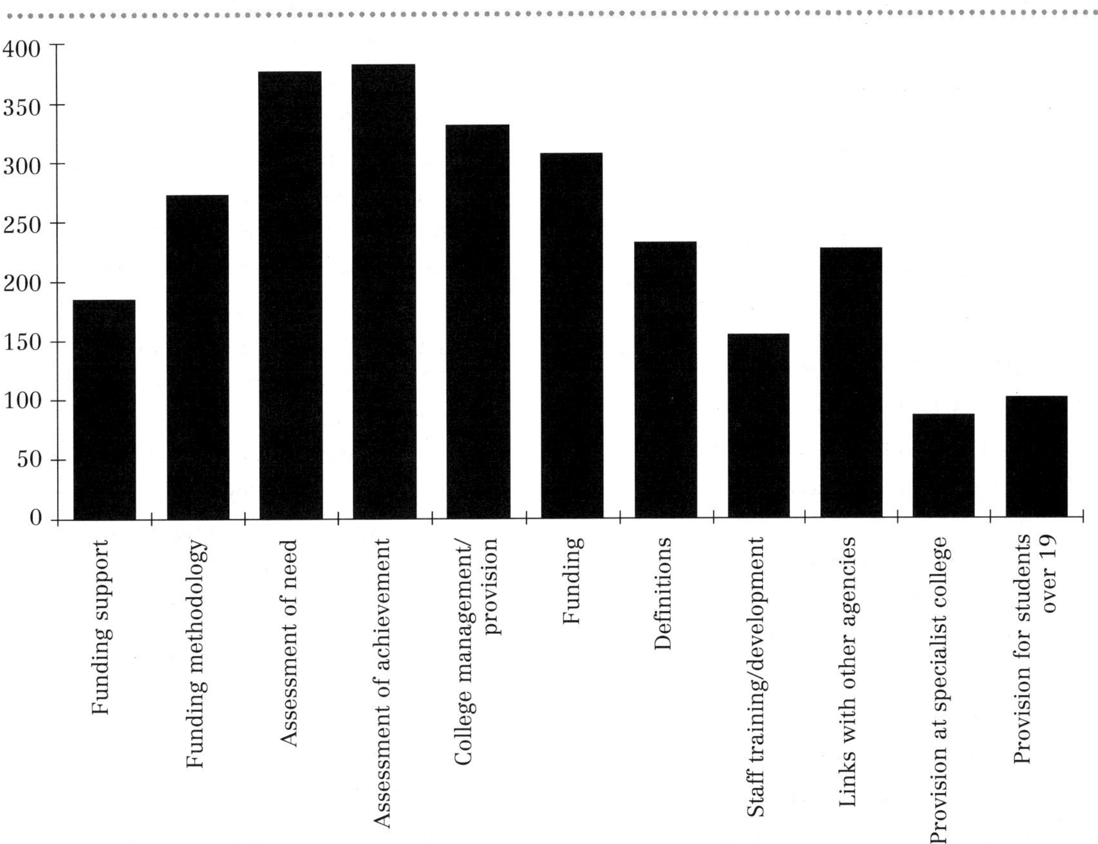

Figure 2. Responses to the call for evidence by type of respondent

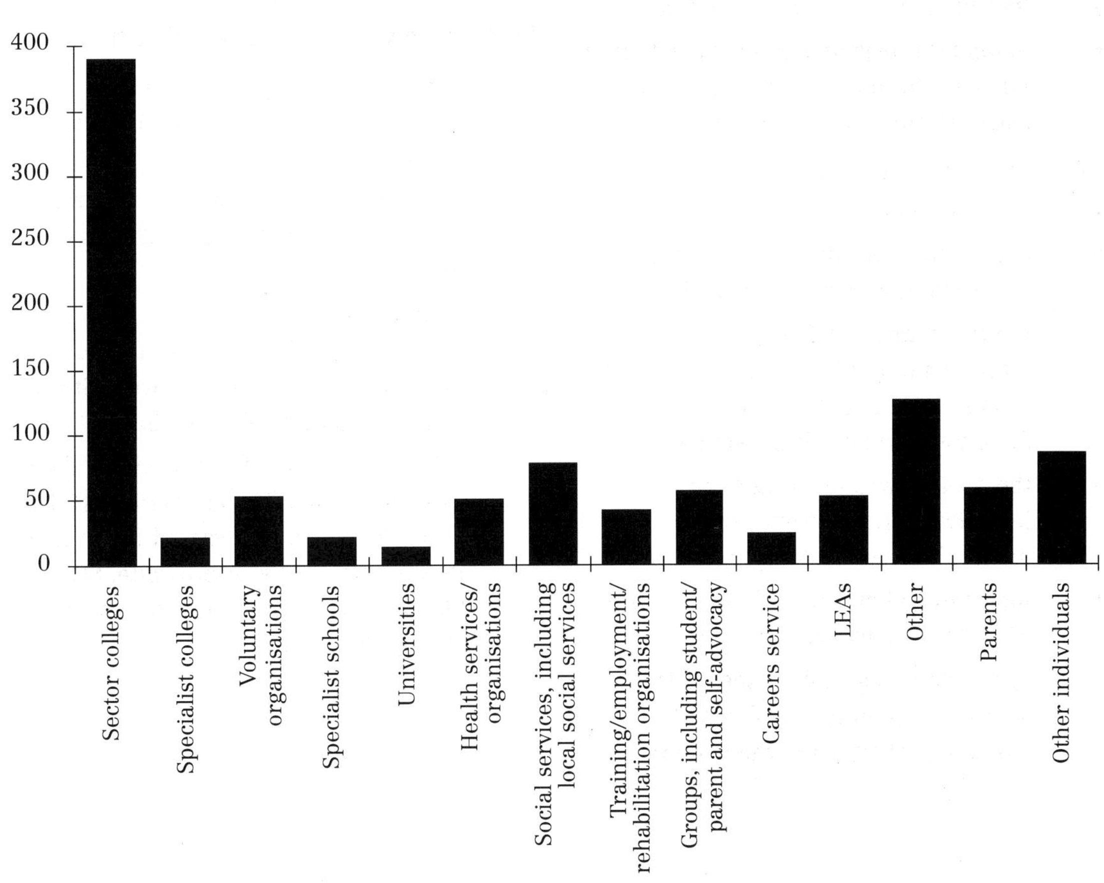

Committee Publications

Disability, Learning Difficulties and Further Education: Call for Evidence from the FEFC Committee, FEFC, Coventry February 1994

Disability, Learning Difficulties and Further Education: Work in Progress by the Council's Committee, FEFC, Coventry May 1995

Beachcroft Stanleys *Duties and Powers: The Law Governing the Provision of Further Education to Students with Learning Difficulties and/or Disabilities: A Report to the Learning Difficulties and/or Disabilities Committee*, London, HMSO, 1996

J. Bradley, L. Dee and F. Wilenius *Students with Disabilities and/or Learning Difficulties in Further Education: A Review of Research Carried out by the National Foundation for Educational Research,* Slough, National Foundation for Educational Research, 1994

Nigel Meager, Ceri Evans and Sally Dench (of The Institute for Employment Studies) *Mapping Provision: The Provision of and Participation in Further Education by Students with Learning Difficulties and/or Disabilities: A Report to the Learning Difficulties and/or Disabilities Committee*, London, HMSO, 1996

SCPR *Student Voices: The Views of Further Education Students with Learning Difficulties and/or Disabilities: Findings from a Series of Student Workshops Commissioned by the Learning Difficulties and/or Disabilities Committee,* London, Skill: National Bureau for Students with Disabilities, 1996

Printed in the United Kingdom for
The Stationery Office
Dd. N14771, C10, 4/97, 78166